Tobias & Rebecca
Honored to be included at your table!

Lisa Soledo-Johnson
10-13-19

IT BEGINS AT THE
table

140 Recipes to
inspire love
for Every Nation,
Tribe, and Tongue

LISA SOLDO-JOHNSON

To my children,

Remember when you go into the world to keep your eyes and ears wide open. And be kind. Love one another. Take care of each other. Tell the truth. Always do your best. Listen to the big people and the little people. Explore new paths and have fun. Know that you are loved like crazy. Give thanks for all your blessings. Above all else, love and you will do wonderful things in this world.

- Rebecca Puig, Designer and Owner of Sugarboo & Co.

To Duane, Jean-Marc, Isabella, Lexi and BJ
You inspire me to love this journey called life.
My passion to create a genuine connection with the world through food is even more meaningful when you are at the table.

It Begins at the Table. Copyright © 2019 Lisa Soldo-Johnson. All rights reserved. Printed in Korea. No part of this book may be used or reproduced in any manner whatsoever without written permission except in the case of brief quotations embodied in critical articles and reviews.

FIRST EDITION

ISBN 978-0-578-44390-4

Library of Congress Control Number: 2019909501

This book is for entertainment purposes. The publisher and author of this cookbook are not responsible in any manner whatsoever for any adverse effects arising or indirectly as a result of the information provided in this book.

IT BEGINS AT THE *table*

140 Recipes to *inspire love* for Every Nation, Tribe, and Tongue

LISA SOLDO-JOHNSON

Table of Contents

Foreword / ix

Introduction / xi

How This Book Works / xvii

Chapter 1: Breakfast and Smoothies / 1

Chapter 2: Small Bites / 13

Chapter 3: Soups and Salads / 37

Chapter 4: Poultry / 67

Chapter 5: Beef, Lamb, Pork / 85

Chapter 6: Fish and Seafood / 121

Chapter 7: Vegetables and Sides / 139

Chapter 8: Spices and Sauces / 175

Chapter 9: Desserts and Baking / 191

Chapter 10: Beverages / 217

Chapter 11: Multicultural Stories and Pantries / 231

America: The Great Melting Pot / 232

Assyria: An Ancient Love Affair / 235

Iran: A Celebration of Food and Life / 238

Nowruz: A Persian New Year's Celebration / 243

Israel: Abundant Aromas from the Mediterranean / 245

China: Uncomplicated Meals / 248

Russia: Big Flavors using Simple Ingredients / 252

Mexico: Vibrant Food in a Vibrant Culture / 256

Chapter 12: Cultural Gathering Menus and Countdown Schedule / 261

Dedication / 281

Acknowledgments / 283

Universal Conversion Chart / 285

Index / 287

Photo credit, David Sherman

Foreword

Cookbooks come in all shapes and sizes, serve many purposes and have many different objectives. At the end of the day, the end goal is about creating a meal. Being a chef, it is difficult for me to admit that the best meals are more about the experience than the food. Sharing a meal with one person or a group can be an unforgettable, even life-changing, event. When made with love and intention, the food takes on a life of its own. Lisa has managed to write a cookbook that is so much more; that has addressed so many experiential touch points where most others have missed. Her love for people shines through her inspiring words and reflects a genuine intent to put all else aside and to gather over the love of a great meal. Written with painstaking attention to detail and the utmost respect for each culture, Lisa has created a niche that we did not realize was missing in the world of cooking. This is a must-read for people across the globe and once read, treasured, flagged for favorites, underlined for quotes and passed on through generations.

David Fhima Chef & Owner of Fhimas' Minneapolis Restaurants

Nutritional Curators for the Minnesota Timberwolves and Lynx, WNBA World Champions

Introduction

"Love is like a butterfly. It goes where it pleases, and it pleases wherever it goes."
- Author Unknown

I began this book with my mother in mind. It wasn't until the doctor diagnosed her with dementia that I felt an urgency to capture on paper the recipes she had stored in her memory and had yet to teach me. A race against time and the quest to embrace my family heritage of nostalgic foods would soon find a deeper meaning through the pages of this book. Like a good story, traditional recipes throughout the world and in every culture, are often lost in the dustbin of history, never embraced by the next generation.

I can remember the first time I moved out on my own, far from the comforts of a family dinner table where my mom served homemade meals. A powerful day of awakening arrived when I grappled with determining "Should I add oil to the pan before I fry the bacon or not?" That's when I understood there was much more to grasp about this cooking thing than I had expected: I realized that cooking means learning from others while trusting our own imaginations. I learned that the food at our dinner tables and the people around it can be transformative. And, I learned that love is the essential ingredient in this ongoing process.

It Begins at The Table is a book about the power of food and the power of love. Looking beyond our differences and celebrating what makes us the same. Opening our minds and our dinner tables to someone from another culture and seeing with our hearts rather than our eyes. I have learned a lot since my initial attempt at frying bacon.

It's a compelling opportunity — to take a fresh look at the world around you, seeing people through a new lens and discovering the beauty of someone whose nationality, food, and customs are distinct from yours. Even an unexpected glimpse at people on the other side of the globe can cultivate a sense of curiosity that challenges our understanding, teaches something new, and moves us to recognize the beauty that each individual and culture contributes to the world. I have discovered another essential truth. When we allow ourselves to look at the heart of a person whose understanding and background have made them unique, a sudden change happens that can affect our world. Like a butterfly whose flight takes them to unpredictable places, we have the privilege of stepping out of our world and into others. This is called the butterfly effect.

The butterfly effect is a colorful and evocative catchphrase for an idea conceived in the imagination of meteorologist Edward Lorenz. His famous cause-and-effect theory states that a seemingly insignificant moment — like the gentle flutter of a butterfly's wings — can alter history, changing the course of human life and our destinies. The enchanting and somewhat alarming notion that somehow something as delicate as a butterfly has the uncanny ability to create providential change in the world — in the lives of the 7.7 billion people who live on planet earth. Is this even possible? I believe it is — and it begins at the table.

> *"Metamorphosis is not about being a caterpillar or a butterfly, but the journey from caterpillar to butterfly."*
>
> Author Unknown

I think about butterflies a lot. Their existence teaches us so much about our own lives. Like the process of metamorphosis, which transforms an unassuming caterpillar into a stunning new creation — a butterfly. I have found that life is an ever-changing experience often formed by the myriad of people who come in and out of our lives. Some stay for a season, others depart in due time, and others remain forever. Each one enriches our lives, making us better human beings, wherever they land. These are the people who enhance and define our lives through friendship, love, acceptance, and even forgiveness. They transform our world. For me, these people — my friends — were almost always born someplace other than the United States; they have brought me the love of diversity that has inspired this book. As these beloved souls enriched my life and taught me to appreciate further the plethora of cultures we are blessed to have, they graciously shared the rich heritage of their recipes with me.

For over 500 years, America has been a nation of migrants, welcoming those in pursuit of a new life. "Give me your tired, your poor, your huddled masses yearning to breathe free." This famous 1883 quote written by American author and poet Emma Lazarus was published one year after Annie Moore, a teenager from Ireland became the first immigrant processed through Ellis Island. Since then, millions of immigrants have entered this country, hoping for a better life. America has been the great melting pot of the world, celebrating what unites us in our shared values as Americans while honoring our uniqueness. But in recent years, we have removed the main ingredient in the pot: Love.

Inside the cocoon of our hearts, there is a longing to connect that tells a redemptive story, and this is where my story begins. I was born in America, but my heritage is Italian and German. My mother was one of the greatest cooks I know. She taught me to cook beginning in my twenties, and often over the telephone as I struggled to recreate one of the many adored recipes that I grew up eating. It wasn't until I was on my own that I took a real interest in cooking, and at that time it was mostly so I didn't starve! Even today, I am still trying to perfect some unwritten recipes my mother was famously known for in my family. The challenge with learning to cook from someone who prepares her food from the feel of the spice shaker as the spice hits the pot is trickier than you might think. Hence, why her recipes were always fantastic and impossible to replicate. But that's what great cooks do. They cook from the soul. I have decided that no one does it quite like mom, and that's okay. We just become different cooks. That's the thing about cooking; it changes with each generation — and sometimes that's how famous family recipes are born.

Since my early days of cooking, my recipe choices and understanding of cultural cuisine are as evolving as the culture in America is today. Much like a traveler determined to see the world hoping to gain insight and understanding of our surrounding cultures, I am always on a journey of discovery in the kitchen — never arriving at a place where there is little left to learn. I like it this way. It keeps me humble and makes life interesting. It's when we stop evolving that we stop living.

Unlike the butterfly just beyond your grasp, if you welcome it, wisdom will land upon your heart and open your mind to the beauty of others.

I find something inexplicably comfortable about being a minority in a sea of people who are visibly and culturally different from me. I almost always feel more at home with a culture that is not my own. They have something to teach me. Something I need to know to become a wiser person. I hope to pass the wisdom and passion for others on to my children, and I hope they teach their children the truth about the goodness of individuals different from themselves. To open your heart and mind with an honest desire to love and accept people for how God made them is the closest thing to heaven on earth we may ever find.

> *"It's the hardened heart that prevents us from seeing the beauty in others. It's the softened heart that sees with love, and love sees farther than your eyes could ever allow you to."*
>
> - John Hagee

I believe that one of the best ways to understand people and see life through their eyes is through their food. So much of my sentiment and inquisitiveness about ethnic groups have stemmed from my friends and their cooking. The love and passion they express for their cultural heritage — through their language, their traditions, and their food have been my greatest teacher.

This eclectic selection of global recipes is a repository of ideas inspired by myself and my friends including their unique, often ancient cultural stories that will take you on a journey of insight and understanding of the world without ever leaving your kitchen table. You don't need a trip to Iran to taste a classic eggplant khoresht or an adventure in Israel to discover the best lamb kabobs — both can be easily created at home. From simple ideas to inspiring dishes.

I have also included some of the wisdom that chefs have discovered in kitchens across the world for generations. Through these friends, you'll encounter a taste of cuisine and life from seven countries, including Assyria, Iran, Israel, China, Russia, Mexico, and the United States of America.

> *"We must never forget the profound impact we have on one another.*
> *We all belong to one race; the human race."*
>
> - Yanni

These recipes represent traditional dishes according to individual family recipes best known in each region of the world, and new creations. Every recipe thoughtfully prepared with a fusion of ingredients combined with those from other countries that will take you on an exciting culinary journey from your kitchen to your dinner table.

I have done my best to recreate the recipes in this book for you as close to their original form from the friends who have shared them. However, traditional methods change from generation to generation and person to person, often bringing forth new ideas on classic dishes. After all, how many families make the same apple pie? So, too, it is with these recipes. Each cook adds a unique fingerprint to the cooking process to create a variation of the former that best suits their taste.

Just as there are over seventeen thousand different species of butterflies in the world including variations in colors, markings, and shapes; every culture has a rich heritage of ideas and traditions that breathe life into the human experience. Food, family, friendship, and love; each written on the DNA of our humanity, have a universal and age-old meaning that erases distance and differences. At the heart of our existence, we are all the same.

As for the butterfly effect, keep in mind, much like the stranger before you, nothing in a caterpillar tells you it will be a butterfly. That is something you must understand on your own through the transforming metamorphosis of your heart. The simple act of sharing a meal with someone new and inquiring about their culture, with an open desire to learn, is to gain wisdom and understanding. A cause and effect that can change the course of your life and maybe even your destiny. The butterfly effect exists, and it begins at the table.

How This Book Works

It Begins at the Table divides by meal courses with recipes organized in order of breakfast and smoothies, small bites, soups and salads, poultry, beef, lamb, and pork, fish and seafood, vegetables and sides, spices and sauces, desserts and baking, and beverages. Following these chapters is a special section called Multicultural Stories and Pantries, which includes inspiring stories of the individuals and their countries featured in this book as well as a list of ingredients commonly used in each country's cuisine.

A special section called Cultural Gathering Menus has eight menu suggestions and a countdown planning schedule for hosting a successful dinner gathering with friends and family. Dinner gatherings are a unique opportunity to learn how to cook delicious dishes from around the world and open your heart and your dinner table to someone from another culture.

CHAPTER 1

Breakfast and Smoothies

Türk Kahvalti - Turkish Breakfast / 3

Basimo Classic Vegetarian Breakfast / 4

Turkish Menemen Egg Scramble / 5

Shakshouka / 7

Energy Blast Breakfast Granola / 9

Popeye's Muscle Builder / 10

Elderberry Smoothie / 10

Creamy Chocolate Oat Milk and Turmeric Smoothie / 11

Türk Kahvalti - Turkish Breakfast

by Laurie Kerkinni - USA

Breakfast is one of the most important meals of the day for the Turkish people. It provides an opportunity to come together at the table and connect with those who sit around it before the day begins. A traditional Turkish Breakfast called Kahvalti (kah-VAHL'-tuh) which means "before coffee" is a leisurely meal served in many Middle Eastern and Mediterranean cultures. The meal is never precisely the same and food can vary by culture and region. As they say in Turkish, "Sabahın tadını çıkarın!" or "Enjoy the morning!" A classic Kahvalti includes an abundance of shareable foods which can be easily prepared ahead including:

- Eggs: Soft boiled eggs or Menemen - Turkish egg scramble (page 5)
- Bread: Pita or Yufka - unleavened Turkish flatbread (page 209)
- Stuffed grape leaves: Dolmas or Aprah du zayto (page 15)
- Cheese Borek: Cheese stuffed phyllo (page 196)
- Hummus (page 23)
- Zaatar (page 179)
- Cheeses: Feta, Kasseri (goat cheese), Civil peyniri (or string mozzarella)
- Cured Meats: salami or pastrami
- Other staples include mixed olives, tomatoes, cucumbers, fresh fruit, honey and jams, yogurt, Fresh herbs, olive oil and of course - freshly brewed black tea.

Preparation Time: 20 minutes   **Cook Time:** 10 minutes

Ingredients:

- Fresh salty cheese
- Stuffed grape leaves
- Eggs
- Cured meats
- Cheese Borek
- Mixed olives
- Tomatoes, cut into wedges
- Cucumbers, sliced
- Fresh fruit
- Hummus
- Yogurt
- Fresh herbs: basil, tarragon, mint
- Zaatar
- Olive oil
- Fresh bread
- Honey or fruit jam
- Turkish tea: black tea
- Salt and cracked pepper

Method:

1. Prepare the ingredients as needed. Group the foods individually or together on serving plates to create a spread of food in the middle of the table.
2. Set the table with enough plates, cups, and silverware to accommodate the number of guests at your table.
3. Brew the tea and serve it hot with sugar or honey. Enjoy!

Wisdom from Laurie's Kitchen:

It is important to use the freshest ingredients and the best quality cheese, meats and olives when serving a Turkish breakfast.

Most of the ingredients can be prepared a day or so in advance so you can plate each of the foods just before breakfast is served, brew a fresh pot of tea, and sit to enjoy the Kahvalti with your guests.

Lisa's Note:

Laurie and I became friends over three decades ago. This food guru is filled with an invaluable source of information on healthy eating. She is a walking encyclopedia of food and cooking knowledge. Laurie and her husband created a downloadable app called "Healthy Pantry by Nxtnutrio" that allows you to avoid allergens, common questionable ingredients, and GMO's by scanning ingredients before you buy them. What's unique about Laurie's style of cooking is her studied approach to every ingredient she puts into her recipes. Look for more of Laurie's recipes in this book.

Basimo Classic Vegetarian Breakfast

by Laurie Kerkinni - USA

Laurie and her family own the successful Basimo Beach Cafes in Clearwater Florida. They are avid healthy food enthusiasts who wanted to bring their vision of "healthy food" to residents and visitors of this beautiful beach town. Since the opening of their restaurants, people from all over the globe, including a few celebrities, have frequented their cafes to experience what delicious tastes like.

Basimo's Classic Vegetarian Breakfast is one of my favorite dishes on their menu.

Preparation Time: 10 minutes   **Cook Time:** 12-15 minutes   **Makes:** 2 servings

Ingredients:

- 3 kale leaves, roughly chopped
- 1-2 garlic cloves, thinly sliced
- 2 tablespoons olive oil
- ½ teaspoon Celtic sea salt, plus more if needed
- Cracked pepper
- 1 medium tomato, sliced
- 2-4 eggs

Method:

1. Chop the kale and set aside.
2. Heat the oil and garlic in a large skillet over medium heat for 2 minutes or until garlic is slightly browned.
3. Add the kale and lightly sauté just until the leaves are coated with oil and have softened slightly. Sprinkle with salt and cracked pepper and push the kale to the side of the skillet.
4. Lay the tomato slices in the pan, sprinkle with salt, and sauté for 30 seconds, turning once. Remove the kale from the pan and place the leaves on 2 separate plates. Lay the tomatoes on top of the kale.
5. Boil 3 cups water in a small pan. Gently crack the eggs into the water, carefully stirring the perimeter of the eggs to coagulate whites to poach. Using a slotted spoon, remove the eggs from the water and lay on a paper towel to drain excess water. Gently lay the eggs on top of the tomato. Sprinkle with salt and fresh cracked pepper.
6. Serve with avocado, fruit, and toast.

Wisdom from Laurie's Kitchen:

The energy that goes into the food in our cafes is what makes us successful. It stems from love, consideration, and commitment! Love because we love making delicious Basimo food. Consideration because we consider our sourcing and our ingredients. Commitment because we believe everybody deserves abundant health – and that is our commitment when we choose our ingredients and our methods of food preparation.

Turkish Menemen Egg Scramble

by Lisa Soldo-Johnson - USA

Breakfast is an essential part of the Turkish culture with individualized versions of Turkish Breakfast taking center stage at many Middle Eastern and Mediterranean breakfast tables across the globe. Menemen (men-EH'-me) is a traditional Turkish egg scramble made of fresh vegetables simmered in their juices and topped with scrambled eggs that naturally seep through the vegetable as they cook. The result is a juicy, flavorful Turkish inspired breakfast scramble that is easy to make, and your family will love.

Preparation Time: 10 minutes **Cook Time:** 20 minutes **Makes:** 4 servings

Ingredients:

- 6 tablespoons butter
- 1 large onion, diced
- 2 large tomatoes, chopped
- 1 red bell pepper, seeded and chopped
- 1 large Anaheim pepper, seeded and chopped
- 1 teaspoon salt
- ½ teaspoon black pepper
- ½ cup hot water
- 6 eggs
- Pinch of paprika

Method:

1. Melt the butter in a large skillet over medium heat. Sauté the onions 3 to 4 minutes or until translucent.
2. Stir in the tomatoes, red pepper, Anaheim pepper, salt, pepper, and water. Bring to a boil, cover, reduce the heat to medium-low and simmer 10 minute or until the peppers soften, stirring occasionally.
3. Meanwhile, scramble the eggs in a small bowl. Gently pour the eggs into the center of the vegetables without stirring. If needed, nudge the eggs to move through the vegetables by moving the pan around on the stove lightly. Add a pinch of paprika across the top of the eggs, cover, and simmer 8 to 10 minutes or until the eggs are cooked.

Wisdom from Lisa's Kitchen:

Serve Menemen as part of a Turkish breakfast or with bread and hot tea.

Did You Know?

Santa Claus is from Turkey. Born around 280 A.D. in Patara, near Myra in modern-day Turkey, a monk named St. Nicholas was born. He became famous for his piety and kindness; spending his inherited wealth helping the poor and sick.

Shakshouka

by Vivi Mizrahi - Israel

Shakshouka has a long, rich history, beginning hundreds of years ago in North Africa. It came to Israel through Maghrebi Jews who fled the country in the mid-20th century as part of the mass Jewish exodus from Arab and Muslim lands. Since then, this traditional poached egg dish has become a staple in Israeli and Arab cuisines, enjoyed for both breakfast and evening meals. You can prepare shakshouka in a variety of ways. Some Arab cultures include potatoes, beans, spicy sausage, a variety of spices, and other ingredients. While in Israel, some recipes are strictly vegetarian, adding more tomatoes, peppers, and spices. No matter how you prefer your shakshouka, the benefit of this dish is the simplicity of a one-pan meal that is healthy, delicious, and easy to prepare. For those who are gluten-free and dairy-free, this dish is perfect for you too!

Preparation Time: 10 minutes

Cook Time: 20 minutes

Makes: 3-6 servings

Ingredients:

- 2 tablespoons canola oil
- 1 cup onion, diced
- 1 medium red bell pepper, roughly chopped
- 1 medium orange bell pepper, roughly chopped
- 2 cups mushrooms, thinly sliced
- 2 cups diced tomatoes
- 2 tablespoons tomato paste
- 1 teaspoon paprika
- ¼ cup hot water
- Salt and pepper
- 6 eggs
- 1 tablespoon chopped parsley, for garnish

Method:

1. Heat the oil in a large skillet over medium heat. Sauté the onions for 3 to 4 minutes or until translucent.
2. Add the bell peppers and mushrooms, sautéing for 5 to 7 minutes until softened. Stir in the tomatoes.
3. Dissolve the tomato paste and paprika with the hot water and pour the liquid over the vegetables, stirring to combine. Simmer for 5 minutes or until the sauce begins to reduce. Add salt and pepper to taste.
4. Using the back of a spoon, create 6 evenly spaced ¼-inch divots in the sauce where the eggs will be placed. Gently crack eggs into the divots. Cover and lower the heat to medium-low and simmer until the egg whites have hardened — leaving the yolks soft. Garnish with parsley.
5. Serve by scooping around the eggs with a large spoon and lifting the vegetables, sauce, and eggs onto individual plates.
6. Serve with pita bread, cottage cheese, whole wheat toast, and seasonal fruit.

Energy Blast Breakfast Granola

by Lisa Soldo-Johnson - USA

I created Energy Blast Breakfast Granola as a simple solution to a healthy morning meal. Toss it into a bowl of yogurt, add it to oatmeal, enjoy it as a cereal with milk, or eat by itself. This mix travels well, too. Pack some in your kids' lunch box and bring a container to work for a healthy midday energy boost. Customize the recipe by using your favorite combination of fruits, nuts, and seeds. A quick and easy breakfast and snack solution rolled into one stellar batch of nutritious yumminess.

Preparation Time: 10 minutes **Bake Time:** 25 minutes **Makes:** 6 cups

Ingredients:

- 2 cups organic old-fashioned oats
- ½ cup almonds, whole or chopped
- ½ cup walnut, whole or chopped
- ½ cup Brazil nut, whole or chopped
- ½ cup cashews, whole or chopped
- 2 tablespoons pumpkin seeds
- 2 tablespoons pine nuts
- 2 tablespoons coconut oil, melted
- ⅓ cup coconut nectar
- 1 tablespoon Bourbon vanilla paste, Madagascar
- 1 tablespoon cinnamon
- 1 cup dried fruit, (apricots, raisins, cranberries, etc.)

Method:

1. Preheat the oven to 350°F.
2. Combine the oats, almonds, walnuts, Brazil nuts, cashews, pumpkin seeds, and pine nuts in a large bowl.
3. In a separate bowl, whisk the coconut oil, coconut nectar, vanilla bean paste, and cinnamon.
4. Pour the liquid over the nuts and seeds and stir until completely coated.
5. Pour the granola on to a baking tray and spread out evenly. Bake 20 to 25 minutes, turning granola half way through the baking process. The granola is done when it turns light golden brown. Remove granola from the oven and cool.
6. Stir in the dried fruit and transfer to an airtight container. Granola will keep in the refrigerator for up to 2 weeks.

Did You Know?

Pine nuts grow inside pine cones.

Popeye's Muscle Builder

by Jean-Marc Johnson - USA

My son, Jean-Marc, created this smoothie recipe using a few simple ingredients. The result was fantastic. He calls it Popeye's Muscle Builder because it includes L-glutamine, which promotes healthy muscle growth and decreases muscle waste. I'm very excited to include this recipe in my book, and even more pleased that my son created his first masterpiece in a glass!

Preparation Time: 5 minutes

Makes: 2 servings

Ingredients:

- 2 cups vanilla almond milk
- 1 banana, frozen
- 1 cup mango chunks, frozen
- 1 cup fresh spinach
- 2 Medjool date
- 1 tablespoon L-glutamine

Method:

1. Place all the ingredients in a blender and blend on high until smooth.

Elderberry Smoothie

by Lisa Soldo-Johnson - USA

I created this refreshing elderberry smoothie to add an extra boost of natural health to the day. Elderberries are a proven natural remedy for fighting off and shortening cold and flu symptoms and boosting the immune system. Use my freshly made elderberry syrup blended with dairy-free milk and fresh fruits for an enjoyable smoothie your entire family will love.

Preparation Time: 5 minutes

Makes: 2 servings

Ingredients:

- 4 cups vanilla almond milk
- 3 tablespoons almond or cashew butter
- 3 cups raspberries, fresh or frozen
- 1 medium ripe banana, fresh or frozen
- 2 Medjool dates
- 2 tablespoons lemon juice
- 4 tablespoons elderberry syrup (page 185)

Method:

1. Place all the ingredients in a blender and blend on high until smooth.

Wisdom from Lisa's Kitchen:

Elderberry syrup (page 185) is easy to make and often more affordable than in stores.

Creamy Chocolate Oat Milk and Turmeric Smoothie

by Lisa Soldo-Johnson - USA

I love to incorporate chocolate oat milk into my smoothies. The delicious dairy-free beverage blends beautifully with a variety of ingredients, including a powerful anti-inflammatory spice called turmeric. Many cultures around the world use turmeric in their foods for its aromatic flavor and healing benefits. Enjoying a glass of delicious health is one of my favorite ways to start the day.

Preparation Time: 5 minutes

Makes: 2 servings

Ingredients:

- 2 cups chocolate oat milk
- 2 frozen bananas
- 2 tablespoons almond butter
- 2 Medjool dates
- 1 teaspoon turmeric powder

Method:

1. Place all the ingredients in a blender and blend on high until smooth.

Wisdom from Lisa's Kitchen:

Chocolate oat milk is easy to make and can be used in a variety of recipes including smoothies, popsicles, baking, and more. Find my recipe for homemade chocolate oat milk on page (page 220).

CHAPTER 2

Small Bites

Aprah Du Zayto - Assyrian Stuffed Grape Leaves / 15

Zeytoon Parvardeh - Pomegranate Walnut Dip / 17

Shrimp and Egg Pot stickers / 19

Fresh Figs with Maple Bacon Glaze / 20

Bacon-Wrapped Medjool Dates / 21

The Perfect Hummus / 23

Persian Guacamole / 24

Borani-e esfanaj - Yogurt and Spinach Dip / 25

Warm Bacon Eggplant Dip / 27

Creamy Cashew Cheese / 29

Binge-Worthy Nut Brittle / 31

Persian Dolmas Stuffed Grape Leaves / 32

Wine & Herb Marinated Carrots / 35

Aprah Du Zayto - Assyrian Stuffed Grape Leaves

by Suheyla Kerkinni - Assyria

Everyone who eats a Suheyla's table will tell you that Aprah Du Zayto is one of her specialties. When Suheyla's stuffed grapes leaves make an appearance at any gathering, it's not long before they are gone. I especially love this vegetarian version of Assyrian stuffed grape leaves. She uses simple, uncomplicated ingredients like onions, rice, and tomato paste infused with herbs and spices tucked tightly into tender, juicy grape leaves to create a delightful appetizer or side dish.

Preparation Time: 30 minutes **Cooking Time:** 1 hour **Makes:** 12 servings

Ingredients:

- 10 cups water, divided
- 16-ounce jar grape leaves
- 3 medium onions, chopped
- ½ cup olive oil
- 1 6-ounce can tomato paste
- 1 teaspoon granulated sugar
- 1 tablespoon ground allspice
- ½ teaspoon cayenne pepper
- ¾ teaspoon salt
- ½ teaspoon pepper
- 2 cups long grain rice
- ⅓ cup lemon juice
- ¾ cup chopped parsley
- 2 ½ cups water, more as needed
- 1 lemon halved

Method:

1. In a medium saucepan, heat the oil over medium-high heat. Add the onions and sauté for 5 minutes or until the onions are translucent.
2. Add 2 ½ cups of water, tomato paste, sugar, allspice, cayenne pepper, salt and pepper. Bring to a boil.
3. Add the rice, then reduce the heat to medium-low and simmer until liquid is mostly absorbed. Stir frequently to prevent from sticking to pan.
4. Stir in lemon juice and parsley and remove from the heat to cool.
5. In a medium saucepan, bring 6 cups of water to a boil. Remove half of the grape leaves from the container and gently rinse under cold water to remove some of the salt. Gently unroll the leaves and carefully place them in boiling water for 2 minutes.
6. Using a slotted spoon, remove the grape leaves from the water and place them in a colander to drain and cool. Gently separate leaves one-by-one without breaking them. Drape around the edges of the colander until you are ready to use.
7. Cut off stems and place a vine leaf on a cutting board with the rough side up and the stem end facing you. Spoon one tablespoon of rice mixture across the leaf towards the stem end (adding a little more if leaf is large). Fold stem end over rice mixture and begin to roll slightly. Fold in sides of leaves to close rice into leaf, then begin rolling tightly to the top of leaf, making sure the sides stay tucked in. Repeat this process until all the leaves are filled.
8. In a medium non-stick pot, place a layer of grape leaves on the bottom of the pot before adding the Aprah to prevent any burning that may occur during the cooking process. Set (Aprah) rolled grape leaves on the bottom of the pot, layering them on top of each other until they are all in the pot. Pour 1 ½ cup water over grape leaves.

continued on next page →

9. Cut a piece of parchment paper the size of the pot and place it over the grape leaves. Set a plate on top of the paper to give it weight during the cooking process.
10. Cover the pot and cook on medium heat for 30 minutes or until all the liquid is absorbed. Be sure to add more water if it dries out during the cooking process.
11. When Aprah is tender, remove the pot from the heat and allow to cool in its covered pot for 2 hours or more.
12. Arrange Aprah on a serving platter and squeeze half of the lemon juice over the grape leaves. Slice the remaining lemon half and use to decorate the platter. Serve Aprah Du Zayto at room temperature.

 Wisdom from Suheyla's Kitchen:

The stuffing measurements will typically fill half of the leaves in a 16 ounce jar. You can double the stuffing recipe if you prefer to use all the leaves at one time or refrigerate remaining leaves in the container for up to 2 weeks.

Serve at room temperature as an appetizer or a side dish.

Zeytoon Parvardeh - Pomegranate Walnut Dip

by Sohiela Mirsharif - Iran

Zeytoon Parvardeh is a traditional Persian dip served as an appetizer or a side dish. The striking combination of earthy walnuts, salty olives, fresh herbs and spices tossed with sweet and sour pomegranate molasses pairs beautifully with bread and crackers, or as a complement to meat and rice.

Preparation Time: 20 minutes   **Bake Time:** 10 minutes   **Makes:** 4 servings

Ingredients:

- 1 cup walnuts, toasted and finely chopped
- 2 cups green pitted olives, finely chopped
- 4 cloves garlic, minced
- ½ cup fresh mint, finely chopped
- ¼ teaspoon golpar (Angelica)
- ½ teaspoon salt
- ½ teaspoon pepper
- 4 tablespoons pomegranate molasses (see recipe)
- ¼ cup pomegranate seeds

Method:

1. Preheat the oven to 350° F
2. Place the walnuts on a baking sheet and toast for 10 minutes. Transfer nuts to a cutting board to cool. Chop the nuts into small pieces and add them to a medium mixing bowl.
3. Add chopped olives, garlic, mint, golpar, salt and pepper. Toss together until well combined.
4. Spoon pomegranate molasses into olive mixture and stir until evenly coated. Cover and refrigerate overnight or until ready to serve.
5. Just before serving, stir in the pomegranate seeds, reserving a few as garnish.

Wisdom from Sohiela's kitchen:

Toasting the walnuts brings out the earthy flavor and reduces bitterness. Serve with lavash bread, crackers, or as a side dish to meats and rice.

Shrimp and Egg Pot stickers

by Rachel Huang - China

Throughout history, China reigns supreme for making some of the best pot stickers in the world. I have found that no matter which culture you are from, everyone loves a good pot sticker. When Rachel taught me how to make her shrimp and egg pot stickers, also known as Chinese dumplings, I knew it would be a family favorite. The combination of ingredients in this recipe are simple, light, and quite honestly, irresistible. Feel free to explore other combination of meat, seafood, and vegetables to create your own unique pot sticker dish.

Preparation Time: 30 minutes **Cooking Time:** 30 minutes **Makes:** 30 pot stickers

Ingredients:

- 3 large eggs, beaten
- 1 teaspoon salt, divided
- 2 tablespoons fresh chives, chopped
- 18 medium raw shrimp, chopped
- ¼ teaspoon white pepper
- 12 tablespoons olive oil
- 30 round Gyoza wrappers
- 1 cup water

Sauce:

- 2 tablespoons water
- 1 tablespoon oyster sauce
- ½ tablespoon soy sauce
- ¼ tablespoon granulated sugar
- ⅛ tablespoon fresh ginger
- ⅛ tablespoon sesame oil
- ⅛ tablespoon spicy chili oil

Wisdom from Rachel's Kitchen:

If you are entertaining, you can prepare the pot stickers ahead of time by assembling, laying flat on a tray, and refrigerating up to 24 hours or until you are ready to cook. However, pot stickers are best if cooked the same day, so the wrappers do not dry out.

Method:

Pot stickers:

1. Whisk the eggs and ⅛ teaspoon of salt together in a small bowl.
2. Heat the oil in a medium-size skillet over medium-high heat. Pour the eggs into the skillet and scramble lightly. Transfer the eggs to a cutting board, chopping them into small pieces. Transfer the eggs to a medium bowl and set aside.
3. Add the chives, shrimp, and remaining ½ teaspoon salt, and pepper to the bowl and toss lightly with a fork.
4. Lay out the Gyoza (dumpling) wrappers on a flat surface. Place 1 tablespoon of the filling in the center of each Gyoza wrapper, being careful not to add too much filling or the wrappers will not close properly.
5. Working quickly and using your finger, moisten the edges of each wrapper with water. Fold each wrapper in half over the filling and press the edges closed to seal. Finish by pinch-pleating the edges together (making sure there are no gaps or openings around the edges). Lightly flatten the bottom of each pot sticker on your work surface so they will stand up inside the pan when searing.
6. Heat the oil in a non-stick pan over medium heat. Set the pot stickers in the oil standing up. Brown the bottoms of the pot stickers for 2 minutes or until the bottoms are lightly golden.
7. Pour in ⅓ cup water, cover and increase the heat to medium-high, steaming for 3 to 6 minutes or until the wrappers are soft and evenly cooked.
8. Gently remove the pot stickers from the pan and arrange on a plate and serve with Rachel's Secret Sauce (page 182) or soy sauce.

Sauce:

1. Whisk the oyster sauce, soy sauce, granulated sugar, fresh ginger, sesame oil, and spicy chili oil in a small bowl and serve with pot stickers.

Fresh Figs with Maple Bacon Glaze

by Lisa Soldo-Johnson - USA

When fresh figs are in season and I am entertaining, this appetizer is usually cooking in my kitchen. The combination of sweet maple glaze and salty smoked bacon spooned over fresh, soft, sweet figs is surprisingly easy to make and impressive when served. For a beautifully colorful presentation, I recommend using both purple and green figs when available. Undoubtedly, this is a beautiful dish that gets rave reviews every time it is served.

Preparation Time: 10 minutes   **Cooking Time:** 15 minutes   **Makes:** 12 servings

Ingredients:

- 24 fresh figs, purple and green
- ¼-pound hickory smoked bacon
- 3 tablespoons bacon drippings
- ¼ cup light olive oil
- ½ cup green onions, chopped
- ¼ cup rice wine vinegar
- 4 tablespoons organic maple syrup
- 1 teaspoon Dijon mustard
- 1 teaspoon salt
- ½ teaspoon ground black pepper

Method:

1. Fry the bacon in a large skillet over medium-high heat until it is pliable but not crispy. Remove the bacon from pan and place on a paper towel. Reserve 3 tablespoons of bacon grease for the glaze and discard the rest.

2. Using the same skillet, add the reserved bacon grease, olive oil, and scallions. Sauté over low heat for 30 seconds. Whisk in the vinegar, syrup, mustard, salt, and pepper and continue to simmer for 1 minute. While the glaze is simmering, chop the bacon into small pieces and add to the glaze, stirring to combine. Remove the skillet from the heat and transfer contents to a serving bowl to cool.

3. Starting at the top, cut each fig crosswise towards its base without cutting through the fruit. Leave ½ inch uncut at the bottom. Arrange the figs on a serving platter and carefully peel open each fig to make room for the glaze.

4. Just before serving, stir the glaze and lightly spoon 1 teaspoon of glaze mixture inside and over each fig. Serve immediately.

Wisdom from Lisa's Kitchen:

Serve figs with blue cheese, goat cheese or your favorite soft cheese and crackers.

Bacon-Wrapped Medjool Dates

by Laurie Kerkinni -USA

I'm a huge fan of salty and sweet, especially when it comes to finger foods. Laurie's bacon wrapped Medjool dates have found a permanent place as my go-to appetizer when I need a quick and easy dish. Tender Medjool dates stuffed with a crunchy almond and creamy gorgonzola cheese wrapped in salty bacon is as drool-worthy as it sounds. I recommend making a double batch because they won't last long on the plate.

Preparation Time: 15 minutes **Cooking Time:** 30 minutes **Makes:** 12 servings

Ingredients:

- 12 Medjool dates, pitted
- 12 almonds
- 12 pieces of dolce gorgonzola cheese, ½-inch cubes
- 6 slices nitrate-free bacon

Method:

1. Preheat the oven to 350° F.
2. Place one almond and one cube of cheese inside each pitted date.
3. Wrap halved bacon slice around date width-wise, overlapping the ends and securing with a toothpick.
4. Lay the dates in a glass baking dish with the toothpick pointing up.
5. Bake for 30 minutes or until the bacon is crispy. Serve warm as an appetizer or dessert with tea.

Wisdom from Laurie's Kitchen:

The best time of year to prepare this appetizer is when the dates are harvested domestically. Harvest time in the United States runs from October through January.

You can prepare the dates ahead of time and bake them shortly before they are ready to be served.

The Perfect Hummus

by Laurie Kerkinni - USA

Hummus is a healthy plant-based protein-packed dip created with chickpeas and tahini. It has been made by cultures around the world for centuries. The approach to making the perfect hummus is as unique as the person who creates it. Laurie makes her dip using organic garbanzo beans and tahini, plenty of fresh garlic, and a precise balance of lemon juice and seasoning. The secret to perfect hummus is adjusting the ingredients until you achieve the ideal balance of flavor and texture. Though it takes a bit of practice, the results are well worth it!

Preparation Time: 15 minutes

Makes: 4 cups

Ingredients:

- 2 (15.5-ounce) can garbanzo beans, drained (organic)
- ½ cup tahini, raw or toasted
- 8-12 cloves fresh garlic, minced
- 3 tablespoons extra virgin olive oil, cold pressed
- 2-3 lemons, juiced
- 1 ½ teaspoons cumin powder
- ¼ teaspoon cayenne pepper
- 2-5 teaspoons Himalayan or Celtic salt
- ½ teaspoon fresh cracked pepper

Method:

1. Place the drained beans in a food processor with the tahini and ¼ cup warm water. Pulse a few times to lightly combine ingredients. Add in 6 minced garlic cloves and process on high until the beans become creamy.
2. Leaving the food processor running, drizzle in the olive oil, juice from 2 lemons, 1 teaspoon cumin, cayenne pepper, and 2 teaspoons salt. Stop the machine and taste the hummus. To adjust the flavor, blend in the remaining salt, garlic, and lemon juice, adjusting the measurements as desired. Add the cracked pepper and blend on high until the hummus is very creamy.
3. Serve with preservative-free pita bread or pita chips, corn chips, or vegetables.

Wisdom from Laurie's Kitchen:

This is a recipe you must create to taste by gradually adding the ingredients. Some lemons hold more juice while some are tarter. Garlic can be potent or mild, and cumin powders vary in quality and flavor. The final flavor should make *you* want to keep eating it. That's when you know it's right.

Garbanzo beans and chickpeas are used interchangeably but are the exact same legume.

Persian Guacamole

by Sohiela Mirsharif - Iran

Sohiela introduced me to her Persian Guacamole during a dinner gathering at her home. I instantly fell in love with her unique approach to guacamole. The combination of fresh Anaheim pepper and fragrant basil paired with tender mozzarella introduces an unusual, new taste and texture experience to this classic dip.

Preparation Time: 10 minutes

Makes: 6 servings

Ingredients:

- 4 ripe avocados, cut into 1-inch cubes
- 1 cup mozzarella cheese, cut into ½-inch cubes
- 16 large basil leaves, chopped
- 1 Anaheim pepper, seeded and diced
- 2 tablespoons fresh lime juice
- 1 teaspoon salt

Method:

1. Place avocados in a medium bowl. Using a large fork, mash the avocado into small chunks.
2. Add the mozzarella cheese, basil leaves, Anaheim pepper, lime juice and salt. Stir to combine the ingredients. Squeeze extra lime juice on the top to prevent it from turning brown.
3. Cover and refrigerate until you are ready to serve.

Wisdom from Sohiela's kitchen:

Serve with pita bread, corn or flour chips, tacos, or as a side to fish or meat.

Borani-e esfanaj - Yogurt and Spinach Dip

by Sohiela Mirsharif - Iran

I've made Sohiela's Borani-e esfanaj many times when I am hosting a get-together. The simplicity of fresh, healthy spinach, cucumbers, and yogurt takes only minutes to assemble and is a crowd-pleaser every time.

Preparation Time: 10 minutes **Cook Time:** 10 minutes **Makes:** 4 servings

Ingredients:

- 12 cups fresh spinach
- 2 cups plain Greek yogurt
- 1 teaspoon salt
- ½ teaspoon black pepper
- 4 small Persian cucumbers, peeled and finely chopped

Method:

1. Place the spinach in a steamer. Cover and steam the spinach for 5 minutes or until completely wilted.
2. Pour spinach into a colander to drain the water allowing it to cool to the touch.
3. Using your hands, squeeze the spinach a few portions at a time to remove as much of the liquid as possible.
4. Lay the spinach on a cutting board, chopping it into ½ inch pieces before transferring it to a bowl.
5. Add in yogurt, salt and pepper, stirring the mixture until the dip is well combined. Adjust the seasoning to your taste, cover, and refrigerate until you are ready to serve.
6. In a separate bowl, add the cucumbers, cover and refrigerate.
7. Just before serving, drain any liquid from the cucumbers and stir into the dip. Spoon the Borani-e esfanaj into a beautiful serving bowl and serve.

Wisdom from Sohiela's Kitchen:

Adding the cucumbers just before serving keeps them crisp and prevents excess liquid from forming.

Serve with pita bread, chips, vegetables, or as a side to rice and meat.

Use as a stuffing for chicken breasts or fish.

Warm Bacon Eggplant Dip

by Lisa Soldo-Johnson - USA

When I think of a warm bacon dip, winter comfort food usually comes to mind. That was until I created this bacon eggplant dip in the summer and comfort food took on a whole new season. Maybe it's the combination of tender eggplant, salty bacon, and sweet shallots paired with a freshly baked loaf of bread and a favorite glass of wine enjoyed over a beautiful summer sunset that speaks to me. Whatever the season, I hope you find this recipe as comforting and delicious as I do.

Preparation Time: 15 minutes   **Cook Time:** 30 minutes   **Makes:** 5 servings

Ingredients:

- 1 large eggplant, peeled and diced into ½-inch pieces
- 7-8 slices bacon
- 1 medium shallot, minced
- ¾ teaspoon garlic powder
- ½ teaspoon sea salt
- ½ teaspoon black pepper
- 4 tablespoons olive oil, plus more if needed.

Method:

1. Fry the bacon in a single layer in a large skillet over medium heat until soft-cooked. Transfer the cooked bacon on to a paper towel to drain, reserving the bacon fat in the pan.
2. Add the olive oil, eggplant and shallots to the bacon fat and cook until the eggplant becomes soft, adding more oil if needed to prevent the eggplant from sticking to the pan.
3. While the eggplant is cooking, cut the bacon strips into ½ inch pieces, removing and discarding any large fatty areas. Add the bacon back into the skillet and toss together. Continue to cook until the eggplant is very soft.
4. Sprinkle in garlic powder, salt and pepper, tossing until the mixture is evenly combined.
5. Serve hot with crackers, bread, as a topping over steak, eggs, or use as desired.

Wisdom from Lisa's Kitchen:
This dip makes a wonderful stuffing for chicken, fish or meats.

Creamy Cashew Cheese

by Lisa Soldo-Johnson - USA

Many years ago, I learned to make nut cheese, and it is still one of my favorite dairy-free recipes. Cashews, in my opinion, make the most delicious nut cheese of all. Unlike almonds or other hard nuts, you don't have to pre-soak cashews, and they quickly process into a smooth, creamy spread that is ready to eat in under 10 minutes.

Preparation Time: 10 minutes

Makes: 1 ½ cups

Ingredients:

- 2 cups raw cashews, unsalted
- 1 tablespoon lemon juice, freshly squeezed
- 1-½ teaspoon sea salt
- ½ - ¾ cup filtered water

Method:

1. Add the cashews, lemon juice, salt, and water to a high-speed blender. Process on high until creamy.
2. Serve with chips, crackers, vegetables, and pita bread. Refrigerate up to one week.

Wisdom from Lisa's Kitchen:

Cashew cheese makes a delicious gluten-free, dairy-free sauce for pizza.

Did You Know?

Cashews have a poisonous shell to prevent animals and pesticides from consuming the cashew still on the fruit. Roasting the cashews destroys the toxins, making them edible and delicious.

Binge-Worthy Nut Brittle

by Laurie Kerkinni - USA

You will understand why I named Laurie's nut brittle, "binge-worthy" as soon as you taste it! The combination of crunchy nuts and dried fruits dehydrated in a sweet cinnamon honey glaze is divine. The recipe makes 16 cups of nut brittle but believe me: the mix will be gone long before you wish it were. Consider making a double batch the second time around.

Soaking Time: 10 hours
Preparation Time: 15 minutes
Dehydrating Time: 72 hours
Makes: approximately 16 cups

Ingredients:

- 4 cups almonds, soaked
- 3 cups pecans, soaked
- 3 cups organic sulfite-free raisins, soaked
- 2 bags frozen cranberries, soaked
- 3 cups organic pumpkin seeds
- 1 ½ cups unsweetened organic coconut flakes
- 1 tablespoon Vietnamese cinnamon
- 1 teaspoon salt
- 4 cups solid honey (not liquid)

Method:

1. Place the almonds in a bowl with 6 cups of filtered water to soak on the counter overnight. Drain and remove the skins from half of the almonds by pinching nut to slide them off.
2. Place pecans in separate small bowl with 3 cups of water to soak for 4 hours. Drain, rinse, and set aside.
3. Place raisins and cranberries together in 3 cups of water to soak for 4 hours. Drain, and set aside.
4. Place pumpkin seeds in a bowl with 1 cup of water to soak for 2 hours. Drain and set aside.
5. Place almonds, pecans, raisins, cranberries, pumpkin seeds, and coconut flakes in a large bowl and stir to combine.
6. Add honey, cinnamon and salt, stirring to combine.
7. Using a dehydrator, set the temperature to 115°F/46°C. Using 4-5 Teflex-lined dehydrator trays, spread the nut brittle over each sheet covering most of the tray, but not to the ends. To prevent brittle from sticking together, be sure to separate pieces so they do not touch while dehydrating.
8. After 24 hours, remove the Teflex sheet and place the nut brittle back on screened trays. Continue to dehydrate an additional 48 hours. Remove the trays from the dehydrator, allowing them cool. Store the nut brittle in glass jars and store in a cool dark place.

Wisdom from Laurie's Kitchen:

Since this delicious nut brittle takes a few days to make, I make a double batch because it disappears so quickly.

You can also make nut brittle in the oven by baking it on the lowest oven temperature for 6 to 8 hours or more depending on how dry you like your fruit.

Persian Dolmas Stuffed Grape Leaves

by Mitra Murphy - Iran

Dolmas are a traditional appetizer or side dish served in Iran. The flavor and ingredients of dolmas can vary depending on the region and individual family recipe. Mitra's version of Persian stuffed grape leaves incorporates a delightful balance of ground beef and onions infused with the flavors of aromatic herbs. This deliciousness is tucked into tender grape leaves and topped with zesty tomato sauce. Dolmas pair beautifully with basmati rice, cucumber yogurt salad, kabobs, or served as a hearty appetizer.

Preparation Time: 45 minutes   **Cooking Time:** 40 minutes   **Makes:** 12 servings

Ingredients:

- 3 tablespoons olive oil
- 1 medium onion, thinly sliced
- 1-pound ground beef, 85% lean/15% fat
- 1 cup beef broth
- 32-ounces tomato sauce, divided
- ¼ teaspoon turmeric
- ½ teaspoon salt
- ¼ teaspoon pepper
- 8 tablespoons lime juice, divided
- 1 cup basmati rice, rinsed
- 1 tablespoon dried savory
- ¼ cup fresh tarragon, chopped or 1 tablespoon dried
- 1 bunch parsley, finely chopped
- 1 bunch cilantro, finely chopped
- 1 bunch green onions, finely chopped
- 16-ounce jar grape leaves
- ¼ cup granulated sugar

Method:

1. Heat the oil in large non-stick pot or skillet over medium-high heat. Sauté the onions until they are slightly translucent. Add ground beef and continue to sauté until lightly browned.
2. Stir in beef broth, 16 ounces of the tomato sauce, turmeric, salt, pepper, 4 tablespoons of lime juice and rice, stirring to combine.
3. Stir in savory, tarragon, parsley, cilantro, and scallions, mixing thoroughly. Reduce the heat to medium-low and cook for 20 to 30 minutes or until the rice is al dente. Stir often during the cooking process so the stuffing does not stick to the bottom of the pot. Remove the pot from the heat and set aside.

Assembly:

1. Gently rinse 24 grape leaves under cold water to remove excess salt. Cut off the short stem from each leaf and lay the leaves over the edge of a large bowl to separate and make it easier to assemble dolmas.
2. Lay a grape leaf onto a cutting board with the rough side up and the stem end towards your body. Spoon 2 teaspoons of stuffing mixture onto the leaf close to the stem end (add a little more if the leaf is large). Fold ½ inch of the stem end over the rice mixture, rolling slightly before folding in the sides, then continue to roll to the end of the leaf. Set aside on a plate and continue until all the filling is used.
3. In medium non-stick pot, place a few grapes leaves flat on the bottom of the pan. Lay the stuffed grape leaves on the bottom, layering them on top of each other until they are all in the pot.
4. In small bowl, whisk remaining 16 ounces of tomato sauce and remaining 4 tablespoons of lime juice with sugar. Pour tomato sauce over the grape leaves, cover, and simmer on medium-low heat for 20 minutes or until the grape leaves and rice are tender. Check occasionally and add more tomato sauce, beef broth or water if

needed to keep the liquid from evaporating. Make sure not to overcook the dolmas or the tomato sauce will burn. Serve warm or refrigerate to serve cold.

Wisdom from Mitra's Kitchen:

Serve as an appetizer, side or main dish with meat and salad.

Pots and cooktops vary and can affect the cooking time, so adjust accordingly.

Adding a layer of grape leaves to the bottom of the pot before the dolmas prevents any burning that may occur during the cooking process.

Refrigerate extra grape leaves in its jar for up to one month.

Wine & Herb Marinated Carrots

by Lisa Soldo-Johnson - USA

Wine and Herb Marinated Carrots have always been one of my favorite vegetable appetizers. The herb-infused wine and mustard marinade permeates the carrots to create an irresistible pickled flavor that is hard to stop eating. They also make an excellent complement for sandwiches, chopped and tossed into a salad, or as a delicious, healthy midday snack.

Preparation Time: 20 minutes   **Cooking Time:** 20 minutes   **Makes:** 12 servings

Ingredients:

- 6 large carrots, cut into ¼-inch matchsticks, 3-inches long
- 1 cup dry white wine
- 1 cup white wine vinegar
- ½ cup water
- ¼ cup olive oil
- 1 tablespoon granulated sugar
- 1 teaspoon salt
- 2 bay leaves
- ¼ cup chopped fresh oregano, or 1 teaspoon dried
- ¼ cup chopped fresh parsley
- 1 large garlic clove, minced
- ¼ teaspoon red pepper flakes
- 1 tablespoon honey mustard

Method:

1. Heat the white wine, white wine vinegar, water, olive oil, sugar, salt, bay leaves, oregano, parsley, garlic, and red pepper in a saucepan over medium-high heat. Cover and bring to a boil, lower heat and simmer for 10 minutes.
2. While the marinade is simmering, prepare the carrots by peeling and cutting them into ¼ inch matchsticks, 3 inches long.
3. Using a mesh strainer over a medium bowl, pour the marinade into the strainer, pressing the herbs with a spoon to strain out excess liquid. Return the liquid to the saucepan and whisk in the honey mustard.
4. Gently lay the carrot sticks into the saucepan, submerging them into the liquid as much as possible. Cover the pot and bring carrots to a simmer over medium-high heat for 10 minutes or until they are crisp but tender.
5. Using a slotted spoon, remove the carrots from the liquid and transfer them to an airtight container. Pour the liquid over the carrots and once cooled, cover and refrigerate overnight to marinate.
6. Bring carrots to room temperature, drain liquid, and serve as an appetizer or snack.

Wisdom from Lisa's Kitchen:

You can prepare the carrots and marinate them in the refrigerator for up to two weeks, making it a perfect menu item to serve at an upcoming gathering or enjoy as a daily snack.

CHAPTER 3

Salads and Soups

Arugula with Garlic, Ginger, and Tamari Mushrooms / 39

Sweet Mediterranean Herb Salad / 40

Israeli Tabouli / 41

Asian Coleslaw / 43

Cruciferous Salad with Creamy Poppy Seed Dressing / 45

1938 Tender Leaf Lettuce with Warm Bacon Vinaigrette / 46

Pomegranate Seasonal Salad / 47

Lentil Salad with Pomegranate Dressing / 49

Salad Shirazi / 51

Kale Caesar Salad with Pomegranate / 52

Spicy Fish and Seafood Soup / 55

Now, *This* is Chicken Noodle Soup! / 56

Clo Hay Red Lentil Soup / 57

Tlavhe Red Lentil Soup / 59

Albondigas - Mexican Meatball Soup / 61

Ashe Berenj - Persian Rice Soup / 63

Ten-Minute Egg Drop Soup / 65

Arugula with Garlic, Ginger, and Tamari Mushrooms

by Laurie Kerkinni - USA

The earthy combination of garlic, ginger, and tamari-soaked mushrooms create a beautiful balance of autumn flavors next to a bed of peppery arugula and gritty Parmigiano-Reggiano. The pungent taste of these mushrooms is incredibly versatile and pair nicely with grilled steak or fish, in a stir fry, or as a topping with mashed potatoes and gravy. The possibilities are endless.

Preparation Time: 10 minutes   **Passive Time:** 30 minutes   **Makes:** 4 servings

Ingredients:

- 4 cups arugula lettuce
- 2 large Portobello mushrooms, sliced ¼-inch (or 1 cup small Portobello's, sliced)
- 6 tablespoons olive oil, plus 1 teaspoon, separated
- 2 tablespoons tamari
- 1-2 minced garlic cloves
- 3 teaspoons freshly grated ginger
- Parmigiano-Reggiano, grated or slivered over the salad
- ½ teaspoon coarse sea salt

Method:

1. Whisk together the tamari, garlic, ginger, and 6 tablespoons olive oil in a medium bowl. Add the mushrooms and coat them with the sauce. Marinate for 30 minutes, coating the mushrooms with the sauce as it marinates.
2. Just before serving, add the arugula to a mixing bowl and drizzle remaining 1 teaspoon olive oil. Sprinkle salt over the lettuce before tossing. Separate the arugula into individual bowls or on a large serving platter.
3. Gently lay the mushrooms on the side of the arugula, being careful not to break the mushrooms.
4. Shred desired amount of the parmesan over the top of the lettuce and mushrooms. Serve immediately or chill until ready to serve.

Sweet Mediterranean Herb Salad

by Lisa Soldo-Johnson - USA

This classic salad combines tender lettuce, creamy goat cheese, crunchy candied pecans, and sweet fresh figs tossed in a light agave dressing. When fresh figs are out of season, replace them with pears, mandarin oranges, raspberries, or your favorite fruit.

Preparation Time: 15 minutes   **Cooking Time:** 15 minutes   **Makes:** 4 servings

Ingredients:

- 4 cups baby mixed greens, roughly chopped
- 1 cup whole pecans
- 2 tablespoons butter
- 2 tablespoons light brown sugar
- 8 fresh figs, quartered
- 8 slices goat cheese rounds
- 3 tablespoons fresh tarragon, chopped
- ¼ cup light olive oil
- 2 tablespoons agave nectar
- ½ teaspoon sea salt
- ½ teaspoon fresh cracked pepper

Method:

1. To make the candied pecans, melt the butter in a small non-stick pan over medium heat. Stir in the brown sugar until dissolved. Add pecans and stir until they are evenly coated with the glaze. Spread the pecans on parchment paper to cool. Be sure the nuts are spread out, so they do not touch each other.
2. Wash and roughly chop the lettuce leaves and transfer to a large serving platter.
3. Alternate the figs and goat cheese around the perimeter of the platter, reserving some of the figs for the top.
4. Sprinkle the candied pecans and tarragon over the salad. Cover and refrigerate until ready to serve.
5. Whisk the olive oil, agave nectar, salt, and pepper in a small bowl. Drizzle the dressing over the salad just before it is served. Pour extra dressing in a serving dish to serve on the side.

Wisdom from Lisa's Kitchen:

You can prepare the salad and dressing up to 4 hours in advance if kept tightly covered and refrigerated.

Did You Know?

Figs are actually flowers from the fig tree turned inside out. The seeds inside the fig are hundreds of little flowers.

Israeli Tabouli

by Vivi Mizrahi - Israel

Tabouli is a classic Mediterranean salad made for centuries throughout the world. Like the variation of spellings (Tabbouleh, Tabouleh, or Tabouli), many cultures have adapted their favorite ingredients to use in this dish. Vivi makes her tabouli using bulgur wheat with fresh vegetables and a touch of lemon juice and sea salt. The balance of flavors in her recipe makes a delicious side with meat and rice, or as a light salad.

Preparation Time: 15 minutes   **Passive Time:** 1 hour   **Makes:** 6 servings

Ingredients:

Salad:
- 1 cup bulgur wheat, soaked
- 3 Roma tomatoes, chopped
- 3 green onions, chopped
- 1-½ bunches parsley, finely chopped
- 1 large English cucumber, peeled and chopped, or 6 small Persian cucumbers
- ⅓ cup olive oil
- 4-5 tablespoons lemon juice, more if desired
- 1-½ teaspoons salt

Method:

1. Rinse and soak bulgur in 3 cups of boiling water in a small bowl for 1 hour. Strain water from the bulgur and transfer to a medium bowl to cool.
2. Add the bulgur, tomatoes, green onions, cucumbers, and parsley, tossing to combine.
3. Whisk the lemon juice, salt, and olive oil in a small bowl. Pour the dressing over the tabouli and toss until the salad is evenly coated. Refrigerate for at least 1 hour before serving.

Wisdom from Vivi's Kitchen:

Prepare the tabouli up to 3 hours before you plan to serve it. The flavors in this salad enhance as it marinates in the refrigerator.

Asian Coleslaw

by Lisa Soldo-Johnson - USA

Growing up in the Midwestern United States, you could always count on coleslaw showing up on the menu during summer picnics. Eventually, this favorite shredded cabbage dish became a bit predictable, and it was time for a change. Asian coleslaw explodes with fresh, crunchy vegetables and sweet Asian vinegar dressing that brings a whole new experience to this beloved American classic salad.

Preparation Time: 20 minutes

Makes: 4-6 servings

Ingredients:

- 2 cups green cabbage, thinly shredded
- 2 cups red cabbage, thinly shredded
- 1 red bell pepper, finely sliced
- ½ cup carrots, thinly shredded
- 15 snow pea pods, thinly sliced
- ½ cup cilantro, chopped
- 2 green onions, chopped
- 1 teaspoon Nigella seeds
- ½ cup avocado oil
- ¼ cup rice vinegar
- ½ teaspoon fresh grated ginger
- ¼ teaspoon sea salt
- ¼ teaspoon cane sugar
- ¼ teaspoon crushed red pepper

Method:

1. Toss the cabbage, bell pepper, carrots, snow pea pods, cilantro, onions, and nigella seeds in a large bowl.
2. Whisk the avocado oil, rice vinegar, ginger, salt, pepper, and red pepper in a small bowl. Pour the dressing over the salad and toss until evenly coated. Sprinkle Nigella seeds and gently toss once more before serving.

Wisdom from Lisa's Kitchen:

You can prepare the salad up to a day in advance and add the dressing right before it is served.

Did You Know?

You can dye Easter eggs blue by boiling 4 cups of water with 1 cup of red cabbage. Once the water is cooled, add 2 tablespoons of white vinegar and soak the eggs until you achieve the shade you prefer.

Cruciferous Salad with Creamy Poppy Seed Dressing

by Laurie Kerkinni - USA

This creamy dairy-free cruciferous salad is one of my favorite recipes to make when I need a crowd-pleaser. The combination of shaved Brussels sprouts, broccoli, kale, dried cranberries, and a lightly sweet dairy-free poppy seed dressing is a surprisingly delightful combination. The beauty of this salad is how well it keeps in the refrigerator for 2 to 3 days. If you are having a dinner party or want to prepare the family dinner ahead of time, this is the perfect salad. Add the dressing just before serving.

Preparation Time: 20 minutes

Makes: 6-8 servings

Ingredients:

- 4 cups broccoli florets, shredded
- 8 brussels sprouts, shredded
- 6 kale leaves, shredded
- ¾ cup dried cranberries
- 1 tablespoon olive oil
- 3 cups Vegenaise
- 3 tablespoons Grade B pure maple syrup
- 1 tablespoon apple cider vinegar
- 1 tablespoon poppy seed
- ¾ teaspoon sea salt

Method:

1. Cut florets from stalks and thinly slice the stems and head using a sharp knife. Transfer to a large bowl.
2. Cut off the butt end of the Brussels sprouts, removing and discarding the bruised or yellowed outer leaves. Slice the Brussels sprouts thinly and add to the bowl.
3. Chop the kale leaves and stems finely into small bite-size pieces, adding to the bowl.
4. Sprinkle cranberries over the greens and drizzle the oil over the salad before tossing to lightly coat the leaves evenly.
5. Whisk the Vegenaise, syrup, vinegar, poppy seed, and salt in a small bowl. Pour the dressing over the salad and toss. Refrigerate until ready to use.

Wisdom from Laurie's Kitchen:

You can prepare the salad without the dressing the day before you plan to serve it, then add the dressing just before you are ready to enjoy it.

Store the dressing in a container and only use the amount needed for the quantity of salad you are serving. Store the dressing in the refrigerator for up to 5 days.

You can use balsamic vinegar or champagne vinegar in place of apple cider vinegar.

The dressing makes a great sauce for grilled or fresh vegetables, fish, and tacos.

Did You Know?

The best time to eat kale is after the first frost because the flavor profile is at its best.

Natural foods that stay fresh the longest are usually the healthiest for you.

1938 Tender Leaf Lettuce with Warm Bacon Vinaigrette

by Lorraine Soldo - USA

My mother often made this salad for us growing up. It was one of her favorites because this tender salad brought back the endearing food nostalgia of her childhood growing up on a farm during the Great Depression. In those days, food was scarce, and her family felt blessed to have it. Meals involved simple dishes made from honest ingredients and not a lot of fuss. Nothing was wasted, not even the oil from the bacon which was used to make the dressing for this salad. Sometimes the best recipes are born within the boundaries or our resources and a generous sprinkle of imagination.

Preparation Time: 15 minutes   **Cooking Time:** 15 minutes   **Makes:** 4 servings

Ingredients:

- 16 leaves, butter leaf lettuce
- 2 green onions, chopped
- 5 pieces nitrate-free bacon
- ¼ cup bacon fat
- ¼ cup white vinegar
- ¼ cup water
- ¼ cup granulated sugar

Method:

1. Heat a skillet over medium heat and fry the bacon until slightly crispy. Drain on a paper towel. Turn off heat and leave the bacon fat in the pan to make the dressing.
2. Rinse, pat dry, and tear lettuce leaves into small bite-size pieces. Transfer to a serving bowl.
3. Chop the bacon into ½-inch pieces, adding them to the salad along with the chopped onions.
4. Return the skillet to medium-high heat. Whisk in the vinegar, water, and sugar until the sugar is dissolved. Bring to a boil for 1 minute and remove the pan from the heat. Spoon 4 to 5 tablespoons of dressing over the lettuce and toss to coat evenly. Add more dressing if desired. Refrigerate the remaining dressing for up to 5 days.

Wisdom from Lorraine's Kitchen:

You can prepare the salad without the dressing ahead of time and refrigerate until ready to serve. Warm the dressing right before adding to the salad.

Did You Know?

In 1938, the Nestle's Crunch candy bar was invented.

Hershey's Krackel bar and Mott's Apple Juice were both introduced to the market.

Pomegranate Seasonal Salad

by Ameneh Gounilli - Iran

Pomegranate Seasonal salad is a flavorful combination of crisp romaine lettuce, juicy pomegranate seeds, a sprinkle of fresh dill, and a splash of lemon juice, and olive oil. What I love about Ameneh's approach to salad is her technique in cutting and washing the lettuce. The result is always clean, crisp lettuce leaves that highlight the flavors in the dish.

Preparation Time: 15 minutes

Makes: 4-6 servings

Ingredients:

- 3 large heads Romaine lettuce
- ½ cup pomegranate seeds
- 3 tablespoons fresh dill, roughly chopped
- 3.5-ounces fresh lemon juice
- 2.5-ounces light olive oil
- ¾-teaspoon sea salt
- Cracked pepper

Method:

1. Remove and discard the butt end and the outer layer of the Romaine lettuce. Cut the lettuce into 1 inch pieces, slicing across the lettuce. Transfer it to a large bowl filled with cold water reaching just above the lettuce. Move the lettuce back and forth to remove any dirt or debris and pour the leaves and water through a colander to remove excess water. Transfer the lettuce into a salad spinner to remove as much water as possible. Pour the lettuce into a large serving bowl.
2. Add the pomegranate seeds and dill to the top of the salad.
3. Squeeze the lemon juice over the salad and top with olive oil and salt. Toss the salad until evenly coated.

Wisdom from Ameneh's Kitchen:

Remove and discard all the outer leaves of the lettuce until you reach the younger unblemished ones. These are the leaves that make your salad taste fresh and flavorful.

I like to prepare my lettuce by cutting and rinsing it in a bowl because it creates a crisp, cold salad with excellent texture and taste.

Did You Know?

Turmeric is the ingredient in curry that gives it a vibrant yellow color.

Turmeric can help decrease inflammation.

Consider using turmeric for cake frosting and other food needing yellow coloring. The artificial food coloring, Yellow #5, is derived from petroleum making turmeric a much healthier option for adding color to your food.

Lentil Salad with Pomegranate Dressing

by Suheyla Kerkinni - Assyria

Lentil salad with pomegranate dressing is a gorgeous legume salad made from tender lentils, fresh vegetables and herbs, and a sweet, tangy pomegranate dressing that turns up the flavor and gives your taste buds reason to celebrate. I like to serve this dish with chicken, fish, or meat while enjoying the leftovers the following day for a light and flavorful lunch.

Preparation Time: 15 minutes **Cook Time:** 30-45 minutes **Makes:** 12 servings

Ingredients:

Salad:

- ¾ cups green lentils
- 3 medium tomatoes, diced and drained
- 1 Anaheim pepper, diced
- ½ red pepper, diced
- ¼ cup chopped yellow onions
- 1 avocado, diced
- ½ cup basil, chopped
- ½ cup parsley, chopped
- ½ cup mint, chopped
- ½ cup dill, chopped
- 4 green onions, chopped

Dressing:

- 4 tablespoons olive oil
- 4 tablespoons fresh lemon juice
- 4 tablespoons pomegranate molasses
- ¼ teaspoon cayenne pepper (optional)
- 1 teaspoon sea salt
- ½ teaspoon black pepper

Method:

1. Boil the lentils in a pan of water 1 inch above them for 5 minutes. Reduce the heat to medium-low, cover, and simmer until tender. (Cooking time can range between 30 to 45 minutes, depending on the age and variety of lentils you use.) Drain in colander and set aside to cool.
2. Whisk the olive oil, lemon juice, pomegranate molasses, cayenne pepper, salt, and pepper in a small bowl.
3. Add the lentils, tomatoes, peppers, onions, avocado, basil, parsley, mint, dill, and green onions to a large bowl. Pour the dressing over the salad and toss together gently until combined. Refrigerate until ready to serve.

Wisdom from Suheyla's Kitchen:

It is important to chop the ingredients very small to achieve the right texture.

Did You Know?

Green and brown lentils are the most common lentils used, since they retain their shape and flavor after cooking.

Lentils do not need to be soaked before cooking.

Salad Shirazi

by Ameneh Gounilli - Iran

Salad Shirazi is a traditional Persian dish named after a city in Iran called Shiraz, located in the south of Iran. It is known as the city of poets, literature, wine, and flowers. That may explain why this dish is so beautiful. The juicy tomatoes, crunchy cucumbers, and fresh mint splashed with lemon juice and sea salt create a refreshing salad that is simple to make and perfect for any meal.

Preparation Time: 15 minutes

Makes: 6 servings

Ingredients:

- 5 Persian cucumbers, thinly sliced ⅛-inch
- 3-4 Roma tomatoes, thinly sliced ¼-inch
- ¼ cup white onions, thinly sliced ⅛-inch
- 6 small fresh mint leaves, chopped, optional
- 2 tablespoons cilantro, chopped, optional
- 6 tablespoons extra light olive oil
- ½ teaspoon sea salt
- ¼ teaspoon fresh cracked black pepper
- 4 tablespoons fresh lemon juice

Method:

1. Neatly lay sliced cucumbers in the middle of a serving plate.
2. Layer the sliced tomatoes around the perimeter of the plate, surrounding the cucumbers.
3. Sprinkle the chopped herbs over the top of the salad, leaving more in the center than the sides.
4. Whisk the lemon juice, salt, and olive oil until combined. Drizzle the dressing over the salad and serve immediately or refrigerate until ready to serve. Refrigerate any unused dressing for up to 5 days.

Wisdom from Ameneh's Kitchen:

Salad Shirazi is always beautifully decorated on the serving platter. Depending on the plate you choose, you can arrange the ingredients in any design you prefer.

Did You Know?

"Nooshe jan" in the Persian language, Farsi, means "Have a nice meal!"

Kale Caesar Salad with Pomegranate

by Laurie Kerkinni - USA

There are countless times when I have ignored adding kale to my grocery cart because it just didn't appeal to my palate the way other salad lettuces do. That is until I tried Laurie's Kale Caesar Salad. Now, fresh organic kale to prepare this addictively good salad with a creamy Caesar dressing is at the top of my shopping list every time I head to the market.

Preparation Time: 15 minutes

Makes: 3-4 servings

Ingredients:

- 8 large organic kale leaves, de-veined and finely chopped
- ¼ cup quinoa, uncooked
- 1 pomegranate, seeded
- 2 ½ tablespoons lemon juice
- 2 ½ tablespoons lime juice
- 2 cloves garlic, minced
- 1 tablespoon Worcestershire sauce
- 1 tablespoon balsamic vinegar
- 1 teaspoon Dijon mustard
- ¼ teaspoon dry mustard
- ½ teaspoon salt
- ¼ teaspoon pepper
- ⅔ cup olive oil
- 2 eggs, coddled
- 3 anchovy fillets, minced (optional)

Method:

1. Toss the kale, quinoa and pomegranate in a bowl.
2. Whisk the lemon juice, lime juice, garlic, Worcestershire sauce, balsamic vinegar, Dijon mustard, dry mustard, salt, and pepper in a bowl. Whisk in the olive oil until emulsified.
3. Coddle the eggs by heating 3 cups of water to a boil. Drop in eggs (still in shell) and let stand for 1 minute. Remove eggs from the water and let cool. Once cooled, crack open and whisk eggs into dressing.
4. Mash the anchovies and whisk them into the dressing or set aside for garnish.
5. Drizzle desired amount of dressing over salad, toss, and refrigerate remaining dressing for up to one week.

Wisdom from Laurie's Kitchen:

Kale is listed on the Dirty Dozen list of foods with the most pesticides. When choosing fruits and vegetables, like kale, reduce your exposure to pesticides by purchasing organic whenever possible.

Prepare this salad ahead of time (without the dressing) and store in the refrigerator for a delicious, healthy salad that is ready to enjoy the next day.

Spicy Fish and Seafood Soup

by Suheyla Kerkinni - Assyria

There is something extraordinarily heart-warming about spicy fish and seafood soup. The eclectic combination of fish and seafood simmers into a comforting broth infused with a delightful aromatic flavor and a subtle kick of spice that complements this soup beautifully.

Preparation Time: 30 minutes   **Cooking Time:** 35 minutes   **Makes:** 8 servings

Ingredients:

- ¼ cup olive oil
- ¾ teaspoon crushed red pepper
- 3-4 garlic cloves, minced
- 8-ounces sliced mushrooms
- 1 red pepper, sliced into ¾-inch pieces
- 2 stalks celery, chopped
- 1 jalapeño pepper, seeded and sliced
- 2 medium potatoes, peeled and cutting into ¾-inch cubes
- 14.5-ounce can diced tomatoes
- 2 bay leaves
- 1 teaspoon salt
- ½ teaspoon pepper
- 1 ½ cup white wine
- 4 cups fish broth or vegetable broth
- ½-pound cleaned clams
- 1-pound cleaned muscles
- 1 ½ pounds salmon or any firm fish, cut into 1-inch pieces
- 1-pound scallops or medium shrimp (tail off)

Method:

1. Prepare the ingredients while the shellfish soak for 30 minutes in a bowl of cold salt water.
2. Heat the oil in a soup pot over medium heat. Add the garlic and crushed red pepper, sautéing 30 seconds to infuse the oil. Add the mushrooms and continue to sauté for 3 minutes.
3. Add the red peppers, celery, potatoes and jalapeños, sautéing for 3 minutes. Add in the diced tomatoes, bay leaf, salt, and pepper, sautéing for an additional 5 minutes.
4. Add the wine and sauté for 2 minutes before adding the broth. Reduce the heat to low, cover, and simmer for 10 minutes.
5. Add the clams and mussels into the soup. Cover, increase the heat to medium-low, cooking 5 to 7 minutes or until the clams and mussel shells have opened. Remove and discard the clams and mussels that did not open.
6. Add the salmon or fish and cook 3 minutes before adding the scallops and shrimp and cooking an additional 2 minutes. Remove the pot from the heat, discard the bay leaves before serving. Serve with garlic toast.

Wisdom from Suheyla's Kitchen:

It is essential to clean your shellfish well to prevent sand from cooking into the soup. Just rinse the clams and mussels, soaking them in a bowl of cold salted water for 30 minutes or more. Mussels sometimes have small fibrous "beards," that should be cut off. Scrub any remaining sediment from the shells before adding to the soup.

Did You Know?

A clam can live close to 35 years if it is not eaten.

Now, *This* is Chicken Noodle Soup!

by Lorraine Soldo - USA

As a child, my mom would make her famous homemade Chicken Noodle Soup when we were feeling under the weather. Now, I make her recipe for my family as often as I can since they love it so much! It is super easy to prepare and only takes a few ingredients. You'll have an entire pot of healthy, comforting soup ready to enjoy in under 2 hours. I usually double the recipe and make enough to freeze in family size containers. Honestly, there is nothing better than having this incredible soup on hand when you are feeling ill or simply want a hot, delicious meal.

Preparation Time: 15 minutes   **Cooking Time:** 1 hour 30 minutes   **Makes:** 8 servings

Ingredients:

- 1 whole organic chicken
- 36 cups water
- 2 teaspoons salt, plus more at the end if needed
- 1 teaspoon black pepper
- 1 cup carrots, peeled and diced
- 1 cup diced celery, organic
- 1 cup diced onions
- 2 bay leaves
- ½ pound extra wide egg noodles, Alberto's brand if available
- ½ cup parsley, roughly chopped

Method:

1. Clean the inside of the chicken thoroughly, removing any veins and debris.
2. Bring the water, chicken, and salt to a boil in a large pot over high heat. Lower the heat to medium, cover and cook for 1 hour.
3. Turn off the heat, remove the chicken from the water and set it aside to cool until the meat peels easily off the bone. Chop the chicken into ½ inch cubes. Transfer the meat back into the pot, turning the heat to medium-high.
4. Add the carrots celery, onions, and bay leaf. Simmer 15 to 20 minutes or until you can pierce the carrots with a fork.
5. If you are using long egg noodles, break them in half and immerse into the soup. Continue to simmer for 25 to 30 minutes or until the noodles are soft.
6. Stir in parsley and simmer 5 minutes before removing pot from the heat. Adjust the flavor by layering in the salt until it reaches a full-bodied flavor, being careful not to make it too salty. Remove the bay leaves before serving.

Wisdom from Lorraine's Kitchen:

The character and flavor of this soup largely depend on adjusting the salt until the flavor comes through, being careful not to add too much or too little. A wonderful full-bodied flavor will be achieved when just the right amount of salt is added.

Organic chicken has more flavor and will create a much better soup.

The most important step in this recipe is to clean the chicken inside and out using cold water. This will prevent any unpleasant cavity particles found inside the chicken from becoming part of your soup. Be sure to clean and sanitize your sink and workspace once the chicken is placed inside of the pot to prevent contamination from the raw chicken.

I use Alberto's extra wide egg noodles. If noodles are too long, break them in half before placing into soup.

If you omit the noodles, it makes a delicious gluten-free chicken vegetable soup.

Clo Hay Red Lentil Soup

by Laurie Kerkinni -USA

Clo Hay red lentil soup is a classic Assyrian soup. Laurie tops hers with black cumin oil for a unique flavor surge with every spoonful. The rich, creamy texture of this dish is enhanced with a squeeze of fresh lemon juice and cracked coriander. Clo Hay is a soup worthy of a second serving every time.

Preparation Time: 5 minutes   **Cooking Time:** 1 hour 30 minutes   **Makes:** 6 servings

Ingredients:

- 2 cups red lentils
- 9 cups water, divided
- ¼ cup rice
- 1 ½ tablespoons salt
- black cumin seed oil
- coriander, fresh cracked, or 2 pinches of ground pepper
- lemon juice, freshly squeezed
- 2 large fresh mint leaves, chopped

Method:

1. Boil the lentils and 7 cups of water in a medium pot over high heat. Reduce heat to medium and simmer 20 minutes, removing foam as it boils.
2. Add the remaining 2 cups water, rice, and salt. Reduce the heat to medium-low and simmer for 1 hour.
3. Ladle the soup into bowls and lightly drizzle the black cumin oil over the soup. Add 3 to 6 twists of fresh cracked coriander or black pepper, and a squeeze of fresh lemon juice around the soup. Top with mint and serve hot.

Wisdom from Laurie's Kitchen:

Include Black Cumin Seed Oil in your diet whenever possible. Scientific research demonstrates that the seeds and the oil from the Black Cumin Seeds, (Nigella Sativa is the botanical name), have remarkable health-supporting properties, including shrinkage of cancerous tumors, aiding digestion, moisturizing skin, balancing hormones, and preventing bug bites.

This seed mentioned in the Book of Isaiah is known as Pharaoh's Oil.

Tlavhe Red Lentil Soup

by Suheyla Kerkinni - Assyria

Tlavhe (pronounced clo-hay) is a traditional Assyrian soup made for generations in Suheyla's family. This creamy red lentil soup gets its unique flavor from the addition of freshly made red pepper paste and dried mint. If you are in the mood for a warm bowl of comfort food, you have found it here.

Preparation Time: 20 minutes   **Cooking Time:** 50 minutes   **Makes:** 6 servings

Ingredients:

- 2 cups red lentils
- 10 cups water
- 1 medium onion, chopped
- 3 garlic cloves, minced
- 4 tablespoons olive oil
- 1 bay leaf
- 4 tablespoons lemon juice
- 2 tablespoons tomato paste
- 2 tablespoons red pepper paste (Chapter 8)
- 1 ½ tablespoons dried mint
- 2 teaspoons black pepper
- ½ teaspoon cumin

Method:

1. Prepare the red pepper paste first.
2. Rinse the lentils in a colander in cold water until the water runs clear. Bring the lentil water to a boil in a large soup pot over high heat. Remove the foam that forms on top of water during the cooking process.
3. Heat the oil in a sauté pan over medium-high heat. Add the onions and garlic, sautéing 5 minutes or until the onions are slightly translucent.
4. Add the onions, bay leaf, lemon juice, tomato paste, red pepper paste, dried mint, black pepper, and cumin to the soup pot and stir to combine. Cover and lower heat to medium-low, simmering 45 minutes or until the lentils are very soft.
5. Remove and discard the bay leaf and transfer the soup in batches to a countertop blender. Blend the soup until creamy.
6. Serve topped with oil, butter, or sour cream and a sprinkle of paprika.

Wisdom from Suheyla's Kitchen:

Homemade red pepper paste gives this soup its uniquely vibrant flavor. The paste is easy to make and stores well in the refrigerator for a few weeks.

Albondigas - Mexican Meatball Soup

by Michael Hernandez - Mexico

Michael shared his mother's, Fermina's, recipe for Albondigas, a hearty Mexican soup packed with juicy meatballs and swimming in a zesty tomato broth. Fermina, often had a simmering pot of Albondigas and homemade tortillas waiting on the stove for the kids after a long afternoon of neighborhood hockey. In so many ways, food is the bridge that brings us back to the warmth and love of our mothers' kitchen.

Preparation Time: 10 minutes   **Passive Time:** 30 minutes   **Makes:** 4-6 servings

Ingredients:

- ½-pound ground chuck
- ½-pound ground pork
- ½ cup long grain rice
- ½ cup plain bread crumbs, or gluten-free bread
- 1 egg
- 1-½ cups finely chopped onions, divided
- 5 garlic cloves, minced
- ½ tablespoon minced fresh or dried mint
- ½ tablespoon minced fresh cilantro
- 2 teaspoon salt, divided
- ½ teaspoon pepper
- ½ teaspoon cumin
- ½ teaspoon oregano
- ½ to 1 teaspoon red pepper flakes (optional)
- ¼ cup olive oil
- 8 cups chicken broth
- 2 cups Roma tomatoes

Method:

1. Combine beef, pork, rice, bread crumbs, eggs, ½ cup onion, 2 minced garlic cloves, mint, cilantro, 1 teaspoon salt, pepper, cumin, and oregano in a large bowl. Using your hands, mix the ingredients together and roll the meat into golf ball size meatballs.
2. Heat a large sauté pan or wide bottom pot over medium heat. When the pan is hot, add the oil and heat for 30 seconds. Add the remaining 1 cup of onions and the remaining 3 minced garlic cloves, sautéing for 5 minutes or until onions are slightly translucent.
3. Stir in the tomatoes and simmer an additional 5 minutes.
4. Lay the meatballs on top of the tomatoes and gently pour the chicken broth over them, being careful not to break the meat apart. Lower the heat to medium-low and simmer for 1 hour. Do not stir the meatballs while they are cooking.
5. Serve with toasted flour or corn tortillas and lime wedges.

Wisdom from Michael's Kitchen:

If you prefer only a subtle kick of heat, reduce the red peppers to ½ teaspoon.

Ashe Berenj - Persian Rice Soup

by Sohiela Mirsharif - Iran

Ashe Berenj (rice soup) is a traditional dish made in Persian kitchens across the world. Sohiela's soup is a comforting blend of rice, legumes, herbs, and meat slow-simmered to create a thick, healthy, flavorful, dish. It represents Persian comfort food at its best. An excellent make-ahead meal that tastes just as delicious the next day.

Preparation Time: 10 minutes
Passive Time: 6 to 7 hours
Cooking Time: 2 hours 30 minutes
Makes: 8-10 servings

Ingredients:

- ½ cup dried great northern beans
- ½ cup dried chickpeas
- ½ cup dried brown lentils
- ¾ cup basmati rice, soaked and salted
- 6 tablespoons avocado oil
- 1 cup onion, finely chopped
- 3 pounds beef shank or beef bone-in chuck short ribs
- 1 teaspoon turmeric
- ½ teaspoon coriander
- ½ cumin
- 3 teaspoon salt
- 1 teaspoon black pepper
- Boiling water
- 3 cups fresh dill, finely chopped
- 2 bunches fresh parsley, finely chopped
- 2 cups spinach, finely chopped
- 2 cups chicken broth, divided (more as needed)

Wisdom from Sohiela's Kitchen:

Only soak the beans for 6 to 7 hours. Over-soaking removes many of the nutrients.

It is important to chop all the herbs very fine, so you don't see the vegetables once the soup is cooked.

Method:

1. Soak the dried beans, chickpeas, and lentils in a large bowl filled with water on the counter for 6 to 7 hours or overnight.
2. In a separate bowl, rinse and soak the rice in salted water for 2 to 4 hours.
3. Heat the cooking oil in a Dutch oven or non-stick pot over medium heat. Sauté the onions and beef shank until the meat is browned on all sides and onions are slightly golden. Stir in the turmeric, coriander, cumin, salt, and pepper. Add the drained and rinsed legumes.
4. Fill the pot with water to cover 2 inches above the meat and legumes. Increase the heat to high and bring to a boil, then lower the heat to medium-low to maintain a strong simmer. Cover and simmer for 1 hour (stirring often so the beans and rice don't stick and burn on the bottom). Tilt the lid on the pot to release pressure as needed.
5. While the soup is simmering, cook the rice al dente in a separate pot and set aside for later use.
6. After the soup has cooked for 1 hour, stir in the cooked rice, chopped dill, parsley, spinach and 1 cup chicken broth. Cover and continue to cook for an additional 1 hour. Remember to stir often to prevent sticking and burning.
7. Remove the beef from the pot and cut the meat from the bone into ½ inch pieces, removing and discarding any fat. Stir meat back into the soup, reserving a few pieces for garnish. Add the remaining 1 cup chicken broth. Adjust the taste with salt and pepper. Reduce the heat to low and simmer for 20 minutes.
8. Serve the soup garnished with the reserved meat, yogurt, chopped parsley, and walnuts if desired. Drizzle lemon juice over the soup once ladled into bowls.

Did You Know?

One tablespoon of dill seed contains more calcium than a cup of milk.

Ten-Minute Egg Drop Soup

by Lisa Soldo - USA

This Ten-minute Egg Drop Soup Recipe is my go-to-choice when I need a quick, healthy, delicious meal in a hurry. I love taking traditional dishes and reimagining them to fit the ingredients and flavor I like best. Add a little shrimp, some mushrooms, or toss in some garlic croutons for added flavor and texture. There is no limit to the variations you can have with this soup other than your imagination.

Preparation Time: 5 minutes   **Cooking Time:** 5 minutes   **Makes:** 4 servings

Ingredients:

- 4 cups chicken broth
- 2 tablespoons tamari
- 1 tablespoon, plus 1 teaspoon cornstarch
- 2 tablespoons water
- 2-3 large eggs
- 2 green onions, chopped

Method:

1. Combine chicken broth and tamari in a pan and bring to a boil over medium heat.
2. While broth is cooking, beat the eggs in a small bowl.
3. Place cornstarch and warm water into a small jar with lid and shake to dissolve. When soup begins to boil, slowly whisk into broth.
4. Slowly drizzle the eggs into the broth with one hand, using the other hand to gently stir the eggs with a fork to form large chunks.
5. Top the soup with the green onions and serve hot.

Wisdom from Lisa's Kitchen:

Be careful not to over whisk the eggs into the soup, so that the eggs will remain chunky

CHAPTER 4

Poultry

Chicken Shoshi / 69

Chicken and Vegetable Pot Pie / 70

Ginger Chicken with Spicy Steamed Cabbage / 72

Spicy Chicken Noodle Bowl / 73

Joojeh Kabobs - Persian Chicken Kabobs / 75

Spicy Marinated Chicken Thighs / 76

Melt in Your Mouth Lemon Butter Chicken / 77

Chicken Saffron / 79

Korean-Style Baked Chicken / 80

Healthy Turkey Chow Mein / 81

Chicken Khoresht Bademjan - Persian Eggplant Stew with Chicken / 83

Chicken Shoshi

by Vivi Mizrahi - Israel

Chicken Shoshi got its name from Vivi's mother-in-law, Shoshi, who was the creator of this delicious sensation. The wonder of chicken Shoshi, as Vivi will tell you is, "It's practically a no-fail dish," and the results are perfectly tender, bursting with flavorful fall-off-the-bone chicken legs that your family will adore. I have written this recipe to serve five people, allowing two chicken legs per serving. But if you have big eaters, you will want to make extra. It's just that good.

Preparation Time: 10 minutes   **Cook Time:** 1 hour 15 minutes   **Makes:** 5 servings

Ingredients:

- 10 chicken legs, skin removed
- 1 ½ large onions, sliced
- 10 cloves garlic, chopped
- 3 tablespoons canola oil
- 3 teaspoons chicken bouillon paste or chicken seasoning.
- 1 teaspoon salt
- ½ teaspoon pepper
- boiling water as needed

Method:

1. Remove the skin from the chicken legs, rinse and set aside.
2. Heat the oil in a large skillet on medium heat. Add the onions and garlic, sautéing for 5 minutes or until the onions become slightly translucent.
3. Lay the chicken legs on top of the onions in a single layer. Pour ½ cup of the boiling water over chicken and simmer 4 to 5 minutes or until the meat begins to brown. Turn the chicken over and continue to simmer until lightly browned on all sides. Add an additional ¼ cup boiling water and chicken bouillon or chicken spice, stirring into the liquid to combine. Top the chicken with salt and pepper. Add enough boiling water to almost submerge the chicken legs, cover and simmer for 15 minutes.
4. Remove cover and stir the chicken and onions to prevent them from sticking to the bottom of the skillet. Cover and continue to cook for 1 hour and 15 minutes, stirring occasionally to prevent sticking. Add boiling water as needed every 20 minutes until the chicken is done, making sure the liquid does not evaporate while cooking.
5. Transfer the chicken to a serving dish, pour the onions and juice over the chicken, and serve hot.

Wisdom from Vivi's Kitchen:

A simple way to remove the skin from the chicken leg is to pull the skin down toward the bone using a dry paper towel, then pull the skin over and off the bone.

The onions on the bottom of the pan enhance the flavor and prevent chicken from burning. Feel free to add more onions if desired.

Be sure to stir and turn the chicken and onions occasionally as it cooks to prevent ingredients from burning.

Chicken and Vegetable Pot Pie

by Lorraine Soldo - USA

As a kid, one of my favorite comfort meals was my mother's homemade chicken and vegetable pot pie. She always knew just how to bring together the perfect crust with tender chunks of chicken and sweet vegetables nestled into a rich buttery cream sauce. Years later, it's still as soothing and delicious as it was back then.

Preparation Time: 30 minutes
Passive Time: 1 hour
Cook Time: 1 hour
Makes: 6 servings

Ingredients:

Crust

- 2 ½ cups all-purpose flour
- 1 teaspoon salt
- 2 sticks unsalted butter, very cold
- 1 cup ice-cold water, divided
- Filling:
- ⅓ butter
- ½ cup onions, chopped
- ¾ teaspoon salt
- ½ teaspoon pepper
- ⅓ cup all-purpose flour
- 2 cups chicken broth
- ⅔ cup milk
- 2 cups chicken breast, chopped into ½-inch cubes
- 10 ounces frozen mixed vegetables

Method:

Filling

1. Melt the butter in a medium pan over low heat.
2. Stir in the onions, salt, and pepper, sautéing until the butter is lightly browned.
3. Sift in the flour, whisking quickly until the mixture is smooth.
4. Whisk in the chicken broth and milk until it becomes creamy. Increase the heat to medium-high and cook until it boils for 1 minute, stirring constantly.
5. Add the chicken and vegetables, stirring to combine. Remove the pan from the heat and set aside.

Crust

1. Whisk together flour and salt in a large bowl.
2. Remove the butter from the refrigerator and dice the cold butter into ½ inch pieces. Transfer them to the bowl. Using a pastry cutter, work the butter back and forth into the flour until the dough forms pea-size crumbles.
3. Pour ½ cup of the ice-cold water over the dough mixture. Using your hands, begin folding the flour and butter mixture over to form the dough. Add more water as needed 1 tablespoon at a time until it forms a solid piece of dough.
4. Divide the dough in half and wrap each piece in plastic wrap. Using your palms, lightly press the dough pieces into a disk shape. Refrigerate for at least one hour before rolling it out.
5. Lightly flour a flat work surface. Remove one dough disk from the refrigerator, unwrap and lay it on top of the flour. Begin rolling the dough by pressing down lightly with a floured rolling pin, rolling it out from the center a few times in each direction. Continue to repeat this process, flouring the surface and your pin as needed until the dough is rolled out into a 12 inch circle.

6. Place the top of the pie plate onto the dough and trim around the edges with the tip of a sharp knife. Loosen the crust from the surface by gently tucking a large spatula under and around the crust until it easily lifts from the surface. Gently fold the crust in quarters to transfer to the pie plate and unfold it, making sure it is centered on the plate. Gently open and press the dough into the pan, folding the overhang of the crust edges under to fit the size of the pan.

Assembly

1. Preheat the oven to 350°F.
2. Pour the filling into the pie shell.
3. Prepare the remaining dough as before. Gently place crust onto the top of the pot pie. Cut off any extra dough hanging from the edges of the pie plate and pinch the edges of both crusts together to seal.
4. Bake for 1 hour or until the crust is golden brown.
5. Remove the pot pie from oven, greasing the top of the crust with soft butter. Set aside to cool for 15 minutes before serving.

Wisdom from Lorraine's Kitchen:

Add a little bit of water at a time when making the dough. Too much water will make the dough sticky and tear apart when rolling out. Too little water will make the dough dry and tough, making it difficult to roll out.

You may choose to lift and rotate your pie dough when rolling it out or keep it in one place while rolling until you transfer it to the pie plate.

The pot pie may drip juice while baking. Place a piece of tin foil on the bottom of your oven to catch the liquid.

Did You Know?

The first pot pie ever made was in Greece where they cooked meats and placed them in open pastry shells. Eventually the Romans added the top crust, making this dish into an actual pie. But it was the English who perfected the process by molding the pastry along the bottom of the pot and calling it a "Pot Pie."

Ginger Chicken with Spicy Steamed Cabbage

by Rachel Huang - China

Occasionally, I come across a recipe that I will make over and over again. This is that recipe, thanks to my friend Rachel who taught me to make her Sichuan-inspired ginger chicken with spicy steamed cabbage. Born in Sichuan, China where food is typically spicy, Rachel prefers to incorporate her own style of subtlety without losing the essence of the dish. Like all of Rachel's recipes, this one is simple, healthy, and delicious!

Preparation Time: 10 minutes   **Cook Time:** 30 minutes   **Makes:** 4 servings

Ingredients:

Ginger Chicken

- 1 tablespoon olive oil
- ¾ cup fresh ginger, julienned
- 1 ½ pounds boneless skinless chicken thighs
- 1 teaspoon turmeric
- ½ teaspoon fish sauce
- ¼ teaspoon stevia
- 1 teaspoon salt, divided
- 1 small Thai Chili peppers, seeded and minced (wear gloves)
- ½ teaspoon Sichuan peppercorn

Sautéed Spicy Cabbage

- 4 cups green cabbage, chopped into 2-inch pieces
- 2 tablespoons olive oil
- 1 teaspoon Sichuan peppercorn
- ½ teaspoon dried red pepper
- 2 tablespoons soy sauce or Tamari
- 1 teaspoon salt
- ⅛ teaspoon sugar
- water as needed

Method:

Ginger Chicken

1. Preheat a skillet on high heat for 30 seconds. Add the olive oil, ginger, and chicken, sautéing for 2 minutes before reducing the heat to medium-low.
2. Sprinkle the turmeric, stevia, ½ teaspoon salt, and Thai Chili pepper over the chicken and stir until the meat is completely coated. Cover and cook for 15 minutes. (Note: Use only 1 seeded Chili pepper for mild heat, or 2 for extreme heat).
3. Stir in the fish sauce, remaining ½ teaspoon salt, and Sichuan peppercorn. Increase the heat to high and sauté for 1 minute.
4. Reduce the heat to low and simmer for 10 minutes to slightly thicken the juice. Remove from heat if juice begins to evaporate. Pour the chicken, ginger and sauce into a bowl and serve with rice.

Spicy Sautéed Cabbage

1. Preheat a skillet on high heat for 1 minute. Add the oil, dried chili pepper, and cabbage. Toss to coat the cabbage in the oil and sauté for 3 minutes to infuse the flavors. (Note: Omit the dried chili pepper if you like it without spice. Use only 1 for mild heat or 2 for spicy)
2. Add the salt, soy sauce, and sugar, tossing to coat cabbage. Add ⅛ cup water, cover and steam for 2 minutes or until the cabbage is slightly soft but still crunchy. Pour the cabbage and any oil onto a plate and serve immediately.

Wisdom from Rachel's Kitchen:

The key to success with this recipe is using dark meat. Chicken thighs keep the dish moist and tender because of the higher fat content in the flesh. White meat dries out faster and does not create the liquid needed to keep it moist and juicy.

In Chinese cooking, we like to keep all the flavors in the food itself rather than the excess liquid.

Fair warning: if you are not a fan of spicy flavors, be sure to remove the seeds (wearing gloves) and use the chili peppers sparingly.

If you don't have Sichuan peppercorn, you can substitute with black peppercorn; however, it will alter the taste slightly but still be delicious.

Did You Know?

According to traditional Chinese medicine, Chinese food has five essential flavors that bring balance to the body: sweet, sour, salty, bitter, and spicy.

Spicy Chicken Noodle Bowl

by Rachel Huang - China

One of the things I love most about Rachel's style of cooking is her creativity when making quick and easy meals. Spicy Chicken Noodle Bowl, inspired by the idea that you can make a delicious meal in under 10 minutes using food already in your refrigerator, so nothing goes to waste. The magic in Rachel's "everything" sauce brings flavor and inspiration to simple meals, making them exciting and appealing new dishes.

Preparation Time: 10 minutes   **Cook Time:** 10 minutes   **Makes:** 4 servings

Ingredients:

- 8.8 ounces Udon noodles
- 2 chicken breasts, thinly sliced
- 1 red bell pepper, cored and thinly sliced
- 1 green chili pepper, cored and thinly sliced
- 2 tablespoons olive oil
- 1 green onion, finely chopped
- 1 tablespoon black cumin or nigella seeds
- 1 cup Rachel's Secret Sauce (page 182)

Method:

1. Prepare Rachel's secret fish sauce ahead of time.
2. Add the noodles to a pot of water to a boil, simmer uncovered for 8 to 10 minutes. Do not overcook. Drain and rinse with cold water.
3. While the noodles are cooking, heat the oil in a skillet over medium-high heat. Sauté the chicken 5 minutes before adding the red peppers and chili peppers. Continue to sauté 5 to 8 minutes or until the chicken is cooked through and the peppers are tender. Add the green onions and black cumin seeds, toss, remove from heat, and set aside.
4. Separate the noodles in 4 bowls, top with chicken, chili peppers, fish sauce, and serve immediately.

Wisdom from Rachel's Kitchen:

To save time in the kitchen, purchase a roasted chicken for this recipe or use leftover chicken from your refrigerator.

Joojeh Kabobs - Persian Chicken Kabobs

by Ameneh Gounilli - Iran

Joojeh Kabobs are a traditional Persian chicken kabob infused with olive oil, lime juice, turmeric, paired with tomato and onion, and then grilled to perfection. They are simple to make and can be prepared ahead of time for the perfect family meal or easy entree for entertaining.

Preparation Time: 30 minutes

Passive Time: 1 hour

Cook Time: 15 minutes

Makes: 6 servings

Ingredients:

- 2 boneless chicken breasts, cut into 2-inch pieces
- 24 cherry tomatoes
- 2 large onions, cut into 2-inch pieces
- ½ cup chopped cilantro
- 12 wood skewers, soaked in water for 30 minutes
- ½ cup olive oil
- ¼ cup lime juice
- 1 teaspoon turmeric
- ½ teaspoon salt
- ½ teaspoon pepper

Method:

1. Whisk the olive oil, lime juice, turmeric, salt, and pepper in a medium bowl.
2. Add in chicken pieces and wearing gloves, massage the marinade into meat until completely coated. Cover and refrigerate for 1 hour or overnight.
3. Preheat the grill for high heat.
4. Assemble the kabobs by threading the chicken, cherry tomato, and onion onto the skewers alternately. Repeat until each skewer is filled, leaving 2 inches open at the bottom and 1 inch at the top of the kabob empty.
5. Lightly oil the grill grate. Place kabobs on the hot grill and cook turning frequently, for 12 to 15 minutes. The chicken is done when the internal temperature of an instant-read thermometer inserted into the center reads at least 165 degrees F (74 degrees C).
6. Transfer Joojeh Kabobs to a plate and serve with basmati rice and Salad Shirazi.

Wisdom from Ameneh's Kitchen:

Soak wood skewers in water before assembling the kabobs to prevent them from burning on the grill.

Be sure to wear gloves while touching the chicken to prevent the turmeric from yellowing your hands and nails.

Did You Know?

Farsi was first recorded in about 500 BCE and is the dominant language of both ancient and modern-day Iran. In Farsi, Joojeh Kabob means grilled chicken.

Spicy Marinated Chicken Thighs

by Suheyla Kerkinni - Assyria

Chicken thighs are one of my favorite cuts of poultry because they are always tender and juicy and cook in no time. Suheyla's spicy marinated chicken thighs are full of flavor and an excellent choice when feeding a large crowd.

Preparation Time: 10 minutes
Passive Time: 4 hours
Cook Time: 30-35 minutes
Makes: 6 servings

Ingredients:

- 3 ½ pounds boneless skinless chicken thighs
- ⅓ cup olive oil
- ½ cup white wine
- ¼ cup lemon juice
- 3 garlic cloves
- 1 tablespoon Italian seasoning
- 1 tablespoon crushed red pepper
- 1 teaspoon salt
- ½ teaspoon black pepper

Method:

1. Whisk the oil, lemon juice, white wine, Italian seasoning, red pepper, salt, and pepper in a large bowl.
2. Rinse the chicken and remove any visible fat and ligaments. Place the chicken into the bowl and coat the meat with the marinade. Cover and refrigerate 4 to 6 hours or overnight.
3. Preheat the oven to 375°F or the grill to medium-high heat.
4. If baking, place the chicken in a glass baking dish and cover with tin foil. Bake for 15 minutes before turning the chicken over. Return the pan to the oven and bake uncovered for an additional 15 to 20 minutes or until the chicken reaches an internal temperature of 165°F.
5. If grilling, place the chicken directly on the grill plates, turning the thighs as needed. Cook until the chicken reaches an internal temperature of 165°F.
6. Transfer the grilled chicken to a serving plate. If baking, spoon the juices over chicken before serving.

Melt in Your Mouth Lemon Butter Chicken

by Laurie Kerkinni - USA

Laurie's lemon butter chicken tops the list of my favorites when it comes to tender, flavorful, fall-off-the-bone chicken. Slow roasted in a blend of butter, olive oil garlic, mustard and lemon for 8 to 10 hours, the slow roasting process permeates the meat with a subtle essence of lemon and butter. I recommend using the juices from the roasting pan to make a flavorful gravy served over a bed of mashed potatoes and a fresh green salad for a complete meal.

Preparation Time: 10 minutes **Cook Time:** 8-10 hours **Makes:** 6 servings

Ingredients:

- 1 5-7-pound whole organic chicken
- 3 tablespoons olive oil
- 2 tablespoons butter
- 8 garlic cloves, minced
- 1 organic lemon rind, grated
- 1 tablespoon Dijon mustard
- 1 teaspoon Himalayan salt
- 1 cup water
- salt

Method:

1. Preheat the oven to 225°F.
2. Heat the oil and butter in a saucepan over medium-high heat until the butter is melted.
3. Add the garlic and sauté for 30 seconds or until the garlic is aromatic.
4. Stir in the lemon juice, lemon rind, Dijon mustard, and salt for 30 seconds and remove from heat.
5. Thoroughly wash and clean the chicken to remove any debris from the body cavity. Place the chicken in a small roasting pan or glass dish. Using your hands, gently separate the thin connective tissue between the skin of the meat and on the chicken. Spoon and spread half the sauce between the chicken skin and meat on both sides of the bird. Use remaining sauce to rub on top and inside of the chicken.
6. Add water to the bottom of the pan, cover with a lid or tin foil, and bake. The chicken will bake slowly for 6 to 8 hours. To keep the bird moist while roasting, spoon liquid from the bottom of the pan over and inside the cavity every 2 hours until the chicken is done. Cook times can vary depending on the size of the chicken. The chicken is done when a thermometer placed into the center of the thickest part of the meat reaches 165°F.

Wisdom from Laurie's Kitchen:

Be careful not to overcook the chicken or the meat will dry out. Cooking times will vary depending on the size of the chicken.

Did You Know?

Naturally occurring sulfur in the garlic interacts with those enzymes, occasionally turning it slightly green or blue when using older garlic. If this happens, it will not affect the flavor of the dish, but it is best to use the freshest garlic whenever possible.

Chicken Saffron

by Sohiela Mirsharif - Iran

Saffron, is a precious nutrient-rich spice used by cultures around the world to aid in building a strong immune system. This super-spice is widely used in Middle Eastern and Mediterranean cooking to add color and flavor to the dish while benefiting from its nutritional value. I love the combination of flavors in this chicken saffron dish. The warm essence of lightly browned onions, garlic, turmeric, and saffron slowly simmer into the chicken for a tender and flavorful dish that serves beautifully over nutty basmati rice and a darkened crunchy tahdig. Saffron can be expensive, so this makes a great dish for special occasions.

Preparation Time: 15 minutes **Cooking Time:** 1 hour 15 minutes **Makes:** 4 servings

Ingredients:

- 4 tablespoons avocado oil, divided
- 1 tablespoon butter
- 1 large onion, thinly sliced
- 2 large garlic cloves, thinly sliced
- 1-pound skinless chicken breasts, cut into ½-inch slices
- 1 cup chicken broth, boiling
- ⅓ cup saffron water (see notes)
- 1 teaspoon turmeric, divided
- 1 teaspoon salt
- ¼ cup barberries

Method:

1. Heat 1 tablespoon avocado oil and the butter in a skillet over medium-high heat until the oil is shimmering. Sauté the onions and garlic 8 to 10 minutes until the onions are lightly browned. Transfer to a dish and set aside.
2. In the same pan, heat the remaining 3 tablespoons of oil over medium-high heat. Add the chicken slices and sauté until chicken is browned on all sides. Stir in the garlic, onions, ½ teaspoon turmeric, salt, and saffron water, simmering for 3 minutes.
3. Bring the chicken broth to a boil in a small pan. Pour the broth over the chicken, sprinkle in the remaining ½ teaspoon turmeric, cover, reduce heat to medium-low and simmer up to an hour (stirring occasionally) or until the liquid is completely absorbed.
4. Soak the barberries in a small dish in warm water for 10 minutes. Drain and lightly toss into the chicken. Serve Chicken Saffron over basmati rice with tahdig (page 159).

Wisdom from Sohiela's Kitchen:

To make saffron water: grind 10 saffron threads into a powder using a mortar and pestle. Add ⅓ cup hot water and soak for 15 minutes.

Always use hot liquid when adding it to a dish. Using cold water can interrupt the cooking process and effect the final flavor of the dish.

Tahdig is formed at the bottom of the pot while the rice is cooking. The longer the rice is kept on the heat the darker the tahdig will become. You can serve this dish with light or dark tahdig.

Purchase good quality saffron at Middle Eastern grocery stores.

Did You Know?

Saffron is more expensive than gold because harvesting it is so laborious.

Korean-Style Baked Chicken

by Lisa Soldo-Johnson - USA

I love the flavors of Korean barbecue. The combination of sweet, salty, and spicy are celebrated flavors to most of us who enjoy a good piece of BBQ chicken. This Asian favorite is made of tender chicken slow baked in a sweet and zesty sauce infused with fresh garlic and salty Nama Shoyu. It's easy to bake in the oven, but feel free to fire up the grill for an authentic BBQ experience.

Preparation Time: 10 minutes **Cook Time:** 45 minutes **Makes:** 6 servings

Ingredients:

- 4 skinless chicken legs
- 4 skinless chicken thighs
- 4 skinless chicken breasts
- ¾ cup agave nectar
- ½ cup Nama Shoyu
- ¼ cup sweet and zesty barbecue sauce
- 3 cloves garlic, minced

Method:

1. Preheat the oven to 350°F.
2. Whisk the agave nectar, Nama Shoyu, barbecue sauce, and garlic in a small bowl.
3. Line a 9x12 baking pan with tin foil. Lay chicken pieces inside the pan in a single layer.
4. Drizzle half of the sauce over the chicken pieces to coat evenly and pour the remaining sauce into a serving bowl. Bake for 45 minutes, turning once in-between.
5. Transfer the chicken to a serving plate and serve hot with reserved sauce.

Wisdom from Lisa's Kitchen:

I chose to use bottles BBQ sauce in this recipe rather than making it from scratch to provide an option for using basic ingredients found in most refrigerators.

If you like a lot of sauce, make a double batch. The extra sauce makes a wonderful complement over steak, fish, potatoes or grilled vegetables. It can be refrigerated up to 1 week.

Healthy Turkey Chow Mein

by Laurie Kerkinni - USA

This classic Chinese dish was one of my mom's favorites when we dined at the local restaurant in town, but most chow mein recipes are made with unhealthy ingredients and packed with preservatives. When Laurie introduced me to her healthy turkey chow mein recipe, I was beyond excited to try one of my mom's favorites without all the bad stuff. Laurie calls it, "The healthiest chow mein known to the culinary world." Works for me!

Preparation Time: 5 minutes **Cook Time:** 20-25 minutes **Makes:** 3-4 servings

Ingredients:

- 1 sweet or yellow onion, thinly sliced
- 4 stalks organic celery, roughly chopped
- 5 tablespoons olive oil, divided
- ½ teaspoon dried or fresh thyme
- 1-pound organic ground turkey thigh
- 2 tablespoons non-GMO cornstarch or tapioca starch
- ¼ cup plus 2 tablespoons organic Tamari, (gluten-free)
- 2 cups fresh bean sprouts
- 4 cups chow mein noodles, (Valley's Own Bakehouse or Gluten-free noodles)
- 4 cups steamed rice

Method:

1. Prepare the rice ahead of time.
2. Heat 3 tablespoons of the oil in a large skillet on medium-high. Add the onion and celery, sautéing 4 to 5 minutes (stirring often) until they begin to soften. Add the thyme and continue to sauté 4 to 5 minutes or until tender. Be careful not to let the onions burn. Push the vegetables to the side of the pan.
3. Add the remaining 2 tablespoons olive oil and the turkey to the skillet and sauté until browned. Mix in the onions and celery until well combined.
4. Whisk ¾ cup warm water and the cornstarch in a small bowl until dissolved. Whisk in the tamari and pour the sauce over the turkey mixture, stirring the sauce into the meat and cooking for 2 minutes. Stir in the bean sprouts, cover, and continue to cook for 2 minutes. You can adjust the flavor by adding more tamari if desired.
5. To serve, place the chow mein noodles in the middle of the plate and top with turkey mixture. Add the rice on the side of the plate and serve immediately.

Wisdom from Laurie's Kitchen:

I recommend doubling the batch because the leftovers are even better the next day!

Chicken Khoresht Bademjan - Persian Eggplant Stew with Chicken

by Mitra Murphy - Iran

Khoresht bademjan, also called Khoresht e bademjan or bademjoon, is traditional Persian stew prepared with eggplant, tomatoes, and either beef, chicken, or lamb meat. This rich, saucy dish is a hardy meal that is served at most traditional Persian dinner parties with basmati Rice and Lavash bread for dipping into the sauce.

Preparation Time: 25 minutes **Cook Time:** 1 hour 25 minutes **Makes:** 6 servings

Ingredients:

- 6 tablespoons cooking oil, divided, plus extra as needed
- 2 large onions, thinly sliced
- 2 garlic cloves, thinly sliced
- 2 pounds skinless chicken thighs
- 1 teaspoon turmeric
- ½ teaspoon ground saffron, dissolved in 4-tablespoons water
- 1 teaspoon salt
- ½ teaspoon pepper
- 1 cup warm water
- 2 cups tomato sauce
- 4 tablespoons lime juice
- 1 teaspoon crushed dried lemon (Sadaf)
- 2-3 medium purple Chinese eggplant
- 2 large eggs, whites only, beaten (optional)
- 20 grape tomatoes, halved

Method:

1. Peel the eggplant and slice lengthwise ½ inch thick. Place the eggplant in a colander and sprinkle both sides with salt to remove the bitter taste. Let sit for 20 minutes.
2. Heat 3 tablespoons of oil in a non-stick skillet over medium heat. Add the onions and garlic, sautéing for 3 minutes before adding the chicken. Continue to sauté for 5 minutes or until the chicken is lightly browned on both sides. Sprinkle the turmeric, saffron water, salt, and pepper over the chicken and stir to combine, sautéing for 1 minute.
3. Pour in 1 cup of warm water, tomato sauce, lime juice, and dried lemon powder. Stir, cover, and simmer on low heat for 30 minutes.
4. Preheat the oven to 350°F.
5. Rinse salt from eggplant slices and pat dry. Heat remaining 3 tablespoons oil in a large skillet over medium heat. Sauté the eggplant in batches until both sides are browned, adding more oil if needed. Remove the eggplant from the oil and set aside.
6. Transfer the chicken and sauce to an oven-proof casserole. Lay the eggplant on top of the chicken widthwise across the pan. Place the tomatoes, flat side down, evenly across the top of the Khoresht.
7. Cover with aluminum foil and bake for 30 minutes. Remove the cover and continue to bake an additional 15 minutes. Remove from the oven and let rest for 15 minutes before serving. Serve over saffron basmati rice.

Wisdom from Mitra's Kitchen:

You will use 2 to 3 Chinese eggplants depending on the size. However, you can substitute one medium regular eggplant if Chinese eggplant is not available.

Did You Know?

Bademjan or bademjoon means eggplant and khoresht means stew in Farsi.

CHAPTER 5

Beef, Lamb, Pork

The Story of Kabobs / 87

Koobideh - Persian Beef Kabobs / 89

Shaami Kabab - Breaded Beef Patties / 90

Ghormeh Sabzi - Persian Herb Stew / 91

Kebab in Puff Pastry / 92

Koofteh Persian Meatballs / 95

Pork Ribs with Ginger and Chili / 96

Israeli Lamb and Beef Kabobs / 97

Maldoum - Syrian Eggplant, Meat, and Tomato / 98

Dobo - Leg of Lamb / 99

Open-Face Hot Beef Sandwich / 101

Tass Kebob - Persian Meat and Potato Casserole / 102

German Sauerkraut and Spareribs / 103

Börek - Meat Filled Pastry / 105

Khoresht Karafs - Persian Celery Stew / 106

Stuffed Bok Choy / 107

Roasted Pork and Green Chili Enchiladas / 108

Russian Stuffed Peppers / 111

Moussaka / 112

Pasta Genovese / 113

Mama Hernandez Tacos / 114

Spicy Sichuan Beef / 117

Beef Khoresht Bademjan - Persian Eggplant Stew with Beef / 118

Moroccan Lamb Chops / 119

The Story of Kabobs

There is a beautiful connection between food and ethnicities that often bind us together in the pages of history. Over time, each culture creates and defines their version of the same dish mainly depending on the climate and ingredients available in those regions. Kabobs have been around for centuries with many cultures laying claim to the ancient grilled meat as part of their culinary heritage. But, where did the kabob originate?

History tells of Persian warriors in medieval times who would use their swords to roast meat over an open fire. The weighty iron sword would become searing hot, cooking the meat evenly from both the outside and the inside. This technique became a traditional cultural method of roasting meats on skewers. This culinary craft passed down through the ages is shared across the world by many cultures. To this day, people often make kabobs using metal skewers with wood handles to create the same authentic grilled meat enjoyed over fifteen hundred years ago.

Koobideh - Persian Beef Kabobs

by Ameneh Gounilli - Iran

In Iran, Kabob Koobideh (beef kabobs) is one of the most popular signature dishes in their culture. This savory dish uses lamb, beef, or a combination of both. Like most traditional recipes, each family has developed their own unique approach to this timeless classic by choosing their preferred combination of meats, spices, and herbs for koobideh.

Since traditional Persian food is carefully prepared using fresh-cut vegetables, herbs, spices, and meats; many times, the recipes can be time-consuming to make. With Kabob Koobideh, prepare your rice and salad in advance, and you will have an authentic Persian dinner on your table in less than an hour.

Preparation Time: 15 minutes   **Cook Time:** 30 minutes   **Makes:** 4-6 servings

Ingredients:

- 1-pound ground beef, 80/20
- ¾ cup grated onion
- ½ cup chopped cilantro
- 1 teaspoon salt
- 1 teaspoon sumac
- 1 teaspoon coriander seeds
- 1 teaspoon turmeric, divided
- ⅛ teaspoon black pepper

Method:

1. Finely grate the onions in a food processor or hand grater and pour into a large bowl.
2. Add the ground beef, cilantro, turmeric, 1 teaspoon salt, sumac, coriander seeds, and cayenne pepper to the bowl and - wearing gloves - mix together until completely combined. Form the meat into small 1 inch cocktail-size meatballs and set aside on a plate.
3. Heat the oil in a large skillet over medium heat. Add the meatballs in batches if the pan isn't large enough to fit all of them at one time, being careful not to overcrowd the pan. Brown meatballs on all sides. While meatballs are cooking, sprinkle remaining 1 teaspoon turmeric, and ½ teaspoon lemon pepper over meat, reserving some of the spices if you are cooking in batches. Pour lime juice over meatballs, reduce the heat to medium-low and simmer for 10 minutes.
4. Pour tomato sauce over meatballs and add the cherry tomatoes, distributing both evenly in the pan. Sprinkle the sauce with remaining 1 teaspoon salt, 1 teaspoon dried dill, remaining ½ teaspoon lemon pepper, and a light sprinkle of turmeric. Add barberries evenly across the meatballs and sauce, cover, and reduce the heat to low, simmering for 10 minutes.
5. Transfer the meatballs and sauce to a large serving bowl. Serve with basmati rice and a salad.

 Wisdom from Ameneh's Kitchen:
Be generous with the turmeric.

Using 80% fat/ 20% lean beef keeps the meat tender. Using leaner beef gives the dish a much drier texture and taste.

Shaami Kabab - Breaded Beef Patties

by Shaya Chatraei - Iran

Shaami kababs are lightly breaded meat patties infused with a combination of fresh ingredients like onion, cilantro turmeric, and egg. Though Shami kebabs originated hundreds of years ago in the Indian subcontinent, many countries including Iran have adopted their version of these exotic meat patties. They are crispy on the outside and tender on the inside. Shaya's version of Shaami kabab is made with potatoes and a splash of lemon juice. You can serve them with a meal, as an appetizer, or light snack.

Preparation Time: 15 minutes   **Cook Time:** Approximately 1 hour   **Makes:** 12 Cutlets

Ingredients:

- 2 medium Yukon Gold potatoes, peeled and halved
- 1-pound ground beef
- 1 large onion, grated
- ¼ cup chopped cilantro
- 3 eggs
- 1 teaspoon turmeric
- 1 teaspoon salt, plus extra for dusting
- ½ teaspoon pepper
- 4 tablespoons olive oil, plus more if needed
- 2 cups Panko bread crumbs
- 1-2 lemons, halved

Method:

1. Bring a pot of water to a boil. Add potatoes and cook for 15 minutes or until tender but still firm. Drain the water and using a potato masher or electric beater, blend the potatoes until smooth. Set aside to cool.
2. Add the potatoes, ground beef, onion, cilantro, eggs, turmeric, salt, and pepper to a large bowl and mix until evenly combined.
3. Using ⅓ cup, shape the meat mixture into pear-shaped patties ½ inch thick. Set patty on a plate and repeat until all of the patties are formed.
4. Heat the oil in a large skillet over medium-high heat. While the oil is heating, coat one patty at a time in the bread crumbs and gently place them into the hot oil. Add more oil if needed
5. Using lemon halves, lightly squeeze juice over each patty and cook 5 to 8 minutes or until golden brown. Turn cutlets over, cover and reduce the heat to low. Simmer for 10 to 15 minutes or until the cutlets are cooked. Squeeze additional lemon juice over cooked cutlets and lightly dust with salt.
6. Remove the cutlets from the oil and set aside on a paper towel to drain oil. Serve warm.

Wisdom from Shaya's Kitchen:

The cutlets should have subtle notes of lemon and salt when the right amount of both is added. Adjust the ingredients as needed.

Ghormeh Sabzi - Persian Herb Stew

by Shaya Chatraie - Iran

Ghormeh Sabzi is a traditional herb stew from Iran. This slow-cooked stew is bursting with a fusion of aromatic herbs, tender lamb or beef, tender beans, and dried lemons or limes that create an authentic Persian-style meal.

Preparation Time: 10 minutes   **Cook Time:** 90 minutes   **Makes:** 4-6 servings

Ingredients:

- 2 pounds boneless lamb or beef stewing meat, cubed ¾-inch
- 1 large onions, finely chopped
- ⅓ cup vegetable oil, divided
- 1 teaspoon turmeric
- 1 ½ cup water
- ¾ cup canned kidney beans, drained
- 1 teaspoon salt
- ½ teaspoon pepper
- 1 large potato, peeled and diced
- 1 ½ cups finely chopped spinach
- 1 cup chopped green onions
- ½ cup chopped parsley
- ¼ cup chopped cilantro
- ¼ cup chopped garlic chives
- 1 tablespoon dried fenugreek
- 3-4 dried limes or 3 tablespoons lime juice
- 4 cups basmati rice

Method:

1. Sauté the oil and onions in a large skillet over medium heat until golden brown. Add the turmeric and simmer for 2 minutes to infuse the onions.
2. Increase the heat to medium-high and add the meat, browning until all sides are seared.
3. Stir in the water, kidney beans, salt, and pepper, cover and reduce the heat to low.
4. In a separate pan, heat the remaining oil on high heat. Add the potatoes and sauté until they are lightly browned. Leaving the oil in the pan, spoon the potatoes into the stew and return the pan to the heat.
5. Add the spinach, onions, parsley, cilantro, garlic chives, and fenugreek seeds to the oil and sauté until the vegetables are slightly wilted. Transfer the ingredients into the stew pot, stirring to combine.
6. Increase the heat to medium-high, add enough water to the pot to cover the stew by 2 inches, stir and bring to a boil for 2 minutes. Reduce the heat, cover and cook on medium-low for 1 hour.
7. After 1 hour, the stew should have a pleasant balance of aromatic herbs and meat with the subtle essence of lime. Adjust the salt and pepper if needed and add 1 to 2 cups of water if the stew is too thick. Cover and continue to simmer for an additional 30 minutes.
8. Prepare the rice 1 hour before the stew is done. Serve Ghormeh Sabzi hot with basmati rice.

Did You Know?

Farsi is the most widely spoken language in Iran. In Farsi, Ghormeh Sabzi translates to, Ghormeh (stewed) and Sabzi (herbs).

Wisdom from Shaya's Kitchen:

The longer Ghormeh Sabzi simmers, the better it tastes. You can leave the stew to simmer on low 2 to 3 hours if time allows.

You can use either dried limes or dried lemons in this recipe. Both can be purchased at Middle Eastern grocery stores or online.

Kebab in Puff Pastry

by Suheyla Kerkinni - Assyria

I'm a huge fan of puff pastry, so when Suheyla told me about her Kebab in Puff pastry, I just had to make it. Tender chunks of lamb, beef, or veal simmered in a red wine sauce and combined with fresh herbs and vegetables. This symphony of flavors bakes into a buttery puff pastry crust for an amazing meal.

Preparation Time: 15 minutes   **Cook Time:** 1 hour   **Makes:** 6 servings

Ingredients:

- 1 ½ pounds boneless lamb, beef, or veal cut into ½-inch cubes
- 3 tablespoons olive oil
- 1 large onion, minced
- 2 medium carrots, peeled and diced
- 2 cups chopped parsley, divided
- 1 teaspoon salt
- ½ teaspoon pepper
- 2 medium tomatoes, diced
- ½ teaspoon dried thyme (optional)
- 1 cup red wine
- 1 cup hot water
- 3 tablespoons butter, plus extra for brushing
- 2 medium potatoes, peeled and diced
- ½ cup frozen peas
- 2 puff pastry sheets, thawed

Wisdom from Suheyla's Kitchen:

I prefer to use lamb because it makes the most tender, flavorful filling. Ask your butcher to cut your meat ahead of time into chunks to save time when preparing.

Method:

1. Heat the oil in a skillet over medium heat. Add the meat and sauté 5 to 6 minutes or until lightly browned.
2. Add the onions, carrots, 1 cup parsley, salt, and pepper, sautéing for 5 minutes, stirring occasionally.
3. Stir in the tomatoes, thyme, and wine, simmering for 3 minutes to infuse the flavors.
4. Add 1 cup of hot water, cover, reduce the heat to medium-low and cook until meat is tender when pierced with a fork. Approximately 45 to 60 minutes for lamb or veal and longer for beef. Add more hot water if liquid absorbs before the meat is tender. The liquid should be absorbed by the time the meat is cooked.
5. While the meat is simmering, heat the butter in a small pan over medium heat. Add the potatoes and sauté 8 to 10 minutes or until lightly browned. Add in the peas and sauté 2 minutes, cover and set aside.
6. When the meat is tender, spoon potato mixture into the pan with the meat mixture and gently stir to combine all ingredients.
7. Preheat the oven to 375°F. Line a baking sheet with parchment paper.
8. Lightly flour a work surface and lay a pastry sheet on the floured surface. Cut the puff pastry in thirds vertically on the seams. Cut the dough in half horizontally to create six squares. Gently roll each pastry square in to 6 inch squares. Divide the meat mixture into 12 servings and spoon it into the center of the pastry square.
9. Bring the ends of the puff pastry together to meet in the middle, closing the filling inside by pinching the sides together down the 4 seams of the pastry and twisting the ends together at the top. Make sure the ends and seams are closed securely. Repeat with the second pastry sheet and lay the puff pastries on the prepared baking sheet. (Use second baking sheet to fit all pastries if necessary.)
10. Bake for 20 to 25 minutes or until the pastry is golden and puffed. Brush the tops with butter and serve hot.

Did You Know?

During the Roman Empire, the Romans used pastry dough to keep meats moist while cooking but would throw away the dough when the meat was cooked.

Koofteh Persian Meatballs

by Ameneh Gounilli - Iran

Koofteh in Farsi means "pounded or ground" because many years ago in Iran, Koofteh was pounded with a large pestle and mortar to give the meat a sticky texture that held it together when cooked. Many cultures around the world have their version of Koofteh prepared with a variety of spices, herbs, and other ingredients that make the meatballs culturally unique from one another. Ameneh's Koofteh has a French influence with the incorporation of lemon pepper that sets this dish apart from other traditional recipes.

Preparation Time: 15 minutes   **Cook Time:** 30 minutes   **Makes:** 4-6 servings

Ingredients:

- 1-pound ground beef, 80% lean/ 20% fat
- ¾ cup onions, grated
- ½ cup chopped cilantro
- 2 teaspoons turmeric, divided
- 2 teaspoons salt, divided
- 1 teaspoon sumac
- 1 teaspoon coriander seeds
- ⅛ teaspoon cayenne pepper
- 3-4 tablespoons olive oil
- 1 teaspoon lemon pepper, divided
- 2 cups tomato sauce
- 2 tablespoons lime juice
- 12 cherry tomatoes
- ¼ cup barberries

Method:

1. Finely grate the onions in a food processor or hand grater. Pour into a large bowl.
2. Add the ground beef, cilantro, turmeric, 1 teaspoon salt, sumac, coriander seeds, and cayenne pepper to the bowl and - wearing gloves - mix together until completely combined. Form the meat into small 1 inch cocktail-size meatballs and set aside on a plate.
3. Heat the oil in a large skillet over medium heat. Add the meatballs in batches if the pan isn't large enough to fit all of them at once, being careful not to overcrowd the pan. Brown meatballs on all sides. While meatballs are cooking, sprinkle remaining 1 teaspoon turmeric and ½ teaspoon lemon pepper over meat, reserving some of the spices if you are cooking in batches. Pour lime juice over meatballs, reduce heat to medium-low and simmer for 10 minutes.
4. Pour tomato sauce over meatballs and add the cherry tomatoes, distributing evenly. Sprinkle the sauce with remaining 1 teaspoon salt, 1 teaspoon dried dill, remaining ½ teaspoon lemon pepper, and a light sprinkle of turmeric. Add barberries evenly across the meatballs and sauce, cover, reduce heat to low and simmer for 10 minutes.
5. Transfer the meatballs and sauce to a large serving bowl. Serve with basmati rice and a salad.

Wisdom from Ameneh's Kitchen:

Be generous with the turmeric. There is no such thing as too much turmeric in this dish.

Using 80/20 beef keeps the meatballs tender. Using leaner beef gives the dish a much drier texture and taste.

Pork Ribs with Ginger and Chili

by Rachel Huang - China

These pork ribs with ginger and chili are good to the bone eating. With only five minutes to prep and thirty minutes on the stove, you will love the incredible flavor that comes through with every bite. Serve it with rice, a bowl of steamed edamame, or your favorite vegetable.

Preparation Time: 5 minutes   **Cook Time:** 30 minutes   **Makes:** 2 servings

Ingredients:

- 1-pound (6 ribs) pork ribs
- 2 garlic cloves, minced
- 1-inch fresh ginger, peeled and minced
- ½ Thai chili pepper, minced
- 1 ½ teaspoon preserved beans with ginger
- ¼ teaspoon salt
- ⅛ teaspoon sugar
- ½ teaspoon soy sauce
- 1 teaspoon cornstarch

Method:

1. Soak the pork ribs in water for 5 minutes to clean. Drain and set them aside in a medium bowl.
2. While the meat is soaking, mix the garlic, ginger, chili pepper, preserved beans, salt, sugar, soy sauce, and cornstarch in a small bowl. Spoon the sauce over the meat and mix until the meat is completely coated.
3. Fill the bottom of a steamer pot with water just below the upper pot. Bring the water to a boil, add the pork ribs to the upper pot, cover, and steam on medium-high for 30 minutes. Be careful not to let the water evaporate from the bottom pot before the meat is done. Add more water if needed. Serve the ribs with rice and a vegetable.

Wisdom from Rachel's Kitchen:

Adding sugar acts like the flavor enhancer MSG but is a much healthier way to increase the flavor of Chinese food.

The cornstarch helps to make the ribs more tender, creating a softer texture to the meat.

Yang Jiang Preserved Black Beans can be purchased in Asian grocery stores or on Amazon. This brand has a higher rating in quality and can be stored in a glass jar in the freezer indefinitely.

Did You Know?

Fermented black beans are made from soybeans that have been dried and fermented with salt and spices including chilies, wine, or ginger.

Israeli Lamb and Beef Kabobs

by Vivi Mizrahi - Israel

Kabobs are a flavorful dish made from ground beef, chicken, lamb — or a combination, and traditionally prepared on a skewer over a hot grill. What I like most about Vivi's Israeli lamb and beef kabobs is her technique of baking rather than grilling. The results are tender, juicy kabobs bursting with taste. This preparation method also gives you more time to prepare the rest of the meal while the kabobs are in the oven. Israeli lamb and beef kabobs - traditionally served with a side of rice and tabouli salad - is a quick and easy meal that can be prepared in under an hour.

Preparation Time: 25 minutes **Cook Time:** 30 minutes **Makes:** 6 servings

Ingredients:

- 2 pounds ground beef
- 1 pound of ground lamb
- 2 cups Italian bread crumbs
- 4 large onions, quartered and minced
- 1 large bunch cilantro, minced
- 4 eggs
- 1 teaspoon cumin
- 1 teaspoon curry
- 1-¼ teaspoon paprika
- 1 tablespoon chicken bouillon powder or paste
- 3 teaspoons sea salt
- 1 teaspoon pepper

Method:

1. In a large bowl combine the bread crumbs, onions, cilantro, eggs, cumin, curry, paprika, chicken bouillon, salt, and pepper.
2. Gently rinse the ground meat with water in a colander and place in the bowl. Using your hands, massage all of the ingredients into the meat, adding more breadcrumbs if the meat is sticky or has too much liquid.
3. Preheat the oven to 350°F.
4. Using the end of a wooden spoon, wrap 3 tablespoons of the meat around the spoon handle to form a 3 inch kabob. Carefully pull the kabob from the stick and lay on a tin foil-lined baking tray. Repeat this process until all of the meat is used.
5. Bake 15 minutes. Turn over and bake an additional 15 minutes.
6. Serve hot with rice and tabouli salad (page 41).

Wisdom from Vivi's Kitchen:

There is a lot of flavor in the stem of the cilantro, so I like to include 2 inches of the stems below the leaves for better flavor.

Using the stick of a round wood spoon when forming the kabobs leaves a hole in the center of the meat which helps it to cook more evenly and keeps the meat tender.

Did You Know?

Cherry tomatoes were originally engineered in Israel in 1973.

Maldoum - Syrian Eggplant, Meat, and Tomato

by Laurie Kerkinni - USA

Syrian cuisine, like most other cultures around the world, passes traditional recipes down through generations that vary between regions and families. Maldoum is a dish originating from the north Syrian city of Aleppo and has found a welcome place in my kitchen. Laurie taught me to make her version of Maldoum - a rustic layered meat and eggplant dish baked to perfection. It is suitable as an appetizer, side dish, or main course with rice.

Preparation Time: 30 minutes
Passive Time: 40 - 60 minutes
Cook Time: 1 hour 10 minutes
Makes: 6-8 servings

Ingredients:

- 2 medium-sized eggplant, sliced
- 1-pound ground beef or lamb, 90/10
- olive oil
- 1 teaspoon allspice
- 1 teaspoon salt
- ½ teaspoon fresh cracked pepper
- 1 egg
- ¼ cup Ritz cracker crumbs
- 5-6 Roma tomatoes, sliced
- 1 large bell pepper, roughly chopped

Wisdom from Laurie's Kitchen:

Sautéing eggplant in a tall soup pot prevents the oil from splashing up on the stove and countertops.

Use gluten-free bread crumbs for a gluten-free option.

Did You Know?

The "Shouting Valley" is the meeting point of four countries: Syria, Lebanon, Jordan, and Israel where people use megaphones to talk to their relatives across the valley.

Method:

1. Slice the eggplant ½ inch thick crosswise. Lay the slices on paper towels and lightly salt. Turn the eggplant over when the water droplets come to the top (15 to 20 minutes). Lightly salt again. When water droplets form, pat the eggplant dry with paper towel.
2. While eggplant is being prepared, mix the meat, allspice, salt, pepper, egg, and cracker crumbs in a medium bowl.
3. Slice the tomatoes ½ inch thick.
4. Heat the oil in a large skillet over medium heat. Using a pastry brush, lightly brush eggplant slices on both sides with egg white and lay them in the oil in a single layer. Sauté 4 to 5 minutes on each side or until they are golden brown. Remove eggplant slices and set them on a paper towel to remove excess oil. Repeat until all of the eggplant is cooked.
5. Preheat the oven to 350°F.
6. Form the meat patties using 1 tablespoon of meat or enough to match the size of an eggplant slice. (If you are using large eggplant, cut the slices in half before assembling.) Place a patty between 2 eggplant slices and set standing up in a 9x11 baking dish. Place a tomato between each set of eggplant patties. Repeat creating 3 rows down the length of the pan until the dish is filled.
7. If you have extra meat, form 2 rolls, gently tucking them between the eggplant patty rows. Top with peppers.
8. Pour water into the bottom of the dish halfway to the top. Bake uncovered for 1 hour. Serve with couscous, bulgur or rice.

Dobo - Leg of Lamb

by Suheyla Kerkinni - Assyria

Dobo is a traditional leg of lamb dish made for generation in Suheyla's family. The process of slow simmering the meat in a seasoned tomato sauce allows the natural juices of the lamb to permeate the flavors with subtle notes of tender lamb, garlic, and allspice. The succulent meat, served over a bed of rice and paired with a fresh green salad, gives you a culinary glimpse into the enthralling flavors of authentic Assyrian cuisine.

Preparation Time: 10 minutes   **Cook Time:** 2 hours 35 minutes   **Makes:** 4-6 servings

Ingredients:

- 3-4 pounds leg of lamb
- 3 tablespoons olive oil
- 4 garlic cloves, minced
- 4-ounces plus 1-tablespoon tomato paste, divided
- 1 tablespoon allspice, whole
- water
- 2 teaspoons salt
- ½ teaspoon pepper
- parsley for garnish

Method:

1. Season the meat with salt and pepper and spread 1 tablespoon of tomato paste on both sides.
2. Heat the oil in a Dutch oven over medium-high heat. Add the meat and brown for 3 to 4 minutes on each side.
3. Add the garlic and allspice and cover the meat with water ¾ inch below the top of the meat. Reduce the heat to medium, cover and cook for 1 hour.
4. Preheat the oven to 250°F.
5. Stir in the remaining 4 ounces of tomato paste, cover and transfer to the oven to roast for 1 hour 30 minutes or longer until the meat is tender. The liquid should remain 1 ½ inches above the meat. Continue to check the water level every 30 minutes, adding more water if needed.
6. Place the meat on a serving tray with sides, strain the sauce into a bowl to remove the whole allspice and garlic cloves, and pour the sauce over the meat to serve. Garnish with parsley and serve with rice.

Wisdom from Suheyla's Kitchen:

Rinse and soak the rice while the Dobo is simmering and begin cooking it one hour before the Dobo is done.

You can roast the Dobo in the oven on a low temperature for 2 hours or longer to enhance the tenderness and flavor of the meat.

Did You Know?

The meat of a sheep in its first year is lamb.

Sheep are exclusively herbivores; they eat a range of grass, clover, forbs, and other pasture plants.

May 7th is National Roast Leg of Lamb Day.

Open-Face Hot Beef Sandwich

by Lorraine Soldo USA

Hot beef sandwiches were a family recipe passed down to my mother by her parents over 70 years ago. This dish became my mom's signature recipe, and she was often encouraged by dinner guests to open a restaurant that only served her famous hot beef sandwich. An old-fashioned down-home comfort food that's easy to make and will make you glad you stayed home for dinner.

Preparation Time: 15 minutes   **Cook Time:** 7 hours   **Makes:** 8-10 servings

Ingredients:

- 4-5-pound rump roast
- 3 tablespoons cooking oil
- Large onion, chopped
- 6 bay leaves
- ¼ cup dried onion flakes
- ½ teaspoon onion powder
- ½ teaspoon garlic powder
- ½ teaspoon dried parsley
- ½ teaspoon salt
- ¼ teaspoon celery powder
- ¼ teaspoon black pepper
- 8-10 slices Rye bread
- Horseradish or Dijon mustard

Method:

1. Preheat the oven to 350°F.
2. Rinse the roast and pat dry. Heat the oil in a sauté pan over medium-high heat. Brown the meat on all sides and transfer to a roasting pan. Roast the meat for 1 hour.
3. Remove the meat from the oven and reduce the heat to 250°F. Lay the meat on a cutting board and cut into ¼ inch slices. Return the meat to the roasting pan, add the onions, bay leaves, and enough water to cover the meat by 1 inch.
4. Sprinkle in the onion flakes, onion powder, garlic powder, dried parsley, salt, celery powder, and black pepper. Gently stir the spices into the water above the meat. Return to oven and bake for 6 hours, checking to see if the meat is tender when pierced with a fork. The internal temperature should reach 160° F. Continue to bake if needed.

Assembly:

1. Using tongs, remove the meat from the roasting pan and set on a cutting board. The meat should be tender enough to shred apart using two forks. If not, use a knife and fork to roughly shred the meat into thin pieces.
2. Make the beef stock into gravy. (page 189).
3. Lay 1 to 2 pieces of Rye bread on each plate and top with a generous pile of beef. Ladle the gravy on top of the beef, spoon a dollop of horseradish sauce or Dijon mustard on top (optional) and serve immediately.

Wisdom from Lorraine's Kitchen:

Slow cooking is required for this dish. The longer the meat cooks the more tender it will be.

Beef, Lamb, Pork | 101

Tass Kebob - Persian Meat and Potato Casserole

by Mitra Murphy - Iran

Tass Kebob is a hearty Persian meat and potato one-pot meal slowly simmered with beef or lamb, fresh vegetables, and aromatic spices. Genuine Iranian down-home cooking uses ground meat patties in place of cubed meat like many traditional Tass Kebob recipes. Enjoy an authentic Persian meal by serving Tass Kebob with basmati rice, Mast-o khiar, and a fresh salad.

Preparation Time: 15 minutes   **Cook Time:** 40 minutes   **Makes:** 4-6 servings

Ingredients:

- 3 tablespoons olive oil
- 1-pound ground beef or lamb
- 1 medium onion, grated
- 1 large onion, halved and sliced ¼-inch thick
- 2 large potatoes, peeled and slice thin, ⅛-inch
- 1 large bell pepper, sliced
- 1 can (16-ounce) tomato sauce
- 2 cups water
- 1 teaspoon crushed dried lemon
- 1 teaspoon turmeric
- 2 tablespoons lime juice
- ½ teaspoon salt
- ½ teaspoon pepper
- 1 large tomato, sliced

Method:

1. Combine the ground beef and grated onions in a medium bowl and form into 6 to 8 patties.
2. Heat the oil in a heavy bottomed non-stick pot on medium-high heat. Lay the patties at the bottom of the pot, browning on each side. Using a slotted spatula, remove the patties from the pot and set aside.
3. Whisk the tomato sauce, water, crushed dried lemon, turmeric, lime juice, salt, and pepper in a small bowl. Pour enough sauce to cover the bottom of the pan and lay meat patties on top of the sauce.
4. Layer in the sliced onions, potatoes, and peppers.
5. Pour the remaining sauce over the casserole, reduce the heat to medium-low, cover and cook 20 to 30 minutes or until potatoes are tender and meat is done. Be sure to check the casserole as it cooks and reduce the heat to low if needed to prevent the meat burning at the bottom of the pot.
6. Lay sliced tomatoes on top, spooning some of the sauce over tomatoes, cover and continue to cook for an additional 10 minutes. Adjust the flavor as needed with salt and pepper. Serve with basmati rice and Mast-o khiar (page 169).

Wisdom from Mitra's Kitchen:

Add a little water if the juice begins to get too low while cooking. You want to have enough sauce when it's cooked to enjoy over the meat and rice.

It is very important to slice the potatoes no thicker than ⅛ inch or they will not cook evenly.

Tass Kebab can burn easily during the cooking process. It is important to reduce the heat and increase the cooking time if the meat begins to overcook before the casserole is done.

Some tomato sauce brands have higher acidity with a bitter taste. You can add up to 1 teaspoon of granulated sugar to the sauce to reduce the acid if needed.

You can use a combination of both beef and lamb.

German Sauerkraut and Spareribs

by Lorraine Soldo - USA

My mom grew up during the Great Depression when food was scarce, and nothing wasted. Preparing meals like sauerkraut and spareribs for a large family was a staple in her home since this dish requires only a few ingredients and not a lot of fuss. Slowly boiled pork spare ribs simmered in water and sauerkraut is an easy to make classic dish served in many German homes around the world. Serve with boiled potatoes tossed in melted butter, salt, and pepper with a side of corn and a salad for an authentic German dining experience cooked in a little over an hour.

Preparation Time: 5 minutes **Cook Time:** 90 minutes **Makes:** 4 servings

Ingredients:

- 3 ½ pounds pork spareribs
- 1 teaspoon salt, divided
- 4-6 cups raw organic sauerkraut
- 4 medium Yukon Gold potatoes, peeled and halved
- 4 tablespoons butter
- 1 teaspoon salt, plus more for spicing
- pepper, for spicing

 Wisdom from Lorraine's Kitchen:

Select ribs that are pinkish-red in color with some marbling and plenty of visible fat on the meat for tenderness and flavor.

The longer pork ribs cook, the more tender the meat will be. Use a fork to test the tenderness. Continue to slow cook up to 30 minutes extra if the meat is not tender enough.

Raw organic sauerkraut is best since it does not have the preservatives or nitrates found in some packaged sauerkraut.

Make extra sauerkraut! A family tradition is to create a sauerkraut sandwich by buttering a piece of white bread, folding in half, and filling it with sauerkraut for a delicious sandwich.

Method:

1. Rinse the ribs in cold water, cut the slab in half and place them in a large pot of water filled just above the ribs. Add ½ teaspoon salt and bring the water to a boil on high heat. Reduce the heat and boil on medium-high for 45 minutes, turning the ribs over at 20 minutes to cook evenly. Using a slotted spoon, remove any fat that come to the top of the water.

2. Add the sauerkraut to the water, reduce heat to medium and cook for an additional 45 minutes.

3. Prepare the potatoes 30 minutes before the ribs are done. Boil 6 cups of water in a medium pot adding the potatoes and remaining ½ teaspoon salt. Reduce the heat to medium-high, boiling for 20 to 25 minutes or until the potatoes are soft when pierced with a fork. Drain the potatoes in a colander.

4. Melt the butter in a pan over medium heat. Add the potatoes and gently stir to coat. Sprinkle in a generous amount of salt and pepper, gently tossing to combine. Remove the pan from the heat, cover and set aside to keep the potatoes warm.

5. When the spareribs are done, carefully remove each slab from the water and transfer them to a colander to drain the excess liquid. Lay the ribs on a cutting board and separate the ribs with a sharp knife. Place them in the middle of a large serving plate.

6. Carefully pour the sauerkraut into the colander to drain out excess liquid. Spoon the sauerkraut around the perimeter of the platter and the ribs.

7. Add the potatoes on top of the sauerkraut and serve hot with a side of corn and a green salad.

Börek - Meat Filled Pastry

by Suheyla Kerkinni - Assyria

Börek has a long history that dates back thousands of years yet is enjoyed even today. Börek is a dish made from thin flaky dough and layered with a variety of meats, cheese, vegetables, or fruits depending on which area of the world has reinterpreted it. Suheyla's borek is packed full of juicy, flavorful beef and vegetables baked into buttery layers of fluffy dough for a savory experience. This dish is sure to be a crowd-pleaser.

Preparation Time: 30 minutes   **Cook Time:** 45 minutes   **Makes:** 8 servings

Ingredients:

- 1-pound ground beef
- 1 ½ stick butter, divided
- 1 large onion, diced
- 1 large bell pepper, seeded and finely diced
- 1 medium tomato, diced
- 1 teaspoon salt
- ½ teaspoon pepper
- ¼ cup chopped parsley
- 1-pound phyllo dough
- 1 large egg, beaten
- ¼ cup milk
- 2 tablespoons sesame seeds

Wisdom from Suheyla's Kitchen:

Keep the unused phyllo dough under a slightly damp cloth or paper towel to prevent it from drying out while you are assembling the borek.

Method:

1. Heat the butter in a large skillet over medium heat. Add the ground beef and sauté 5 minutes. Add the onions and continue to sauté for an additional 5 minutes. Add the peppers and tomatoes, sautéing again for 5 minutes before removing the pan from the heat.
2. Preheat the oven to 350°F. Prepare a 12 x 15 glass baking pan with oil or butter.
3. Melt the butter in a small pan over medium heat. Remove the pan from the heat and whisk in the beaten egg and milk.
4. Unroll the pastry sheets and lay both stacks on a flat surface. Place the baking pan on top of one dough stack. Using the tip of a sharp knife, cut the dough around the outside of the pan so the dough fits in your pan. Discard the outside pieces. Repeat with the second stack and refrigerate one stack of dough until you are ready to use it.
5. Working gently but quickly, lay one sheet of pastry dough on the bottom of the pan. Using a pastry brush, lightly brush melted butter mixture on top of the dough and repeat with another layer of dough. Continue to layer the dough and butter until the first stack of phyllo dough is used.
6. Spoon the meat mixture evenly across the dough.
7. Remove the second stack of dough from the refrigerator and repeat the layering process with the dough and butter. Sprinkle the top with sesame seeds and using a sharp knife, cut the borek into 16 equal squares.
8. Bake for 30 minutes or until the top is lightly browned. Remove the borek from the oven and let it rest 10 minutes before serving.

Khoresht Karafs - Persian Celery Stew

by Sohiela Mirsharif - Iran

Khoresht Karafs is a Persian Celery Stew bathed in the aromatic flavor of turmeric, curry, and mint combined with celery and lamb or beef. The stew slowly simmers to create an eruption of exotic flavors. What makes Sohiela's recipe special is her technique. Each ingredient is prepared individually with just a touch of salt and pepper to enhance its flavor before they are affected by the rest of the characteristics in the dish. I asked Sohiela, "What should this dish taste like?" She smiled and said, "A recipe is perfect when you taste it and can't tell one ingredient from the other, and all you know about the dish is that it's delicious. That's when you know it's right."

Preparation Time: 10 minutes   **Cook Time:** 2 hours 15 minutes   **Makes:** 6 servings

Ingredients:

- 1-pound lamb shoulder or beef, cut into 1-inch pieces
- 6 tablespoons grapeseed oil, divided
- 4 cups organic celery, cut into 1-inch pieces
- 1 ¼ teaspoon salt, divided
- 1-¼ teaspoon black pepper, divided
- 2 tablespoons dried mint
- 1 bunch curly parsley, finely chopped
- 1 ½ cup finely chopped scallions
- 1 ½ cup diced onions
- 1 tablespoon tomato paste
- ½ teaspoon turmeric
- ½ teaspoon curry
- ½ teaspoon paprika
- 9 cups boiling water, divided
- ½ teaspoon lemon juice, fresh squeezed, add more if desired

Method:

1. Heat 2 tablespoons of the oil in a Dutch oven or non-stick pot over medium heat. Add the celery and sauté until the celery becomes translucent. Sprinkle with ¼ teaspoon salt and ¼ teaspoon pepper, stir, transfer celery to a medium bowl and set aside.
2. Add 1 tablespoon of oil, parsley, dried mint and scallions to the pot and sauté for 1 minute or until parsley begins to darken slightly. Lightly sprinkle with ¼ teaspoon salt and ¼ teaspoon pepper and stir to combine. Pour the parsley into the bowl with the celery. Continue using the same pot for each step.
3. Add 2 tablespoons of oil and the meat, browning on all sides. Transfer the meat to a separate bowl and set aside.
4. Add 1 tablespoon of oil and the onions, sautéing until slightly translucent. Transfer the meat back into the pot with the onions. Add the tomato paste, turmeric, curry, paprika, ¼ teaspoon salt, and ¼ teaspoon pepper. Stir until the meat and onions are evenly coated.
5. Pour 7 cups of boiling water over meat, stir and bring to a boil. Cover and reduce heat to medium-low and simmer for 30 minutes.
6. Stir in the celery mixture and remaining 2 cups of boiling water to keep the stew saucy. Cover and cook on medium heat for 1 hour or until the meat and celery are tender when pierced with a fork.
7. Stir in ½ teaspoon lemon juice and ½ teaspoon salt and simmer 10 minutes. Taste and add more lemon juice, salt or pepper if needed. Serve hot with basmati rice.

Wisdom from Sohiela's Kitchen:

When cooking individual ingredients, always add the seasoning at the end to allow the ingredient time to cook in its own flavor.

A famous Persian saying in my family: "Kam Bokhor Hamishe Bokhor" meaning, "Eat a little but always eat."

Stuffed Bok Choy

by Vivi Mizrahi - Israel

Stuffed vine leaves have been around for centuries and still made in kitchens throughout the globe. Stuffed grape leaves, also called dolmas or aprah du zayto, are typically served as an appetizer or side dish. Rather than traditional finger food, Vivi's stuffed bok choy leaves are wholesome and hardy, making this dish an excellent choice as the main course served with a side of rice.

Preparation Time: 25 minutes   **Cook Time:** 55 minutes   **Makes:** 6-8 servings

Ingredients:

- 2 heads bok choy, or 12-16 leaves
- 2 tablespoons canola oil
- 1 cup long grain rice
- 1-pound ground beef or ground turkey
- 1 teaspoon chicken bouillon paste or powder
- 1 teaspoon cumin
- ¾ teaspoon salt
- ¼ teaspoon pepper
- ¼ teaspoon curry powder
- ¾ cup boiling water, divided
- 2 cups tomato sauce
- 4 tablespoons Meyer lemon
- 1 teaspoon salt
- 1 ½ teaspoon granulated sugar

Method:

1. Remove the leaves from the stem, rinse and transfer leaves to a heat proof dish. Pour boiling water over the leaves and soak for 15 minutes or until they are soft and pliable. Drain the leaves in a colander and lay them flat on a cutting board.
2. Heat the oil in a non-stick pan over medium heat. Rinse off the rice, transfer it to the pan and sauté for 3 minutes, stirring continuously.
3. Add the ground meat and stir until combined with the rice. Add ¼ cup boiling water, chicken bouillon, cumin, salt, pepper, and curry powder, stirring continuously 7 to 8 minutes or until the meat is cooked. Remove the pan from the heat and set aside.
4. Take the drained leaves and spoon 1 to 2 tablespoons of the rice stuffing across the larger end of the leaves. Folding the end over the stuffing, begin rolling the leaf while folding the sides into the middle as you roll. Lay the stuffed leaf on the bottom of a large pan and repeat until all the leaves are filled. Keep the stuffed leaves close to each other in the pan.
5. Mix the tomato sauce, lemon juice, salt, and sugar in a small bowl and pour over the stuffed leaves. Pour ½ cup boiling water over the leaves and bring the pan to a boil on medium-high heat. Reduce the heat to low and simmer for 45 minutes. Using a spatula, gently move the leaves around in the pan every 15 minutes to prevent the leaves from sticking to the bottom of the pan. Serve hot with rice.

Wisdom from Vivi's Kitchen:

If the leaves of the bok choy are large (the size of your hand) cut them in half lengthwise and remove the center stem to create two separate leaves.

You can assemble this dish up to a day ahead to time and cook just before you are ready to serve.

Did You Know?

Bok choy is also called a "soup spoon" because of the shape of its leaves.

Roasted Pork and Green Chili Enchiladas

by Michael Hernandez - Mexico

When it comes to Mexican comfort food, it doesn't get better than this. Roasted Pork and Green Chili Enchiladas is a favorite family recipe of Michael's, who learned the art of authentic Mexican cooking as a child from his mother, Fermina. The slow roasted pork bathed in a fragrant spiced broth is then wrapped in a soft flour tortilla before baking under a creamy enchiladas sauce.

Preparation Time: 15 minutes   **Cook Time:** 3 hours 45 minutes   **Makes:** 4-8 servings

Ingredients:

- 3 pounds bone-in pork shoulder roast
- 3 tablespoons olive oil
- 1 large onion, diced
- 3 garlic cloves, minced
- 2 poblano chilis, roasted, peeled and diced
- 1 red bell pepper, diced
- 1 yellow or orange bell pepper, diced
- 4 cups chicken stock
- 1 teaspoon oregano
- 1 teaspoon basil
- 1 tablespoon cilantro, minced
- 1 teaspoon cumin
- 1 teaspoon salt
- 1 teaspoon pepper
- 1 tablespoon freshly minced sage leaves
- 1 teaspoon red chili flakes
- 1 stick butter
- ¼ cup all-purpose flour
- 8 flour tortillas, 8-inch
- 2 cups Monterey jack cheese
- 2 cups cheddar cheese
- Salsa
- Sour cream

Method:

Roast the Poblano Chilis:

1. Gas stove method: Turn a burner to the highest setting and place your peppers directly on the flame. Use a pair of tongs to turn the chilis until the skin is mostly blackened. Set aside to cool before cutting into ¼ inch pieces.

2. Oven method: Preheat the oven to 425°F. Coat the poblano pepper generously with olive oil and place in a cast iron pan or on a baking sheet. Roast each side of the pepper for 6 to 8 minutes, turning with tongs, until the skin is evenly charred. Remove from oven, cover with a dish towel and let the pepper cool for 10 minutes. Gently peel the skin from the pepper, cut off the top and remove seeds. Chop the peppers into 1 inch pieces and set aside.

Prepare the Pork:

1. Preheat the oven to 350°F.

2. Heat a large skillet over medium-high heat. Heat the oil for 20 seconds before adding in onions and garlic, sautéing for 2 minutes. Add the pork shoulder over the onions and cook 3 to 5 minutes until the pork is lightly browned on both sides. Remove the pork and set aside. Add the poblano chilis and bell peppers to the pan and sauté for 2 to 3 minutes to infuse the flavors.

3. Transfer the vegetables and pork to a roasting pan, pour in the chicken stock and cover. Roast 3 hours until the pork is tender and easily pulls apart with a fork.

4. Approximately 15 minutes before the pork is done, stir in the oregano, basil, cilantro, cumin, salt, pepper, sage, and red chili flakes.

5. Remove the pan from the oven and lay the pork on a cutting board. Pour the liquid through a mesh strainer over a 1 quart glass measuring cup or bowl reserving the liquid. Discard the peppers and onions. Using two forks, pull the meat apart into thin shreds, discarding the fat.

Enchiladas Sauce:

1. Melt the butter in a skillet over medium heat. When the butter is hot, whisk the flour into the butter continuously until roux becomes smooth and begins to thicken. Reduce the heat to medium-low and gradually begin to whisk in reserved broth ½ cup at a time, allowing the sauce to thicken a bit before adding more broth. Continue until all of the broth is incorporated and thickens to a sauce.

Assemble:

1. Preheat the oven to 350°F.
2. Combine the Monterey jack cheese and cheddar cheese together in a small bowl.
3. Lay the tortillas on a flat surface and spoon pork (about ½ cup), and cheese in center of each tortilla, distributing fillings evenly between 8 tortillas. Reserve ¾ cup cheese for topping at the end. Fold one side of tortilla over the filling, then fold in the two ends, and roll tortilla over to close. Place the enchiladas, seam side down, in a 9x13 baking pan. Pour the enchilada sauce on top and sprinkle the remaining cheese over top of sauce. Bake for 25 minutes. Let rest for 10 minutes. Top with salsa and sour cream before serving.

Wisdom from Michael's Kitchen:

Double the recipe to make a second pan (unbaked) for your freezer for a quick and easy meal on those busy nights. Keeps in the freezer up to 3 months.

Did You Know?

Millions of monarch butterflies migrate to Mexico every year from the United States and Canada.

Russian Stuffed Peppers

by Natasha Baig and Maya Pugachevsky

For centuries, the foundations of Russian cuisine were often laid by a harsh climate and limited ingredients - giving birth to creativity in the kitchen. True to Russian cuisine, the vibrant flavors and simple ingredients in Russian stuffed peppers come together beautifully to produce an appealing meal that sets this recipe apart from most other stuffed peppers I have tried.

Preparation Time: 30 minutes **Cook Time:** 45 minutes **Makes:** 4 servings

Ingredients:

- 4 medium bell peppers, stemmed and cored
- ½-pound ground turkey
- ½-pound ground beef
- ½ cup cooked rice
- 5 tablespoons olive oil
- 2 cups diced onions
- 1 cup finely shredded carrots
- 6 cups marinara sauce, divided
- 1 bay leaf
- 1 teaspoon salt
- ½ teaspoon black pepper

Method:

1. Bring the rice to a boil in a small pot cooking until done. Set aside to cool.
2. Bring 12 cups of water to a boil in a large pot. Gently submerge the peppers into the water and boil on medium-high heat for 10 minutes to soften. Using tongs, carefully lift each pepper from the water, turning them over to remove any extra water inside the pepper. Set aside to cool.
3. Mix the rice and ground meat together in a medium bowl and divide it into 4 equal portions, filling each pepper with the meat mixture.
4. Heat the oil in a Dutch oven or oven-proof pot over medium-high heat. Add the onions and carrots, sautéing for 5 minutes, and stirring often, until golden brown. Stir in 3 cups of marinara sauce, bay leaf, salt, and pepper. Bring sauce to a boil and cook for an additional 3 minutes.
5. Preheat the oven to 350°F.
6. Gently lay the peppers into the sauce, partly submerging them into the liquid. Pour the remaining 3 cups marinara sauce over the peppers, cover and bake 45 minutes. Remove pot from oven and let rest 10 minutes before serving.

Wisdom from Natasha and Maya's Kitchen:

Use freshly grated carrots instead of pre-grated packaged carrots to keep the dish juicy, tender and flavorful.

You can use your favorite ground meat in place of ground beef if preferred.

Did You Know?

Russia is the only country surrounded by 12 oceans.

Moussaka

by Vivi Mizrahi - Israel

Over the years, Moussaka (mu-sa-ka), influenced by the creative reinterpretation of many Middle Eastern and Mediterranean cultures, has remained a favorite dish across the globe. In Greece, they enjoy the meal served hot, while in Turkey, it is served warm or at room temperature, and in Arab countries, both hot and cold are acceptable. Vivi, who is from Israel, serves her Moussaka with layers of meat and vegetables baked bubbling hot with a mouth-watering cheese topping.

Preparation Time: 30 minutes **Cook Time:** 1 hour 20 minutes **Makes:** serves 6

Ingredients:

- 2 medium eggplants, sliced ½-inch thick lengthwise
- 2 pounds ground beef
- 3 tablespoons olive oil, plus extra for brushing eggplant
- 1 onion, chopped
- 2 garlic cloves, minced
- 1 cup roughly chopped mushrooms
- 5 Roma tomatoes, quartered
- 1 cup cilantro, chopped
- 2 teaspoons chicken bouillon paste
- 1 ½ tablespoon Baharat spice (page 181)
- ½ teaspoon salt, plus extra for salting eggplant
- ½ teaspoon black pepper
- ½ teaspoon cayenne pepper
- 2 cups shredded mozzarella cheese, divided
- 4 eggs

Method:

1. Preheat the oven to 400°F.
2. Spread the eggplant in a single layer on a tray, salt both sides, and let it sit for 30 minutes to remove the bitterness.
3. Heat the oil in a skillet and sauté the onions over medium-high heat for 5 minutes or until translucent. Add the garlic and mushrooms, sautéing for 5 minutes or until soft.
4. Add the ground beef and continue to cool until browned. Drain the oil and return to heat.
5. Stir in the chicken bouillon paste, Baharat spice, salt, pepper, and cayenne pepper. Adjust spices are desired. Remove the pan from the heat and set aside.
6. Lightly pulse the tomatoes in a blender to roughly chop them, being careful not to puree them.
7. Pat both sides of the eggplant with a paper towel to remove water, place on a baking sheet and bake 20 minutes. Turn over and bake an additional 20 minutes before removing from the heat.
8. Layer bottom of a 9x13 greased baking dish with eggplant, tomatoes, cilantro, and meat. Repeat layers until all ingredients are used. Top with 1 ½ cup mozzarella cheese. Reduce the oven heat to 350°F and bake 40 minutes.
9. 10 minutes before moussaka is done, beat 4 eggs, pour over the top of moussaka and top with remaining ½ cup mozzarella cheese and finish baking. Remove from oven and let rest 15 minutes before cutting to let the juices set. Serve hot.

Pasta Genovese

by Michael Hernandez - Mexico

Made famous in Naples, Italy, Pasta Genovese is a flavorful red sauce for pasta, served over a bed of al dente noodles and topped with fresh Parmigiano-Reggiano. Michael's version of this European pasta, made with beef, pork, onions, red wine, herbs, and butter, with a touch of heat, is an inspired take on a classic Italian dish.

Preparation Time: 10 minutes **Cook Time:** 2 hours 40 minutes **Makes:** 6-8 servings

Ingredients:

- ¼ cup olive oil
- 1-¼ sticks cold butter, divided
- 6 cloves garlic, minced, divided
- 2-½ cups onions, diced
- 5 ribs celery, finely diced
- 2 carrots, peeled and finely diced
- 1-pound ground pork
- 1-pound ground beef
- 1 teaspoon red pepper flakes
- 1 teaspoon ground anise seed
- 1 teaspoon ground celery seed
- 1 teaspoon ground sage
- 1 teaspoon salt, more if needed
- 1 tablespoon pepper
- 1 28-oz can tomato sauce
- 2 15-oz cans, tomato puree
- 1 6-oz can tomato paste
- 4 cups water
- ¼ cup granulated sugar
- 1 cup red wine
- 12 large basil leaves, diced
- 1-pound dried pasta, ziti, tortiglioni or rigatoni
- Parmigiano-Reggiano

Method:

1. Heat the olive oil and 10 tablespoons of butter in a large skillet over medium heat. Add the onions, celery, and carrots and simmer for 10 minutes.
2. Add pork and beef, sautéing for 20 minutes or until the meat is cooked. Stir in the chili flakes, ground anise, ground celery seed, ground sage, salt, and pepper.
3. Add the tomato sauce, tomato puree, tomato paste, water, sugar and wine. Stir, cover, reduce heat to low and simmer for 2 hours, stirring occasionally.
4. About 30 minutes before the sauce is done, bring a large pot of water to a boil. Place the pasta noodles in the salted water, reduce heat to medium and cook until pasta is al dente.
5. Remove the pan from the heat and stir in the remaining 10 tablespoons of butter cut into pieces (making sure it is cold), and the basil leaves. Gently stir until the butter is melted.
6. Drain the noodles before tossing them with the sauce. Serve with fresh grated Parmigiano-Reggiano.

Wisdom from Michael's Kitchen:

Simmering the spices in the meat before adding the tomato sauces enhances the flavor of the sauce by allowing the spices to bloom during the cooking process.

Did You Know?

History teaches that pasta was brought to Italy from China by Marco Polo during the 13th century.

Thomas Jefferson, the third president of the United States, introduced pasta to Americans. Upon visiting Naples, Italy, he fell in love with macaroni and shipped crates of this pasta along with a pasta making machine back to the United States. The now famous, macaroni and cheese was served to White House guests at an 1802 state dinner.

Mama Hernandez Tacos

by Michael Hernandez - Mexico

Occasionally, a recipe can bring people together in unexpected ways. Michael's mother, Fermina, was well known for her kind generosity and her exceptional tacos. Mama Hernandez's handmade tortillas envelop savory meat filling sealed and cooked to golden perfection. Her tacos, topped with a vibrant, flavorful mix of lettuce, tomato, and dill pickles, was a big part of Mama Hernandez legacy. When someone was down on their luck, Fermina was always there with a heart full of love and a batch of her tacos. Because of this, she had friends for life.

Preparation Time: 45 minutes
Passive Time: 30 minutes
Cook Time: 25
Makes: 6-8 servings

Ingredients:

Filling:
- 1-pound ground beef, 80 % lean / 20 % fat
- ½ medium onion, chopped
- 3 cloves garlic, minced
- 1 teaspoon cumin
- 1 teaspoon salt
- ½ teaspoon black pepper
- 10 4-inch flour tortillas
- 3 tablespoons oil

Tortillas:
- 2 cups all-purpose flour
- 2 teaspoons baking powder
- 1 teaspoon salt
- 3 ¼ cup solid vegetable shortening, divided
- 1 cup warm water

Toppings:
- ½ cup shredded lettuce
- ½ cup minced dill pickles
- ½ cup diced tomatoes

Method:

Filling

1. Heat the oil in a skillet over medium-high heat. Add the onions and garlic, sautéing 5 minutes or until the onions become translucent. Add the ground beef, cumin, salt, and pepper, sautéing 10 minutes or until the meat is thoroughly cooked. Pour the meat into a colander over the sink to drain excess oil.

Tortillas

1. Combine the flour, baking powder, and salt together in a mixing bowl. Cut in ¼ cup of the vegetable shortening with your fingers until the flour forms crumbles. Add the water ¼ cup at a time to form a dough. (Depending on the flour, you may use less or more water.) Lightly flour a work surface and knead the dough until it becomes soft and pliable. The dough should be tacky but not sticky. Divide the dough into 12 equal pieces, roll into balls and cover with a damp towel for 30 minutes to allow the dough to rise.
2. Using a well-floured work surface and rolling pin, roll the dough balls into flat 4x4 circles to ⅛ inch thick.
3. Heat a non-stick large skillet over medium-high heat. Place a tortilla in the center of the pan and cook approximately 30 seconds or until bubbles appear and the tortilla looks lightly toasted. Turn over and repeat on the other side. Continue this process until all the tortillas are cooked, stacking them on top of each other under a dry towel.

Assemble:

1. Fill each tortilla with 2 tablespoons filling and fold tortilla in half to create a half-moon shape. Secure the taco shell during cooking by threading one toothpick through the top of the shell and one on each side of the shell. Place the taco into a sealed container to keep fresh while you assemble the remaining tacos.

2. Heat remaining 3 cups oil in a large sauté pan over medium-high heat. When the oil is hot, working in batches, gently lay the tacos into the oil and cook until golden brown. Turn over and cook the other side. Remove tacos from oil, set upright on a paper towel with the open side facing down to drain any excess oil.

3. Remove toothpicks and top each taco with 2 tablespoons of topping and a drizzle of hot sauce. Top with shredded cheese and sour cream if desired. Serve warm.

Wisdom from Michael's Kitchen:

Flour and leavening agents are affected by the age of the ingredients, weather, and other factors. When making the tortilla dough, it is always best to add the water slowly and work the dough into the perfect texture, rather than adding the water all at once. Controlling the amount of water allows you to achieve a soft, pliable, tacky dough.

Did You Know?

According to Mexican tradition, Antojitos (snack) tacos are enjoyed at dinner, while seafood tacos are eaten at lunch.

Spicy Sichuan Beef

by Rachel Huang - China

I learned to make Spicy Sichuan beef from Rachel who has mastered the art of simple cooking with big flavor. Typically eaten cold as an appetizer or entree, this beef imparts a stand-alone flavor so inviting that you only need a side of rice and a vegetable to make it a perfect meal.

Preparation Time: 20 minutes   **Cook Time:** 90 minutes   **Makes:** 4 servings

Ingredients:

- 1 ½ pounds beef shank or beef brisket
- 1 teaspoon Sichuan peppercorn oil (page 182)
- 1 garlic clove, minced
- 2 tablespoons Spicy Chili Crisp
- 1 ½ tablespoon Premium Soy Sauce, or Tamari
- ½ teaspoon Chinkiang vinegar, or rice vinegar
- ½ teaspoon granulated sugar
- ¼ cup chopped cilantro
- 1 tablespoon water
- 1 tablespoon chopped green onions

Method:

1. Place the beef in a large pot and cover with water 1-inch above the meat. Bring the water to a boil over medium heat. Cover, reduce heat to low, and simmer for 90 minutes or until done. The internal temperature of the beef should reach 160°F. when done.
2. Remove the beef from the water and set aside to cool. (Save the broth for soup or another recipe).
3. When the beef is cooled, thinly slice the meat across the grain into ⅛ inch slices. Transfer the meat to a wide bowl and set aside.
4. Whisk the oil, ½ teaspoon peppercorn, garlic, Spicy Chili Crisp, soy sauce, Chinkiang vinegar, sugar, water, and green onions in a small bowl. Pour the sauce over the beef and gently toss until the meat is evenly coated, being careful not to break the meat apart. Serve as an appetizer or with rice as a meal.

Wisdom from Rachel's Kitchen:

You can freeze the broth to use as a soup broth.

Adjust the soy sauce to make it saltier or add extra chili crisp to make it spicier.

You can purchase Premium Soy Sauce and Chinkiang Vinegar at Asian grocery stores or online.

Did You Know?

You can make your own Sichuan Peppercorn Oil. (page 182)

Beef Khoresht Bademjan - Persian Eggplant Stew with Beef

by Shaya Chatraei - Iran

In Iran, Khoresht Bademjan made with beef, lamb, or chicken is a traditional eggplant stew enjoyed at many dinner tables. Sometimes a new recipe can seem overwhelming, especially if it's from a culture unfamiliar to the cook. However, this dish is simple to make and uses basic ingredients which helps you to put an impressive authentic Persian meal on the table in about an hour and a half. Since most of that cooking time is hands-off, this gives you plenty of time to make a delicious Salad Shirazi and a bowl of Mast-o Khiar (yogurt and cucumber dip) to complete your meal.

Preparation Time: 10 minutes   **Cook Time:** 30 minutes   **Makes:** 6 servings

Ingredients:

- 3 tablespoons butter, divided
- 2 pounds chuck roast or lamb, cubed
- 2 teaspoons turmeric, divided
- 1 medium onion, diced
- 2 tablespoons minced garlic
- 2 teaspoons cumin
- 3 teaspoons salt
- 1 4-ounce can tomato paste
- 1 32-ounce can crushed peeled tomatoes
- 1 cup chicken for beef broth
- 1 cup water, plus more if needed
- 2 medium purple eggplant, sliced ½-inch thick
- 2 eggs, white only, beaten
- 4 cups basmati rice, cooked
- olive oil

Method:

1. Heat 1-tablespoon of butter in a Dutch oven or large pot over medium heat until melted. Add the meat and ½ teaspoon turmeric and brown on all sides. Transfer the meat and juices to a bowl and set aside.
2. Using the same pot, heat the remaining 3 tablespoons of butter, onions, garlic, cumin, salt, and remaining 1 ½ teaspoons turmeric, sautéing until the onions are translucent.
3. Place the meat and juices back into the pot along with the tomato paste, and crushed tomatoes, stirring to combine before adding the broth and 1 cup of water. Cover and simmer on low heat for 30 minutes.
4. Preheat the oven to 350°F.
5. Heat 3 tablespoons of olive oil in a wide skillet over medium heat. Beat the egg whites in a small bowl and using a pastry brush, lightly coat each side of the eggplant slices one at a time as you place them into the hot oil. (This prevents the eggplant from soaking up the oil when cooking.) Brown eggplant on both sides in batches, adding more oil as needed. Place the cooked eggplant on a paper towel and set aside.
6. Transfer the stew into an ovenproof baking pan and gently lay the eggplant on top of the stew, cover with tin foil and bake 45 minutes. Remove foil and continue to bake an additional 15 minutes. Serve hot with basmati rice (page 159), Salad Shirazi (page 51), and Mast-o khiar. (page 169)

Did You Know?

Smaller eggplants are sweeter and more tender. Choose an eggplant that is heavier for its size. Look for a smooth, shiny skin with no blemishes, cuts, wrinkles or streaking. You can store eggplants in the refrigerator for up to five days.

Wisdom from Shaya's Kitchen:

Eggplant soaks up a lot of oil while it cooks. To prevent this, lightly brush eggplant slices with egg whites before sautéing to prevent excess oil from soaking in to the vegetable.

Moroccan Lamb Chops

by Lisa Soldo-Johnson USA

Like many foods around the world, Moroccan cuisine finds some of its inspiration through a fusion of neighboring countries and cultures. The distinct flavors of Moroccan food boast of flavors like cinnamon, cumin, turmeric ginger, saffron, cloves, anise, nutmeg, and cayenne pepper. I wanted to experiment with these exotic flavors when creating my Moroccan lamb chops, so I formulated a Moroccan blend using the combination I like best. Serve the lamb chops over a bed of couscous with a yogurt cucumber sauce for an authentic Moroccan meal.

Preparation Time: 10 minutes
Passive Time: 1 hour
Cook Time: 8-12 minutes
Makes: 4 servings

Ingredients:

- 8 lamb chops
- 2 garlic cloves, minced
- 4 tablespoons black pepper
- 2 teaspoons ground ginger
- 2 teaspoons cinnamon
- 1 teaspoon turmeric
- ½ teaspoon ground cardamom
- ¼ teaspoon ground cloves
- ¼ teaspoon nutmeg
- 1 tablespoon lemon juice
- 1 tablespoon olive oil

Method:

1. Combine the black pepper, ginger, cinnamon, turmeric, cardamom, cloves, and nutmeg in a small bowl and stir until they are well blended. Stir in lemon juice and olive oil.
2. Rinse and pat dry the lamb chops. Coat the front and back of the lamb chops with the spice blend and transfer the chops to an ovenproof pan and refrigerate for 1 hour.
3. Preheat the oven to broil.
4. Broil the chops 4 to 6 minutes on each side or until the internal temperature reaches 145°F. for medium rare, or 160°F. for medium, depending on your preference. Remove the lamb chops from the oven and serve immediately.

Wisdom from Lisa's Kitchen:

Make a double batch of the Moroccan spice to use on chicken, beef, shrimp, fish, stews and vegetables. Store in an airtight container for up to 6 months.

Be generous when coating the lamb chops with the spice. Lamb chops are small, but the taste shouldn't be.

Did You Know?

Moroccan sheep breeds store most of their fat in their tails. The result is delicious meat without the pungent flavor that Western lambs tend to have. Good lamb meat should be tender and juicy, with a pleasant aftertaste.

CHAPTER 6

Fish and Seafood

Pan Fried Garlic Shrimp / 123

Turmeric Salmon with Capers and Dill / 124

Crowd-Pleaser Crab Dip / 125

Fish Tacos with Pineapple Island Salad and Lime Crema / 127

Russian Baked Cod / 129

Cajun Shrimp Pasta with Shrimp and Andouille / 131

Chimichurri Shrimp / 133

Garlic Cinnamon Tilapia / 134

King Solomon's Sweet Orange Salmon / 135

Salmon Asparagus Pinwheel with Goat Cheese / 137

Pan Fried Garlic Shrimp

by Rachel Huang - China

If you love shrimp, you will love Rachel's pan-fried garlic shrimp. Her straightforward approach to creating flavorful food that wows really stands out in this dish. Serve it just as it is with a side of rice, add it to your favorite pasta, surf and turf meal, or as an appetizer at your next gathering.

Preparation Time: 5 minutes   **Cook Time:** 3 minutes   **Makes:** 4 servings

Ingredients:

- 1-pound medium-large shrimp, shelled and deveined
- 2-3 tablespoons olive oil
- 2 green onions, chopped
- 2 garlic cloves, minced
- ½ teaspoon salt
- ½ teaspoon pepper

Method:

1. Heat the oil in skillet over high heat.
2. Add the shrimp and sauté for 1 minute on each side.
3. Add the scallions, garlic, salt, and pepper and toss together to infuse the flavors.
4. Transfer the shrimp to a plate and serve as an appetizer or as a meal with rice and tea.

Wisdom from Rachel's Kitchen:

Using medium to large size shrimp is best for this dish because it enhances the flavor.

If you choose to use shrimp with shells, have the butcher fillet and devein the backs of the shells so it will be easier to peel after it has been cooked.

Chinese food is a style that is best when you cook and eat each dish as they are prepared

Turmeric Salmon with Capers and Dill

by Ameneh Gounilli - Iran

Turmeric is a healthy yellow spice commonly used in Persian cooking. Though not a traditional recipe from Iran, I fell in love with Ameneh's turmeric salmon because of the vibrant flavors of lemon pepper, capers, dill, and turmeric that permeate the fish as it cooks. The preparation is quick and easy. Keep it simple and serve with a salad and rice. This salmon will be the highlight of the meal.

Preparation Time: 5 minutes **Cook Time:** 20 minutes **Makes:** 4-6 servings

Ingredients:

- 2-pound salmon filet, cut into 2-inch slices
- 4 tablespoons olive oil
- 1 teaspoon turmeric
- 1 teaspoon lemon pepper
- ½ teaspoon pepper
- 4 tablespoons capers
- 4 tablespoons fresh dill

Method:

1. Heat the oil in a non-stick skillet over medium heat. Sprinkle turmeric over the oil and place the salmon skin side down into the pan.
2. Sprinkle the lemon pepper and pepper over the salmon filets and simmer for 3 to 4 minutes until the skin side is nicely seared. Gently flip the salmon over, cover and cook 5 to 6 minutes or until the salmon is mostly cooked. Add the capers and fresh dill to the top of the fish and continue to simmer uncovered for 2 to 3 minutes to infuse the flavors.
3. Serve the salmon hot with rice or sautéed vegetables and a salad.

Wisdom from Ameneh's Kitchen:

Preparing salmon with the skin on one side keeps the moisture locked into the fish as it cooks.

Remove the salmon from the heat before thoroughly cooked as the residual heat will continue to cook it when removed from the pan.

Did You Know?

Turmeric is the ingredient in curry that gives it a vibrant yellow color.

Turmeric can help decrease inflammation.

Consider using turmeric for cake frosting and other food needing yellow coloring. The artificial food coloring, Yellow #5, is derived from petroleum making turmeric a much healthier option for adding color to your food.

Crowd-Pleaser Crab Dip

by Laurie Kerkinni - USA

This flavorful crab dip is perfect for occasions when you need an easy crowd-pleasing appetizer for your next gathering. Made with layers of cream cheese, fresh tomatoes, peppers, and parsley infused with fresh lemon and topped with tender crab meat served alongside crackers or fresh bread.

Preparation Time: 20 minutes

Makes: 12 servings

Ingredients:

- ½ cup finely chopped onions
- 1 garlic clove, minced
- 8 ounces organic cream cheese, softened
- 1-2 teaspoons whole milk or heavy whipping cream
- 1 Roma tomato, chopped
- ½ green pepper, finely chopped
- ¾ cup curly or Italian parsley, finely chopped
- 1-2 teaspoons freshly squeezed lemon juice
- ⅛ teaspoon Celtic salt or Himalayan salt
- 1 cup Trader Joe's Wild Caught Crab Meat

Method:

1. Mix the onion, garlic, cream cheese, and milk in a bowl until well combined. Using a 6 x 6 baking pan, spread the dip evenly the pan.
2. Toss together tomato, green pepper, 2 tablespoons parsley, lemon juice, and salt in a separate bowl and spoon the mix over the cream cheese mixture.
3. Transfer the crab from the can to a small bowl and break apart the meat with a fork until it has an even consistency. Use your fingers to gently sprinkle crab meat over the vegetable mixture.
4. Sprinkle the remaining parsley over the crab meat, cover and refrigerate the dip until you are ready to serve.

Wisdom from Laurie's Kitchen:

Trader Joe's Wild Caught Crab Meat tastes best, but you may substitute another brand.

Serve crab dip as an appetizer with chips or bread.

Refrigerate unused crab meat in an airtight container and use by next day for a crab salad, seafood omelet or in soup.

Fish Tacos with Pineapple Island Salad and Lime Crema

by Lisa Soldo-Johnson - USA

I am a huge fan of fish tacos and love the endless selection of ingredients you can use when making this light, hearty meal. In this recipe, I incorporated some of my favorite flavors including fresh cilantro and cucumbers, crunchy red cabbage, juicy pineapple, and my favorite dreamy lime crema. Serve in a flour or corn tortilla or toss the ingredients in a bowl for a refreshing fish taco salad.

Preparation Time: 15 minutes   **Cook Time:** 2 minutes   **Makes:** 6 servings

Ingredients:

Fish:

- 1-pound fresh cod
- ¼ cup olive oil
- 1 lime, juiced
- ½ teaspoon Chilin-Chili Lime Rub
- ¼ teaspoon salt
- 2 tablespoons chopped cilantro
- fresh cracked black pepper

Pineapple Island Salad:

- 2 cups shredded red cabbage
- 2 cups diced pineapple, use fresh only, not canned
- 1 cup cucumber, peeled and diced
- ½ cup diced red onion
- 1 teaspoon finely chopped jalapeno pepper
- 2 tablespoons lime juice
- ½ teaspoon salt
- 1 package 6-inch soft flour tortillas

Lime Crema:

- 1 cup sour cream
- 1 tablespoon lime juice
- 1 teaspoon lime zest
- ½ teaspoon garlic powder
- ½ teaspoon salt

Method:

1. Combine the goat cheese, dill, surf and turf spice, and capers in a small bowl and mix well.

2. Lay the salmon filet on top of a piece of plastic wrap, cutting it long enough to fold over entire filet. Using the smooth side of a mallet, gently tap the fish until it flattens out to ½ inch thick, being careful not to break the fish apart.

3. Fold the top of the plastic wrap away from the fish and spread the goat cheese mixture over the entire top of the filet. Lay the asparagus on top of cheese across the width of the fish with the tops slightly extended past the top edge of the fish. Cut off and discard the bottoms of the asparagus that extend past the fish. Gently press the asparagus into the cheese to prevent from slipping when you roll the filet together.

4. Starting at the widest end, begin to slowly roll the filet, pressing the fish tightly together as you roll and moving the plastic wrap away as you roll. Continue to tightly roll the filet into itself until you get to the thin end of the fish.

5. Carefully wrap the filet tightly with the plastic wrap, giving the fish a gentle squeeze to compact it together and transfer to the freezer for 30 to 60 minutes. This will stiffen the fish and cheese for ease of cutting.

6. Just before removing the fish from the freezer, bring a steamer pan of water to a simmer over medium-high heat. Remove the filet from the freezer, unwrap it on a cutting surface and using a serrated knife, gently cut the fish into 1 inches slices or 4 equal portions down the length of the filet, depending on your preference. Be careful not to squeeze the filling out of the pinwheels as they are cut.

7. Gently transfer the pinwheels to the steamer part of the pan and cover. Steam salmon for 1 to 2 minutes or until fish has turned a light pink. Using a spatula and your fingers, gently remove the pinwheels from the steamer being careful or it will fall apart. Serve immediately.

continued on next page →

Wisdom from Lisa's Kitchen:

Make a double batch of this recipe as part of easy meal prep for the week. Keeps in the refrigerator for up to 3 days and travels well for lunch on the go.

Lime crema can be enjoyed with a variety of foods and makes a delicious veggie or chip dip, a side with rice or grains, and pairs nicely with fish and chicken.

Russian Baked Cod

by Natasha Baig & Maya Pugachevsky - Russia

One of the things I appreciate about Russian cuisine are the basic ingredients and simple techniques used to create a uniquely delicious dish. The tradition of serving fish as an appetizer was introduced to me by my friend Natasha and her mother Maya whose Russian roots taught them to master the art of a tenderly baked cod in a zesty tomato sauce. This dish is best to serve cold or at room temperature. Enjoy it as an appetizer or an entree with your favorite side dish or salad.

Preparation Time: 10 minutes   **Cook Time:** 35 minutes   **Makes:** 6-8 servings

Ingredients:

- 2-pounds fresh cod fish, skin removed
- 1 ½ teaspoon salt, divided
- 1 teaspoon pepper, divided
- 8 tablespoons avocado oil, divided, more if needed
- 4 tablespoons all-purpose flour
- 1 medium onion, chopped
- 1 cup shredded carrots, roughly chopped
- 6-ounces tomato paste
- 1 large bay leaf
- 1 teaspoon granulated sugar
- ¾ cup water
- ½ lemon, optional

Method:

1. Rinse the cod under cool water and pat dry. Sprinkle the fish with ½ teaspoon salt, and ½ teaspoon pepper on each fillet and transfer to an airtight container. Cover and refrigerate overnight before cooking. This creates a better flavor in the fish. Remove the fish from refrigerator 1 hour before preparing to bring it to room temperature.
2. Heat 6 tablespoons of the oil in a skillet over medium-high heat.
3. Flour each side of the fillets, adding them to the hot oil. Fry the fish for 3 minutes on each side or until lightly browned.
4. Gently transfer filets to a 9 x 12 baking dish and set aside
5. Preheat the oven to 350°F.
6. Heat remaining 2 tablespoons of oil in a medium pan over medium-high heat. Add onions and carrots, sautéing 3 to 4 minutes or until soft (adding more oil if needed). Stir in the tomato paste, bay leaf, sugar, salt, pepper, and water. Bring the sauce to a boil, remove from heat and pour over the fish.
7. Bake for 25 to 30 minutes or until fish is done. The cod is ready when it easily pierces with a fork and flakes along the center of the fillet.
8. Remove the cod from oven and give it a squeeze of lemon juice over the fish. Set it aside to cool or serve hot as a main dish with rice and Salad Olivier (page 141). If you are serving it as a traditional Russian appetizer, cover the fish and refrigerate until it is cold.

Wisdom from Natasha and Maya's Kitchen:

Russian Baked Cod is traditional prepared a day ahead and served as a cold appetizer with vodka.

Cajun Shrimp Pasta with Shrimp and Andouille

by Lisa Soldo-Johnson - USA

I was inspired to create this dish when I visited Jamaica and fell in love with their Cajun-influenced pasta dishes. This creamy Cajun pasta is packed full of flavor and has the perfect kick of heat depending on how much Cajun spice you sprinkle in. Make it your own by adding your favorite ingredients like lobster or chicken in place of shrimp or sausage, mushrooms and peppers instead of corn and tomatoes, or use them all. The possibilities are limitless!

Preparation Time: 10 minutes **Cook Time:** 30 minutes **Makes:** 2-4 servings

Ingredients:

- 2 cups uncooked penne pasta
- 2 tablespoons butter
- 3 tablespoons all-purpose flour
- 1-¼ cup milk
- 1-½ teaspoon salt, divided
- ½ teaspoon pepper
- 1 pinch nutmeg
- ½ cup parmesan cheese
- 2 tablespoons olive oil
- 2 green onions, chopped
- ½ cup chopped tomatoes
- ½ cup frozen corn
- 16 cooked shrimp, tailed
- 2 Andouille sausage, sliced
- 1-2 teaspoons Cajun seasoning (page 180), adjust to taste
- 3 tablespoons chopped cilantro

Method:

1. Melt the butter in a sauté pan over medium-high heat. Whisk the flour in quickly to form a paste.
2. Pour ⅓ cup milk into the pan and whisk vigorously until creamy. Add another ⅓ cup milk and continue to whisk. Add the remaining milk and whisk until the sauce is creamy and smooth. Whisk in ½ teaspoon salt, pepper, and nutmeg. Add the cheese to sauce and stir until melted. Remove the pan from the heat and set aside.
3. Heat the oil in a sauté pan over medium-high heat. Add the onions and sauté for 20 seconds to infuse the oil. Stir in tomatoes and corn, sautéing for 2 minutes.
4. Add in the shrimp, sausage, and noodles, tossing to combine. Stir in the sauce and reduce the heat to medium. Cook for 3 minutes, continuing to stir as needed.
5. Stir in the Cajun seasoning and remaining 1 teaspoon salt, stirring until ingredients are well combined. Add more seasoning if preferred. Sprinkle in cilantro and toss lightly.

Wisdom from Lisa's Kitchen:

Begin by using less Cajun seasoning to ensure the dish doesn't become too spicy. Add additional seasoning at the end if desired.

You can customize this recipe using your favorite meats and vegetables.

Did You Know?

The invention of Chocolate Milk came from Jamaica. In the early 1700s, the locals gave Sir Hans Sloane, an Irish botanist, some cocoa to drink. The taste was too strong, so he decided to mix it with milk to make it more palatable, and upon his return to England, it was sold as medicine for many years.

Chimichurri Shrimp

by Michael Hernandez - Mexico

Chimichurri Sauce is a zesty marinade used in both Central and South American cooking for meats and seafood. Michael's homemade chimichurri sauce is simple to make and yields a much more authentic flavor than store-bought versions. Chimichurri Shrimp can be served as an appetizer or as a main dish. The shrimp pairs well with other seafood, meats, pastas, and salads.

Preparation Time: 10 minutes   **Cook Time:** 6 minutes   **Makes:** 6 servings

Ingredients:

- 1 pound large or jumbo shrimp, shelled and deveined
- 1 cup olive oil
- ¼ cup champagne vinegar
- 3 garlic cloves
- 1 tablespoon lemon juice
- 1 tablespoon lime juice
- 2 tablespoons chopped parsley
- 1 tablespoon chopped cilantro
- 1 tablespoon chopped fresh basil
- 2 teaspoons dry mustard powder
- 1 teaspoon fresh thyme
- 1 teaspoon dried oregano
- 1 teaspoon red pepper flakes
- 1 teaspoon salt
- 1 teaspoon pepper

Method:

1. Place all the ingredients, except oil, in a blender and puree until smooth.
2. With the blender running, slowly pour the oil in a steady stream.
3. Continue blending for 15 seconds to fully incorporate the oil.
4. Transfer 1 cup of the sauce to a serving bowl, reserving the rest for basting or marinating the shrimp.
5. Preheat an outdoor grill to 500°F. Soak wooden skewers in water for 10 minutes.
6. Thread the shrimp on skewers to cook.
7. Cook shrimp for 2 to 3 minutes per side until they are no longer translucent. Serve hot with chimichurri sauce on the side.

Wisdom from Michael's Kitchen:

The mustard powder will prevent the sauce from separating.

For a more intense chimichurri flavor, marinate the shrimp in the reserved sauce in the refrigerator for as little as 1-hour or overnight.

Garlic Cinnamon Tilapia

by Laurie Kerkinni -USA

Tilapia is a delicate meaty fish that adapts nicely to a wide variety of dishes and is also relatively inexpensive. Laurie introduced me to her garlic and cinnamon tilapia many years ago, and since then I have made it again and again. The combination of garlic salt and cinnamon creates a surprisingly delightful flavor that pairs beautifully over a bed of nutty quinoa or wild rice and your favorite vegetable.

Preparation Time: 5 minutes   **Cook Time:** 12-15 minutes   **Makes:** 2 servings

Ingredients:

- 2 tilapia fillets
- 1 teaspoon olive oil
- ½ teaspoon garlic salt
- ½ teaspoon cinnamon

Method:

1. Preheat the oven to 375°F.
2. Rinse the filets and pat them dry.
3. Line a broiling pan with a piece of lightly oiled tin foil large enough to tent over the fish. Lay the tilapia in the center of the foil. Drizzle olive oil over each filet and sprinkle each side with garlic salt, and cinnamon. Fold tin foil over the fish and close tightly on all sides.
4. Bake for 12 to 15 minutes or until the fish is white and flakey.
5. Using a spatula, carefully remove the fish from the tin foil and transfer to individual serving plates. Serve immediately.

Wisdom from Laurie's Kitchen:

You can add asparagus, mushrooms, or other vegetables in with the fish while it is baking. The tin foil will help to steam the vegetables.

King Solomon's Sweet Orange Salmon

by Vivi Mizrahi - Israel

Vivi introduced me to her King Solomon's Sweet Orange Salmon years ago, and it has since become one of my favorite ways to prepare salmon. A delightful combination of citrus orange, salty tamari, and a sweet brown sugar marinade creates a moist, flavorful fish that pairs beautifully with Israeli couscous, sautéed vegetables or over a bed of mashed potatoes or fresh greens. It's a meal fit for a king.

Preparation Time: 10 minutes   **Bake Time:** 30 minutes   **Makes:** 4-6 servings

Ingredients:

- 1 large salmon filet, skinless
- 3 tablespoons orange juice
- 3 tablespoons red wine vinegar
- 3 tablespoons soy sauce or tamari
- 3 tablespoons olive oil
- ½ cup light brown sugar

Method:

1. Rinse salmon fillet and place the fish in a 2 inch deep baking pan large for the filet to lay flat.
2. Whisk the orange juice, red wine vinegar, soy sauce, olive oil, and brown sugar in a small bowl. Pour the liquid over top of the salmon filet and cover the pan with tin foil. Refrigerator for 1 hour or up to 12 hours.
3. Preheat the oven to 350° F. Bake salmon for 20 minutes, turning over and continuing to bake an additional 10 minutes or until fish is tender and flaky. Serve hot with the marinade spooned over the top.

Wisdom from Vivi's Kitchen:

Double the marinade measurements for extra sauce to pour over the salmon, salad, potatoes, or other side dish.

Salmon Asparagus Pinwheel with Goat Cheese

by Lisa Soldo-Johnson - USA

Salmon pinwheels are the ultimate quick and easy fish recipe perfect for any occasion. This gorgeous dish is light and satisfying, and the fish steams to perfection in two minutes or less. You can also customize this recipe by using your favorite ingredients. Not a goat cheese lover? Substitute cream cheese. Flavor with your ideal combination of herbs and spices — trade in the asparagus for another steam-able vegetable or toss in a few butterflied shrimps. The possibilities are endless.

Preparation Time: 15 minutes   **Cook Time:** 2 minutes   **Makes:** 4 servings

Ingredients:

- 1 8-inch piece of salmon filet
- ½ cup goat cheese
- 1 teaspoon fresh dill or ½ teaspoon dry
- ½ teaspoon surf and turf spice
- 1 tablespoon capers
- 3-4 asparagus spears, cut to the width of filet

Wisdom from Lisa's Kitchen:

Have your meal prepared and plated before you begin steaming the fish, so it is ready to be eaten as soon as the fish is done.

Serve the salmon pinwheels with wild rice, white rice, couscous, quinoa, and your favorite side and a fresh green salad.

Feel free to substitute the spices with others that complement the salmon.

Did You Know?

Preparing for a larger crowd? You can assemble salmon pinwheels through step 5 and freeze up to 3 days in advance if the salmon has not been pre-frozen.

Method:

1. Combine the goat cheese, dill, surf and turf spice, and capers in a small bowl and mix well.
2. Lay the salmon filet on top of a piece of plastic wrap, cutting it long enough to fold over entire filet. Using the smooth side of a mallet, gently tap the fish until it flattens out to ½ inch thick, being careful not to break the fish apart.
3. Fold the top of the plastic wrap away from the fish and spread the goat cheese mixture over the entire top of the filet. Lay the asparagus on top of cheese across the width of the fish with the tops slightly extended past the top edge of the fish. Cut the bottom of the asparagus off that extends past the fish. Gently press the asparagus into the cheese to prevent them from slipping when you roll the filet together.
4. Starting at the widest end, begin to slowly roll the filet, pressing the fish tightly together as you roll and moving the plastic wrap away as you roll. Continue to tightly roll the filet into itself until you get to the thin end of the fish.
5. Carefully wrap the filet tightly with the plastic wrap, giving the fish a gently squeeze to compact it together and transfer to the freezer for 30 to 60 minutes. This will stiffen the fish and cheese for ease of cutting.
6. Just before removing the fish from the freezer, bring a steamer pan of water to a simmer over medium-high heat. Remove the filet from the freezer, unwrap it on a cutting surface and using a serrated knife, gently cut the fish into 1 inches slices or 4 equal portions down the length of the filet depending on your preference. Be careful not to squeeze the filling out of the pinwheels as they are cut.
7. Gently transfer the pinwheels to the steamer part of the pan and cover. Steam salmon for 1 to 2 minutes or until fish has turned a light pink. Using a spatula and your fingers, gently remove the pinwheels from the steamer being careful or it will fall apart. Serve immediately.

CHAPTER 7

Vegetables and Sides

Persian Salad Olivieh / 141

Orzo with Red Pepper, Mushrooms and Spinach / 142

Kuku Sabzi - Persian Frittata with Fresh Herbs / 143

Caesar Tossed Herb Roasted Potatoes / 145

Japanese Soba Noodles with Ginger Peanut Sauce / 146

Schloof - Suryani Eggplant and Tomatoes / 147

Shirin Polo - Persian Jeweled Rice / 149

Couscous with Mushroom and Spinach / 151

Lamb Rice / 153

1890 Slow Baked Pinto Beans / 154

Chinese Smashed Cucumbers / 155

Garlic Green Beans with Shallots and Barberries / 157

Basmati Rice with Potato Tahdig / 159

Balogh - Assyrian Side Dish / 161

Mexican Fiesta Salad / 163

Mast va laboo - Persian Yogurt and Beet Dip / 164

Torshi Liteh / 165

Sesame Garlic Veggie Trio / 167

Russian Salad Olivier / 168

Mast o Khiar with Shallots and Garlic / 169

Kashk-o bademjan / 171

Sweet and Spicy Steamed Cauliflower / 173

140 | It Begins at the *Table*

Persian Salad Olivieh

by Shaya Chatraei - Iran

When it comes to tasty comfort food, it doesn't get better than this. Salad Olivieh is a Persian chicken salad made with potatoes, pickles, real mayo, and sour lemon juice to create a creamy, crunchy, rich flavor and texture that is hard to stop eating. Traditionally served as a side with meals, it could also be enjoyed on a sandwich or as a light lunch or mid-day snack.

Preparation Time: 20 minutes
Passive Time: 2 hours
Cook Time: 1 hour
Makes: 6-8 servings

Ingredients:

- 1 3-pound whole chicken, boiled (or 4 cups diced chicken meat)
- 3 large Yukon gold potatoes, peeled, boiled, diced
- 3 large eggs, hardboiled, peeled, chopped
- 2 cups diced dill pickles
- 3 cups real mayonnaise
- ¼ cup lemon juice
- ⅛ cup olive oil
- 1 teaspoon salt, plus more if needed
- ½-teaspoon pepper, plus more if desired
- Cherry tomatoes, halved
- Black olives, whole or halved

Method:

1. Add the cleaned chicken and salt to a pot with enough water to cover 3 inches. Cover and bring to a boil. Reduce the heat and cook on medium heat for 1 hour. Remove the chicken to cool. Remove and discard the skin and bones from the meat. Dice 4 cups of the chicken, saving remaining meat and broth for another use. Transfer the shredded chicken to a large bowl.
2. While the chicken is cooking, boil the potatoes and eggs in separate pots. Remove them from the water to cool before peeling and chopping the eggs and potatoes. Add them to the bowl with the chicken.
3. Add the diced pickles to the bowl.
4. Whisk the mayonnaise, lemon juice, olive oil, salt, and pepper in a small bowl. Pour the dressing over the chicken salad and toss until evenly coated. Adjust the flavor with salt and pepper if desired. Cover and refrigerate a minimum of 2 hours to allow the flavors to infuse.
5. Transfer to a serving bowl or plate and garnish with tomatoes and black olives. Serve as an appetizer or side dish.

Wisdom from Shaya's Kitchen:

To save time in preparation, you can use a pre-roasted chicken. Just be sure it will give you enough chicken meat required for the recipe.

The beauty of Salad Olivieh is you can garnish and decorate it any way that pleases you.

Orzo with Red Pepper, Mushrooms and Spinach

by Suheyla Kerkinni - Assyria

Orzo is a favorite grain used by many cultures including Italy, Greece, Germany, Mediterranean, and Middle Eastern cooking. This pasta-like grain is one of those blank-slate ingredients, allowing the flavors and spices of the dish to take center stage. Suheyla's orzo recipe is special because of its versatility. It is light, flavorful and pairs beautifully with chicken, fish, or meat.

Preparation Time: 10 minutes   **Cooking Time:** 25 minutes   **Makes:** 6 servings

Ingredients:

- 5 cups chicken broth or water
- 2 cups orzo
- ¼ cup olive oil
- 8-ounces baby Bella mushrooms, sliced
- 3 garlic cloves, minced
- 1 red bell pepper, diced
- 8-ounces fresh spinach, chopped
- salt (as desired)

Method:

1. Bring chicken broth or water to a boil in a saucepan over high heat. Stir in orzo, reduce the heat to medium-high, cover and cook 7 to 8 minutes or until orzo is tender but firm to the bite.
2. While the orzo is cooking, heat a large sauté pan over medium heat. Add the oil and heat for 1 minute before adding the garlic, sautéing for 30 seconds.
3. Add the mushrooms and sauté 6 minutes or until tender. Add the red pepper and continue to sauté for an additional 2 minutes to infuse the flavors.
4. Add the spinach and sauté until just wilted.
5. Remove the pan from heat, pour orzo into a mesh strainer to remove the liquid. Pour the orzo over the spinach and gently toss to mix the ingredients. Sprinkle in a bit of salt to reach your desired flavor. Serve with chicken or fish.

 Wisdom from Suheyla's Kitchen:
You can also use gluten-free orzo in this dish.

Did You Know?

The word orzo is Italian for "barley."

Kuku Sabzi - Persian Frittata with Fresh Herbs

by Shaya Chatraei - Iran

In Persian cuisine, Kuku is a dish made with fried vegetables, herbs, and eggs. Kuku Sabzi is a traditional herb frittata served in Iran as a delicious, healthy side to complement meats, rice, and salad. This dish has a special meaning when served during the Persian New Year. The fresh green herbs symbolize a rebirth while the eggs represent fertility. What a beautiful sentiment given to those who enjoy it for the year to come! Kuku makes a healthy, flavorful side dish packed with herbs and spices you can enjoy any time of the year.

Preparation Time: 10 minutes   **Cooking Time:** 30 minutes   **Makes:** 8 servings

Ingredients:

- 8 tablespoons vegetable oil, divided
- 1 medium onion, diced
- 1 leek or 3 scallions, (green parts only), finely chopped
- 6 eggs
- 1 ½ teaspoon salt
- 1 teaspoon black pepper
- ½ teaspoon turmeric
- 1 tablespoon rice spice (page 180)
- 1 teaspoon baking powder
- 2 bunches cilantro, finely chopped
- 2 bunches dill, finely chopped
- 2 bunches parsley, finely chopped

Method:

1. Heat 2 tablespoons oil in a 10 inch ovenproof skillet over medium heat. Add the onions and leeks, sautéing 8 to 10 minutes or until very soft. Transfer to a bowl to cool.
2. Whisk the eggs, salt, pepper, turmeric, rice spice, and baking powder in a medium bowl. Add in the onions, cilantro, dill, parsley, folding together gently with a wood spoon until just combined. Do not over mix.
3. Using the same skillet, heat the remaining 6 tablespoons oil on medium-low heat. Once oil is hot, gently pour the mixture into the oil, spreading it out to the sides of the pan. Cover and cook 15 to 20 minutes, checking the middle of the Kuku Sabzi for softness. Transfer the pan to the oven and broil for 2 minutes. When a toothpick inserted into the middle comes out clean, gently slide it from the pan on to a round serving plate. Cut into wedges and serve warm.

Wisdom from Shaya's Kitchen:

Prepare the herbs a day ahead if needed and lay them on a paper towel to dry before refrigerating in a covered container.

It is best to hand chop the herbs. Using a food processor makes the herbs wet and releases the flavor and texture of the herbs.

You can make your own rice spice. (page 180)

Did You Know?

In Farsi, Kuku means "vegetarian dish," and Sabzi means "herbs" although, some Kuku's include meat.

Caesar Tossed Herb Roasted Potatoes

by Lisa Soldo-Johnson - USA

Caesar Tossed Herb Roasted Potatoes is a recipe I created after falling in love with the creamy Caesar dressing recipe in this book. I used rosemary and garlic for these potatoes but feel free to use any combination of herbs and spices that appeal to your palate. It's the Caesar dressing that creates the real magic. Serve as a side dish, breakfast potatoes, or an appetizer with extra dipping sauce.

Preparation Time: 20 minutes   **Cook Time:** 40-50 minutes   **Makes:** 4 servings

Ingredients:

Potatoes

- 2 pounds small Yukon gold potatoes, quartered
- 4 cloves garlic, minced
- 2 tablespoons chopped fresh rosemary
- 1 teaspoon sea salt
- ½ teaspoon black pepper
- ¼ cup olive oil

Caesar Dressing

- ⅔ cup olive oil
- 2 large eggs, coddled
- 2 ½ tablespoons lemon juice
- 2 ½ tablespoons lime juice
- 2 cloves garlic, minced
- 1 tablespoon Worcestershire sauce
- 1 tablespoon balsamic vinegar
- 1 teaspoon Dijon mustard
- ½ teaspoon salt
- ¼ teaspoon black pepper
- 3 anchovy fillets, minced (optional)

Method:

Potatoes:

1. Preheat the oven to 400°F.
2. Toss the potatoes, garlic, rosemary, salt, pepper, and olive oil in a medium bowl.
3. Spread the potatoes on a baking sheet in a single layer and bake 40 to 50 minutes or until soft when pierced with a fork. Set aside to cool 5 minutes before adding the dressing.

Dressing:

1. Whisk the lemon juice, lime juice, garlic, Worcestershire sauce, balsamic vinegar, Dijon mustard, dry mustard, salt, and pepper in a small bowl. Whisk in olive oil until emulsified.
2. Coddle the egg by placing the eggs (shells on) in a bowl filled with 3 cups of boiling water for 1 minute. Remove the eggs from the water and let cool completely. Whisk the eggs into the dressing. If you are using anchovies, whisk them now or reserve them for garnish.

Assemble:

1. Transfer the potatoes to a bowl. Pour the desired amount of dressing over the potatoes and gently toss. Serve warm.

Wisdom from Lisa's Kitchen:
The potatoes are delicious both hot and cold.

Use the extra dressing as a dip for vegetables, a marinade for fish, lamb or beef, or spoon it over rice for a delicious side dish.

Did You Know?

The best potato for roasting is thin-skinned, nicely textured, and similar in size.

Japanese Soba Noodles with Ginger Peanut Sauce

by Lisa Soldo-Johnson - USA

Soba noodles made from buckwheat flour are a firm, flavorful noodle traditionally served both hot and cold in Japanese cuisine. My family loves eating this dish as a meal, though they complain I never make enough. It is also a fabulous make-ahead recipe to serve chilled as a side dish or appetizer.

Preparation Time: 5 minutes **Cook Time:** 10 minutes **Makes:** 4 servings

Ingredients:

- 8 ounces soba noodles
- 1 cup water
- 2 tablespoons fresh ginger, grated
- 1 tablespoon minced garlic
- ¼ cup peanut butter
- 2 tablespoons pure maple syrup
- 3 tablespoons Tamari
- 1 tablespoon avocado oil or cooking oil
- ½ red bell pepper, thinly sliced
- ½ cup frozen peas
- 1 teaspoon salt, divided
- ¼ teaspoon crushed red pepper flakes
- 1 teaspoon sesame seeds

Method:

1. Add the soba noodles and ½ teaspoon salt to a pot of boiling water on high heat. Stir to separate the noodles in the water. Return the water to a boil, reduce the heat to medium-high and cook 5 to 8 minutes until soft but not mushy. Drain the noodles in a colander, transfer to a pot of cool water and move back and forth to remove extra starch. Drain and transfer to individual serving bowls.
2. While noodles are cooking, whisk together water, ginger, garlic, peanut butter, maple syrup, and tamari in a small pan over medium-high heat. Bring to a boil, reduce heat to low and simmer 5 minutes.
3. Heat the oil in a separate small pan and sauté red bell peppers on medium high 3 to 4 minute or until tender. Add in the frozen peas, remaining ½ teaspoon salt and red pepper flakes, simmering 2 minutes until the peas are heated through. Pour the sauce over the vegetables and stir to combine.
4. Ladle the sauce over the noodles, top with sesame seeds and serve.

Did You Know?

In Japan, the water that the soba noodles are cooked in is called "Sobayu" and is full of vitamins. Once the noodles are drained, the water is added to the sauce or chilled and enjoyed as a nutritious beverage.

Schloof - Suryani Eggplant and Tomatoes

by Laurie Kerkinni - USA

Schloof, a traditional Suryani dish made with layers of sautéed eggplant and tomatoes cooked in garlic and oil, a sprinkle of Anaheim peppers, and topped with fragrant parsley. The ingredients combine into a beautiful symphony of flavors, unlike any vegetable dish you have eaten. Serve Schloof at room temperature as an appetizer or a side dish with fish, lamb, or beef and jasmine or basmati rice.

Preparation Time: 1 hour **Cook Time:** 45 minutes **Makes:** 6-8 servings

Ingredients:

- 3 eggs, beaten, (whites only)
- 2 large eggplant, sliced ½-inch thick
- 8 cups chopped Roma tomatoes (approximately 15 tomatoes)
- 2 tablespoons olive oil, plus more as needed
- 2 large Anaheim pepper, halved, seeded and roughly chopped
- 8 garlic cloves, chopped
- 1 teaspoon salt, plus more for salting
- 1 bunch curly parsley, chopped

Wisdom from Laurie's Kitchen:

Lightly brushing the eggplant with egg whites prevents a lot of the oil from absorbing into the eggplant while cooking.

This is a make ahead recipe because it is served cold or at room temperature.

Choose fresh tomatoes. Older tomatoes tend to cool down faster and liquify.

Choose the most fragrant parsley for this recipe.

Method:

1. Slice the eggplant ¼ inch thick, set in rows on a paper towels, and lightly salt. Turn the eggplant over when water droplets come to the top (approximately 20 minutes) then lightly salt the other side. When water droplets form, pat dry with paper towel.
2. Add enough oil to fill the bottom of a large skillet ⅛ inch. Heat the oil over medium heat. Brush both sides of the eggplant lightly with egg whites. Lay the eggplant in a single layer and sauté until golden brown. Turn over and repeat browning, adding more oil if needed. Remove the eggplant from the oil and drain on paper towels, discarding oil in the pan.
3. Using the same skillet, heat 2 tablespoons oil on medium heat. Add Anaheim peppers, cover and simmer 3 to 4 minutes or until peppers are lightly toasted and slightly soft. Using a slotted spoon, remove the peppers from the pan and set on paper towel.
4. Add the garlic and salt to the oil and sauté 30 seconds. Increase the heat to medium high, add the tomatoes and sauté 4 to 5 minutes, making sure the tomatoes do not overcook and remain slightly chunky. Remove the pan from the heat.

Assemble:

1. In an 8x8 glass serving dish, layer eggplant, tomatoes (using a slotted spoon), all Anaheim peppers. Repeat with eggplant, tomatoes, and parsley. Set aside to cool for 1 hour before serving or refrigerate until ready to serve.

Shirin Polo - Persian Jeweled Rice

by Soheila Mirsharif - Iran

Shirin Polo (wedding rice) is a gorgeous Persian sweet rice traditionally served on special occasions, holiday celebrations, or weddings. This unforgettable rice dish, created with a vibrant burst of colors and aromatic flavors like candied citrus peel, sweet carrots, pistachios, almonds, raisins, and plenty of sour barberries hold a deep meaning in the Persian culture. Each ingredient represents a sentiment of wealth and happiness for the newly married couple. Saffron, carrots and orange peel represent gold, barberries symbolize rubies, pistachios are beautiful emeralds, and almonds are pearls. There are so many reasons to love Shirin Polo.

Preparation Time: 40 minutes   **Cook Time:** 1 hour 30 minutes   **Makes:** 12 servings

Ingredients:

- 3 cups basmati rice
- 2 teaspoons salt, divided
- 1 cup barberries
- 3 large oranges
- ½ cup thinly julienned carrots
- 4 tablespoons butter, divided
- 1 cup plus 2 tablespoons granulated sugar, divided
- 1 teaspoon cardamom powder
- 1 cup light olive oil, divided
- ½ cup sliced pistachios
- ½ cup slivered almonds
- ½ cup Hunza golden raisins
- 1 cup granulated sugar
- ½ teaspoon ground saffron threads, dissolved in ½ cup hot water

Method:

1. Place the rice in a medium bowl and rinse under cold water 4 to 5 times until the water runs clear to remove dirt and debris. Top the rice with 6 cups of water and 1 teaspoon of salt. Soak for 2 hours to 24 hours.
2. To prepare the orange peel: Using a sharp knife, cut away the outside of the orange peel, then remove as much of the white pith from the skin as possible. Cut the skins into thin strips. Add the orange peels to a pot of boiling water and boil for 2 minutes to remove bitterness. Drain and rinse with cold water.
3. Heat 2 tablespoons butter in a skillet over medium heat. Sauté the orange peel and carrots for 2 minutes. Add the sugar and cardamom, sautéing for 1 minute. Stir in 1 cup water, bring to a boil, and simmer 8 to 10 minutes. Pour the orange peel and carrots into a mesh strainer over a bowl, reserving the syrup for later.
4. Fill a large non-stick 5-quart pot with 10 cups of water and bring to a boil on high heat. Add the drained rice and 1 teaspoon of salt to the water. Parboil the rice for 6 to 8 minutes or just until the rice is slightly soft on the outside grain. You can test this by biting into a grain. Pour the rice into a mesh strainer and rinse with cold water to stop the cooking process.
5. Whisk ½ cup oil, ½ cup water, and 1 tablespoon saffron water. Spoon 2 cups rice into the bowl, stirring until the rice is evenly coated yellow. Spoon the rice over the bottom of a non-stick pot.
6. Spoon a thin layer of rice over the saffron-rice. Continue to add rice in layers by spooning the rice into the middle of the pot in a pyramid shape, allowing the rice to fall towards the sides. Cover and cook for 10 minutes over medium-high heat.

continued on next page →

Wisdom from Sohiela's Kitchen:

If you prefer to serve the dish with the ingredients mixed, you can alternate the layers on a platter with the rice, carrot/orange mixture, barberries, almonds, pistachios, and raisins, serving the tahdig on the side.

Did You Know?

In the Persian language, Farsi, Shirin means "sweet," and Polo means "rice."

---

7. Whisk remaining ½ cup oil, ½ cup water, and the reserved orange syrup in a small bowl, drizzling the liquid over and around the rice.
8. Cover the lid of the pot with a cotton tea towel, tying the ends at the top of the lid. Cover the pot with the lid, reduce the heat to low and steam for 70 minutes.
9. While the rice is cooking, soak barberries in a small bowl filled with cold water for 15 minutes. Drain and set aside. Heat 1 tablespoon butter, 2 tablespoons water, 2 tablespoons sugar, and the barberries, in a skillet over medium heat and sauté for 3 minutes. Transfer to a bowl and set aside.
10. In the same skillet, heat 1 tablespoon butter, add the pistachios and sauté for 30 seconds. Transfer to a bowl and set aside.
11. In the same skillet, heat remaining 1 tablespoon butter, almonds, and raisins, sautéing for 30 seconds. Transfer to a bowl and set aside.
12. When the rice is done, remove the pot from the heat and rest it on a cool damp cloth for 10 minutes to naturally loosen the crust (tahdig) from the pot. Do not remove the lid.

Assemble:

1. You can assemble the rice in any design you like. Here is Sohiela's suggestion.
2. Gently spoon and sprinkle the rice onto a large serving platter one layer at a time, creating a gradual mound at the center, until you reach the yellow rice. Carefully removing the tah-dig at the bottom of the pot and reserving it on a separate plate.
3. Creating a bullseye design from the outside in, spoon the yellow rice on the outside circle.
4. Add a thin circle of the carrots and orange peels on the inside of the yellow rice.
5. Next, add a thin circle of barberries.
6. Then a thin circle of almonds.
7. Leave a ring of the white rice showing.
8. Add a thin circle of the pistachios.
9. Fill in the inside of the bullseye with remaining carrot and orange peel mixture, topped with remaining barberries.
10. Break apart the tahdig and serve it on a separate plate next to the Shirin polo.

Couscous with Mushroom and Spinach

by Lisa Soldo-Johnson - USA

Couscous with mushrooms and spinach is a dish I created, spur of the moment, using only the ingredients I had on hand. I find these are the times when some of the best recipes are born. Since couscous absorbs flavors incredibly well, the combination of chicken broth, garlic, mushrooms, and spinach take center stage. I love the simplicity of this dish. Serve it with grilled fish or chicken for a quick and easy meal.

Preparation Time: 5 minutes   **Cooking Time:** 30 minutes   **Makes:** 4-6 servings

Ingredients:

- 5 tablespoons olive oil, divided
- 1 cup couscous
- 2 cups chicken broth
- 2 garlic cloves, minced
- 2 cups chopped Portobello mushrooms
- ½ teaspoon salt
- 4 cups spinach, roughly chopped

Method:

1. Heat 2 tablespoons oil in a skillet over medium heat. Stir in the couscous sauté 2 minutes. Pour in the chicken broth and bring to a boil. Reduce the heat to low, cover and simmer for 10 minutes.
2. Using a separate skillet, heat the remaining 3 tablespoons oil over medium-high heat. Add the garlic and sauté for 30 seconds to infuse the oil. Add the mushrooms and salt, sautéing 4 to 5 minutes or until softened. Add the spinach and continue to sauté 2 minutes.
3. Transfer the couscous to the sauté pan and stir to combine. Cover and simmer 5 to 10 minutes or until most of the liquid is absorbed. Serve hot as a side dish or warm salad.

Wisdom from Lisa's Kitchen:

Add sautéed chicken or shrimp and serve it as a main course.

Did You Know?

Couscous is not a grain. It is made from semolina flour and sprayed with water before it is rolled out to create a grain-like texture that is manufactured in different sizes.

Lamb Rice

by Vivi Mizrahi - Israel

Shortly after we moved to our new home, I learned to make fragrant lamb rice from my neighbor and friend, Vivi. She and her husband Eli migrated to the United States over two decades ago from Israel. Since that first cooking lesson, my repertoire of Mediterranean food has significantly expanded, but lamb rice is still one of my favorites! This dish is both savory and addictive. It makes an excellent side dish or stand-alone meal paired with a salad or your favorite vegetable.

Preparation Time: 5 minutes
Passive Time: 30 minutes
Cooking Time: 45 minutes
Makes: 8 servings

Ingredients:

- 2 cups long grain rice, washed and soaked in boiling water
- 1-pound ground lamb
- 3 small onions, diced
- 3 tablespoons canola oil (plus more if needed)
- 1 ½ bunches cilantro, chopped
- 1 tablespoon bouillon paste
- 3 teaspoons salt
- ½ teaspoon pepper
- ½ teaspoon cumin

Method:

1. Rinse the rice in a medium bowl until the water runs clear. Cover the rice with boiling water and soak for 30 minutes.
2. Heat 3 tablespoons oil in a skillet over medium heat. Sauté onions for 5 minutes or until they are translucent. Add the lamb, browning meat (adding more oil as needed) until it is almost cooked.
3. Stir in the bouillon paste, salt, pepper, and cumin. Mix in the cilantro and sauté for 30 seconds. Stir in the rice including the water it was soaking in. Cover and simmer on medium heat for 5 minutes or until most of the liquids is absorbed. Lower the heat and simmer for 15 minutes (adding ½ cup boiling water if the liquid has cooked out).
4. Remove the cover and using a large spoon or spatula, pull the bottom of the rice to the top so the rice cooks evenly. Add ½ cup boiling water, cover, reduce the heat to medium-low and simmer for 20 minutes. The lamb rice should remain tender and moist during the cooking process. If it begins to look dry, add ½ cup boiling water as needed. Serve as a side dish or main course with a salad and bread.

Wisdom from Vivi's Kitchen:

Use boiling water to keep the lamb rice from cooling down during the cooking process.

1890 Slow Baked Pinto Beans

by Lorraine Soldo USA

1890 slow baked pinto beans are a dish my German Grandfather created over a century ago and has remained a treasured family favorite ever since. There is just no comparison to the richness achieved when beans are slow-baked in an old ceramic bean pot for hours. The results are a velvety age-old flavor that modern cooking methods could never duplicate. My favorite part of this recipe is the simplicity of ingredients used and the ease of making it. I'm pretty sure my Grandfather would be proud to know his bean recipe is still enjoyed generations later!

Preparation Time: 15 minutes **Cook Time:** 6-8 hours **Makes:** 24 servings

Ingredients:

- 2 cups dried pinto beans
- ¾-pound fresh side pork (do not use bacon)
- 1-½ tablespoons salt, plus more for adjusting flavor
- Water

Method:

1. Preheat the oven to 350°F.
2. Sort the beans to remove broken or shriveled beans and debris. Rinse beans 2 to 3 times until the water runs clear.
3. Cut the side pork into 1 inch pieces.
4. Spoon the beans and pork into the bean pot or deep oven-proof pot, alternating in 4 layers starting with the beans. Fill the pot with water 1 inch above the beans. Sprinkle salt over beans, cover with foil or lid, and bake for 1 hour
5. Reduce the heat to 250°F., stir bringing the bottom beans to the top, cover and bake 5 to 7 hours. Be sure to stir the beans every hour to distribute the juices, adding more water if the liquid evaporates.
6. Remove the pot from the oven and gently stir, layering in salt until the right flavor is achieved. The beans should taste rich, creamy, and slightly salty. Keep covered at room temperature until ready to serve. Refrigerate or freeze leftovers.

Wisdom from Lorraine's Kitchen:

Fresh side pork is where the true flavor comes from in this dish. I do not recommend substitutions. You can order side pork from most local butchers.

Baking times will vary depending on the oven, bean pot, and age of the beans.

You can use an oven-proof pot if you do not have a ceramic bean pot.

Freeze in separate containers that fit 4 to 6 serving to use only what is needed per meal.

Refrigerate up to 4 days; freeze up to 6 months.

Chinese Smashed Cucumbers

by Rachel Huang - China

I had never heard of smashing a cucumber before adding it to a dish until Rachel introduced me to this method. Her technique involves crushing the cucumber to bring out its natural juices while softening the meat inside the skin. This process takes a simple cucumber to a new level of excitement. The added combination of a salty and sweet dressing creates a vegetable loaded with texture and flavor. Serve with steamed fish, beef, lamb, or poultry.

Preparation Time: 15 minutes **Cook Time:** 15-20 minutes **Makes:** 10-12 servings

Ingredients:

- 2 medium cucumbers, thinner skins
- 1 garlic clove, minced
- ½ teaspoon salt
- ¼ teaspoon granulated sugar
- 1 teaspoon Premium Soy Sauce, or Tamari
- 1 teaspoon rice wine vinegar
- 1 teaspoon sesame oil
- 1 tablespoon sesame seeds

Method:

1. Cut off and discard the ends of the cucumbers. Using the side of a large cutting knife, pound one side of the cucumber to partially smash and break the skin. Turn the cucumber to the unbroken side and repeat if the cucumber needs further softening on the inside. Roughly chop into 1 inch pieces and transfer to a bowl.
2. Whisk the garlic, salt, sugar, soy sauce, rice wine vinegar, and sesame oil in a small bowl. Pour the dressing over the cucumbers, toss and refrigerate for 30 minutes.
3. Top with sesame seeds just before serving.

Wisdom from Rachel's Kitchen:

Some cucumbers have thicker tough skin while others have thin softer skin. This method works best with thinner skinned cucumbers.

Garlic Green Beans with Shallots and Barberries

by Lisa Soldo-Johnson - USA

Garlic Green Beans with Shallots and Barberries is a combination of crunchy, buttery, and sour all rolled into one simple dish. Fresh haricot vert sautéed in olive oil, garlic, and shallots and dusted with sour barberries makes the perfect side dish or appetizer.

Preparation Time: 5 minutes   **Cook Time:** 12-15 minutes   **Makes:** 4 servings

Ingredients:

- 2 tablespoons dried barberries
- ⅓ cup olive oil
- 2 tablespoons minced shallots
- 1 tablespoon minced garlic
- ¼ teaspoon Himalayan sea salt, plus more for dusting
- 4 cup fresh haricot vert, ends cut off

Method:

1. Soak barberries in ½ cup warm water while preparing beans.
2. Simmer the olive oil, shallots, garlic, and salt in a small saucepan 3 to 4 minutes over medium-low heat. Remove the pan from the heat and set aside.
3. Boil 1 cup of water in a medium skillet. Steam the green beans 3 to 4 minutes or until beans are soft but crunchy. Strain water from beans and return to heat.
4. Pour olive oil mixture over the beans, toss to coat and sauté for 2 minutes.
5. Drain barberries, add to the beans, toss and continue to sauté for 1 to 2 minutes. Dust the top with a pinch of Himalayan sea salt and serve warm.

Did You Know?

In Iranian cooking, barberries' sourness stands as a symbol that life isn't always going to be a bed of roses.

Basmati Rice with Potato Tahdig

by Mitra Murphy - Iran

The first time I tried Basmati rice with potato tahdig (crust) I absolutely adored it. Tahdig forms at the bottom of a pot by using, potatoes, pita bread, or yogurt and topped with rice to create a hard crust that captures the flavor during the cooking process. This recipe uses thin slices of potatoes to create a crispy, crunchy, golden tahdig. In the Iranian culture, tahdig is everyone's favorite part of the rice. There is a charming tradition of friendly fighting over the tahdig to see who gets the last piece. It's just that good!

Preparation Time: 10 minutes
Passive Time: 2 hours
Cooking Time: 1 hour 20 minutes
Makes: 6 servings

Ingredients:

- 4 cups basmati rice rinsed and soaked
- ¼ cup plus 4-8 tablespoons light olive oil, depending on the pot size
- ½ cup milk
- 1-2 medium Yukon potatoes, sliced ¼-inch thick rounds
- 2 tablespoons hard butter, cut into 8 small pieces
- 2 teaspoons saffron water
- 1 tablespoon plus 2 teaspoons salt, divided

Method:

1. Place the rice in a medium bowl and rinse under cold water 4 to 5 times until the water runs clear to remove dirt and debris. Top the rice with 6 cups of water and 1 tablespoon of salt. Soak for 2 hours to 24 hours.
2. Fill a large non-stick pot with 10 cups of water and bring to a boil on high heat. Add the drained rice and 1 teaspoon of salt to the water. Parboil the rice for 6 to 8 minutes or just until the rice is slightly soft on the outside grain. You can test this by biting into a grain. Pour the rice into a mesh strainer and rinse with cold water to stop the cooking process.
3. Heat the oil in the same pot over medium heat, adjusting the amount of oil used depending on your pot size. The oil should be approximately ⅛ inch from the bottom. Stir in the milk. Cover the bottom of the pot with potato slices. Sprinkle the potatoes with remaining 1 teaspoon of salt.
4. Spoon a thin layer of rice over the potatoes. Continue to add rice in layers by spooning the rice into the middle of the pot in a pyramid shape, allowing the rice to fall towards the sides. Poke 5 to 6 holes into the rice using the end of a wooden spoon at the center and around the rice. Add the butter pieces over the rice evenly.
5. Mix ¼ cup oil with ¼ cup water and gently pour over the rice, being careful not to collapse the pyramid shape. Spoon the saffron water over the rice in a circular direction to create a spiral pattern. Reduce the heat to low.
6. Cover the lid of the pot with a cotton tea towel, tying the ends at the top of the lid. Cover the pot with the lid, reduce the heat to low and steam the rice for 30 to 70 minutes (depending on your cooktop), checking to ensure it doesn't burn.

continued on next page →

Wisdom from Mitra's Kitchen:

Soaking the rice before cooking helps it to stay firm during the cooking process, while preventing the grains from sticking together.

It is important to use a non-stick pot to prevent the potatoes from sticking to the bottom.

Be sure to cook on low to prevent the potatoes from burning.

To make the saffron water, crush 5 to 6 threads with a pestle and mortar. Add 2 tablespoons hot water and stir until dissolved.

7. Remove the pot from the heat and rest it on a cool damp cloth to naturally loosen the tahdig from the pot. You can keep the rice in the pot until you are ready to serve it.

8. To plate the rice, remove the cover from the pot. Use a plate large enough to cover top of the pot, quickly invert the two together, allowing the rice and tahdig to loosen onto the plate. Serve the rice topped with the potato tahdig or cut it into wedges, setting the tahdig on the sides of the rice to serve. Serve hot with kabobs (pages 75, 89) and a salad.

Did You Know?

Tahdig translates to "the bottom of the pot" in the Persian language, Farsi.

Balogh - Assyrian Side Dish

by Suheyla Kerkinni - Assyria

Balogh is a traditional Assyrian side dish made with a healthy combination of split pea, hearty bulgur, fragrant herbs and spices, and packed with flavorful crunchy onions for a delicious side dish that pairs perfectly with meat or fish.

Preparation Time: 15 minutes   **Cook Time:** 30 minutes   **Makes:** about 6-8 servings

Ingredients:

- 8 cups water
- 1-¼ cup red or yellow split peas
- 1 cup #1 fine bulgur
- 2 tablespoons ground coriander
- ½ teaspoon black pepper
- 1 ½ teaspoon salt, divided
- 1 teaspoon crushed red pepper (optional)
- 1 cup minced yellow onions, divided
- ½ cup chopped green onions, divided
- 1 cup finely chopped parsley, divided

Method:

1. Rinse the split peas and add them to a soup pot with the water and ½ teaspoon salt. Bring the water to a boil over medium-high heat and cook for 30 minutes, stirring occasionally.
2. Pour the split pea soup into a large bowl, reserving 1 cup for the end. Stir in the bulgur, coriander, remaining 1 teaspoon salt, black pepper, and red pepper flakes. Let the Balogh set for 15 minutes to thicken.
3. Stir in ¾ cup minced yellow onions, ¼ cup green onions, and ¾ cup parsley until it is well combined. Heat the remaining 1 cup pea soup and stir it into the mixture.
4. Transfer the Balogh to a serving dish and top with remaining ¼ cup yellow onions, remaining ¼ cup green onions ¼ cup parsley and green onions. You can use less of the toppings if desired. Serve hot.

Wisdom from Suheyla's Kitchen:

I reserve 1 cup of pea soup, heated just before adding to the finished Balogh, so the dish is served hot.

Be sure to use #1 fine bulgur for this recipe.

If you prefer a less oniony flavor, reduce the amount of onions.

Mexican Fiesta Salad

by Lisa Soldo-Johnson - USA

Mexican fiesta salad is a crowd pleaser! Made with a vibrant mix of black beans, corn salsa, tomatoes, onion, cilantro, avocado, and a zesty lime dressing. The excitement of the flavors permeates your palate with every bite. It's a perfect make-ahead dish for parties, large gatherings, dinner tonight, or meal prep for the week. Hold off on adding the dressing until just before you serve it and this salad will last in the refrigerator for up to 3 days.

Preparation Time: 15 minutes

Cook Time: 15-20 minutes

Makes: 10-12 servings

Ingredients:

- 2 cups quinoa
- 1 15-ounce can black beans, drained and rinsed
- 2 cups corn salsa, or canned corn
- 1 avocado, cut into ½-inch pieces
- 1-pint cherry tomatoes, halved
- ½ cup red onion, diced
- ½ bunch cilantro, chopped
- 3-4 tablespoons fresh squeezed lime juice
- ½ cup light olive oil
- 1 teaspoon salt

Method:

1. Rinse the quinoa in a bowl until the water runs clear. Drain and transfer to a medium pot filled with 4 cups of water. Bring to a boil, cover, reduce heat to medium low and simmer 15 to 20 minutes or until the water is absorbed. Transfer quinoa to a large bowl to cool completely.
2. Add the black beans, corn salsa, avocado, tomatoes, red onions, and cilantro to the bowl.
3. Whisk the olive oil, lime juice and salt in a small bowl. Pour the dressing over the quinoa and toss until the salad is completely combined. Refrigerate until ready to serve.

Wisdom from Lisa's Kitchen:

Add grilled chicken or shrimp to make it a main course or light lunch.

Serve it inside fish tacos or toss some in an egg scramble for a delicious Mexican-inspired meal anytime of the day.

Mast va laboo - Persian Yogurt and Beet Dip

by Mitra Murphy - Iran

Mast va laboo is a Persian yogurt and beet dip introduced to me by Mitra. This dish is an unexpected delight made with creamy yogurt, fresh beets, and cool mint. It's also a gorgeous dish with a stunning pink color created by the beets. Serve as a side dish with kabobs or an appetizer with bread.

Preparation Time: 15 minutes   **Cooking Time:** 1 hour   **Makes:** 4 servings

Ingredients:

- 2 large uncooked red beets
- 1 cup plain Greek yogurt
- 2 tablespoons granulated sugar
- 2 tablespoons fresh mint
- ½ teaspoon salt
- ½ teaspoon pepper

Method:

1. Steam the beets with the skin on for 1 hour. Remove the beets from the pot and set aside to cool.
2. Remove the skin from the beets by running under cool. Using your hands to peel away and discard the skin.
3. Cut the beets into ½ inch cubes on a cutting board and transfer the beets to a bowl. (Be sure to rinse the board immediately to prevent staining.) Refrigerate beets until ready to serve.
4. In a separate bowl, whisk the yogurt, sugar, salt, and pepper. Refrigerate until ready to serve.
5. Just before serving, pour the yogurt sauce over the beets and gently mix together until the beets are evenly coated. (The sauce will turn pink.)
6. Garnish with fresh mint and serve with Persian bread, Indian naan, or pita bread as an appetizer or side dish.

Did You Know?

An Assyrian text dated 800 BC, describes beets growing in the Hanging Gardens, one of the seven wonders of the ancient world.

Torshi Liteh

by Sohiela Mirsharif - Iran

In Persian cuisine, Torshi is a pickled vegetable dish served as a complement to meals that typically include kabobs, rice, yogurt dips, and other traditional dishes. Although there are many ways to make torshi, I particularly love Sohiela's version because it highlights a savory spice called Angelica (golpar), adding a distinct aromatic flavor to the vegetables.

Preparation Time: 1 hour
Passive Time: 24 hours
Cook Time: 5 minutes
Makes: about 4-6 jars (1 pint each)

Ingredients:

- 1 cup celery, finely chopped
- 2 large carrots, peeled and shredded
- ½ head cauliflower, chopped into extra small florets
- 1 cup potatoes, diced
- 4 large eggplant, chopped into 1-inch cubes
- 1 teaspoon ginger, minced
- ½ cup parsley, minced
- 2 tablespoons fresh tarragon, finely chopped
- 2 tablespoons turmeric
- 2 tablespoons pickling salt
- 2 tablespoons coriander seeds
- ½ teaspoon coriander powder
- 2 tablespoons black caraway or nigella seeds
- 2 tablespoons crushed Angelica (golpar)
- 1 cup apple cider vinegar, plus more to cover torshi in jar

Method:

1. Wash and chop the vegetables. Spread them out on a clean towel or tablecloth to air-dry for 24 hours before preparing the recipe. Wash the herbs but do not chop. Lay them flat to air dry with the vegetables.
2. The following day: Sterilize canning jars in boiling water. Drain and let cool. Chop the herbs. Place the eggplant in a large pot covered with 1 cup vinegar or enough to cover eggplant completely. Bring to a boil over medium-high, reduce heat to medium and simmer for 5 minutes. Drain in a colander.
3. Place the eggplant, vegetables, herbs and spices into a large mixing bowl. Using a wooden spoon, stir until evenly mixed.
4. Spoon torshi into the jars, patting down gently to remove some of the air space. Leave 1 inch space at the top for the vinegar.
5. Gently pour vinegar over the torshi, allowing the liquid to flow through the vegetables and settle just above the vegetables, leaving ½ inch space on top. Place lid on jar and seal tightly. Refrigerate for 2 weeks before using.

Wisdom from Sohiela's Kitchen:

When preparing torshi, use the freshest ingredients and completely dry all the vegetables and herbs before starting so it will keep well.

It is best to dry vegetables and herbs out of reach from pets to avoid contamination of animal hair or dander that may float in the air.

The spice, Angelica (Golpar) is what gives this recipe a distinct flavor. It can be purchased in most Middle Eastern grocery stores or online.

Torshi improves over time. The longer it ferments in the vinegar the better. Torshi can last for years if refrigerated or on a shelf if processed in a water bath.

Sesame Garlic Veggie Trio

by Lisa Soldo-Johnson - USA

Some of my favorite recipe creations happen spontaneously. I like to incorporate international flavors into most of my meals so my family can experience food from a different culture. Garlic Sesame Vegetable Trio includes enoki mushrooms often used in Chinese cuisine for soups and stews. Combine with crunchy haricot vert and sweet peppers to make a healthy flavorful side dish for fish, beef, and poultry. Or serve it with a bed of quinoa or rice for a simple, yet tasty vegetarian meal.

Preparation Time: 10 minutes
Cooking Time: 15 minutes
Makes: 4 servings

Ingredients:

- 1-pound fresh green beans, trimmed
- 4 mini sweet peppers, seeded and slice
- 1 cup enoki mushrooms, trimmed
- 1 tablespoon sesame oil
- 1 tablespoon grapeseed oil
- 1 shallot, finely chopped
- 3 garlic cloves, thinly sliced
- 2 teaspoons sesame seeds
- Coarse sea salt
- Fresh cracked pepper

Method:

1. Boil 6 cups of water in a medium saucepan over high heat. Add the green beans, peppers, and mushrooms. Parboil for 3 to 4 minutes or until slightly soft when pierced with a fork.
2. While the vegetables are cooking, heat the oils in a sauté pan over medium heat. Add the garlic and shallots, sautéing until just aromatic (2 to 3 minutes).
3. Drain the vegetables and transfer them to the sauté pan. Sprinkle in the sesame seeds, salt, and pepper. Toss and continue to sauté for 2 to 3 minutes or until the vegetables are tender but not too soft. Adjust the flavor with additional salt and pepper if desired.
4. Serve with Spicy Sichuan Beef (page 117) and a side of rice or quinoa, or your favorite meat or fish.

Wisdom from Lisa's Kitchen:

Be careful to overcook the Enoki mushrooms or they will become tough and fibrous.

Did You Know?

Enoki mushrooms have been used for centuries in Asian culture to boost the immune system, reduce body fat, prevent allergies and more.

Russian Salad Olivier

by Natasha Baig and Maya Pugachevsky

Russian Salad Olivier has been a staple in Russian cuisine since its inception over a century and a half ago. Playfully blended with basic ingredients including chicken, potatoes, vegetables, and pickles, this hearty potato salad is a dish commonly found on many Russian dinner tables. Although the original recipe was much more complicated, time and resources played a role in changing the ingredients used to make this classic favorite. In Russian communities around the world, Salad Olivier remains one of the main dishes served during New Year's Eve celebrations.

Preparation Time: 20 minutes   **Cook Time:** 40 minutes   **Makes:** 6-8 servings

Ingredients:

- 1-½ pounds boneless skinless chicken thighs, baked and chopped into ½-inch cubes
- 2 large Yukon gold potatoes, baked, cooled, peeled and chopped into ½-inch cubes
- 3 large eggs, hardboiled, peeled, chopped
- 1-¼ cups diced dill pickles
- 1 cup chopped green onions
- 15-ounce can mix peas and carrots, drained
- 1 ½ cup olive oil mayonnaise
- 1 teaspoon salt, plus more if desired

Method:

1. Add the chicken, potatoes, eggs, pickles, onions, peas and carrots, salt, and mayonnaise in a large bowl and gently stir to combine, being careful not to smash the vegetables. Refrigerate until ready to serve.

Wisdom from Natasha and Maya's Kitchen:

Place potatoes under cold water before peeling.

If using fresh carrots and peas, cook them the night before and refrigerate to cool before chopping the carrots the next day.

Did You Know?

Over time, regions of the world, including Europe, Iran, Israel, Mongolia and Latin America have created their own version of Salad Olivier.

Mast o Khiar with Shallots and Garlic

by Shaya Chatraei - Iran

Mast-o-Khiar is a Persian dish made with yogurt (mast) and cucumber (khiar) and served with meat and rice. Though there are many ways to make this dish, Shaya's recipe uses cucumbers, mint, garlic, and shallots infused and chilled in creamy yogurt. Mast o Khiar also pairs nicely over fajitas, in sandwiches, as a dip with crackers and vegetables, spooned over gazpacho soup, or any recipe that is complemented by yogurt and cucumbers.

Preparation Time: 10 minutes

Makes: 6 servings

Ingredients:

- 2 cups plain Greek yogurt
- 1 English cucumber or 3 Persian cucumbers, peeled and diced
- 1 small garlic clove, minced
- ½ shallot, minced
- 2 tablespoons dried mint, plus extra of garnish
- 1 teaspoon sea salt
- ½ teaspoon black pepper

Method:

1. Mix the yogurt, shallots, mint, salt, and pepper in a medium bowl.
2. Add the cucumbers and blend until they are evenly distributed into the sauce.
3. Spoon Mast o Khiar into a serving bowl and decorate the top with dried mint and/or rose petals.
4. Cover and refrigerate until ready to serve.

Wisdom from Shaya's Kitchen:

For the freshest results, wait to add the cucumber until right before you serve it. This will prevent the dip from becoming watery.

One way to extend the life of Mast o Khiar is to lightly sprinkle the prepared cucumbers with salt and allow them to drain in a colander for 30 minutes before adding to the yogurt, preserving the quality of this dish for a day.

Mast o Khiar is best when eaten the same day. The cucumbers lose liquid over time, creating a watery consistency in the yogurt.

Did You Know?

Greek yogurt has twice the protein of regular yogurt.

Kashk-o bademjan

by Sohiela Mirsharif - Iran

Human nature teaches us to eat with our eyes first. Sohiela's Persian cuisine is a gorgeous presentation of Kashk-o bademjan, a traditional Persian eggplant dip infused with garlic, onions, spices, and the addition of a yogurt whey called kashk. This sets the dish apart from other bademjan (eggplant) recipes and adds a delicate touch of creaminess. Sohiela embellishes her presentation with flower designs using tiny mint leaves and kashk, colored with and without saffron, to create the yellow and white flowers. It's a delicious work of art. Serve Kashk-o bademjan as an appetizer with a Persian bread called lavash or toasted pita bread.

Preparation Time: 20 minutes **Cook Time:** 1 hour 30 minutes **Makes:** about 6-8 servings

Ingredients:

- 5 large eggplants, peeled and sliced lengthwise ¼-inch thick
- 4-6 egg whites, whisked
- 1 cup olive oil, more as needed
- 4 garlic cloves, minced
- 1 large onion, thinly sliced, divided
- 1 cup chicken broth
- 7 tablespoons kashk (page 177), divided
- 1 teaspoon sea salt, divided
- 1 teaspoon turmeric, divided
- ½ teaspoon paprika
- 3 tablespoons dried mint, powdered
- fresh mint

Method:

1. Whisk egg whites in a small bowl. Heat ¼ cup oil in a skillet over medium heat. Lightly brush both sides of the eggplant with egg whites and lay them in the hot oil. Lightly sprinkle with salt and turmeric, turning over when browned and repeating on the other side, adding more oil if needed. Transfer the eggplant to paper towels to absorb the oil.

2. Using the same skillet, heat 2 tablespoon oil in a wide skillet over medium-low heat. Sauté the onions 5 to 10 minutes or until the they begin to turn brown. Add the garlic and sauté for 30 seconds. Sprinkle ½ teaspoon salt, ½ teaspoon turmeric, ½ teaspoon paprika, and 3 tablespoons dried mint, sautéing for 20 seconds.

3. Remove the skillet from the heat and layer the eggplant on top of the onions, pour in the chicken broth, cover and cook over low heat for 30 minutes or until the liquid is absorbed.

4. Using a colander, strain any visible oil from the eggplant. Transfer the eggplant mixture to a bowl and mash with a potato masher or fork into a creamy texture. Stir in 3 to 5 tablespoons kashk until blended. Transfer the Kashk-o bademjan to a decorative serving plate to garnish. Serve warm with lavash or toasted pita bread wedges.

Garnish:

1. To create flowers: Mix 2 tablespoons kashk and ¼ teaspoon turmeric in a small bowl. Spoon the mix into a plastic sandwich bag and cut off the tip. Fill another bag with remaining 2 tablespoons plain kashk. Decide how many flowers you want to add to the top. Squeeze individual circles over the top of the Kashk-o bademjan using both colors to create the inside of a flower.

2. Using smaller mint leaves, place small sprigs next to kashk for the leaves of the flower. Sprinkle nigella seeds on top and/or around the

continued on next page →

inner flowers to create a seed-look to the flowers. You can also use any dark colored (subtle-flavored) herb you have on hand to create the seeds on the flowers.

 ### Wisdom from Sohiela's Kitchen:

Use a mortar and pestle to powder the dried mint.

To speed up the process of cooking the eggplant, use two skillets at the same time.

Lightly brushing the eggplant with egg whites prevents the eggplant from soaking in a lot of the oil while it is cooking.

You have the option of roasting the eggplant brushed with olive oil on 400°F. for 40 minutes or until golden brown.

Persian food is always decorated beautifully when it is served to guests. Feel free to be creative when decorating this dish.

If you don't want to make your own kashk (boiled yogurt), it can be purchased at most Middle Eastern grocery stores.

Sweet and Spicy Steamed Cauliflower

by Lisa Soldo-Johnson - USA

Sweet and Spicy Steamed Cauliflower is a quick and easy side dish recipe that pairs beautifully with meat, fish, and seafood. It also makes a delicious appetizer served hot or cold. Make it a vegetarian meal by placing over a bed of quinoa or couscous.

Preparation Time: 5 minutes
Passive Time: 10 minutes
Cook Time: 10 minutes
Makes: 4 servings

Ingredients:

- 3 cups cauliflower
- 2 tablespoons coconut amino
- ⅛ teaspoon red pepper flakes

Method:

1. Steam the cauliflower for 7 to 10 minutes or until tender and transfer to a bowl.
2. Toss the cauliflower with the coconut amino and red pepper flakes. Let marinate for 10 minutes before serving.

Did You Know?

A single floret of cauliflower contains 10% of your daily vitamin C needs.

Steaming cauliflower preserves the most amount of nutrients.

CHAPTER 8

Sauces and Spices

Sauces and Spices / 176

Kashk Yogurt Cream / 177

Za'atar / 179

Rice Spice / 180

Cajun Spice / 180

Bahārāt - Middle Eastern Spice Blend / 181

Rachel's Everything Sauce / 182

Sichuan Peppercorn Oil / 182

Chinese Spicy Chili Sauce / 183

Elderberry Syrup / 185

Pomegranate Molasses / 186

Lime Crema / 186

Creamy Caesar Dressing / 187

Yogurt Cucumber Sauce / 187

Real Deal Cocktail Sauce / 188

No Fail Gravy / 189

Red Pepper Paste / 189

Sauces and Spices

Making specialty spices and sauces at home means you no longer have to limit your meals to the basic flavors and seasonings most of us have in our pantries already. One of the challenges I have faced in making international cuisine is the eclectic selection of specialty spices and seasonings sometimes needed in those dishes. If you are anything like me, you've had days when you start cooking a recipe knowing that you have all the right ingredients on hand, only to find out that your spice bottle (you know, the one you need at just that moment) is empty. This inspired me to create useful sauce and spice combinations to have on hand whenever needed. Since then, culturally inspired cooking in my kitchen has grown a new set of wings.

Kashk Yogurt Cream

by Sohiela Mirsharif - Iran

Kashk is a fermented dairy made from boiled yogurt and water and is widely used in Iranian cuisine. Kashk is most notably used in a traditional Persian dish called Kashk-o bademjan but can easily be used to increase the depth of flavor in soups, stews, roasted vegetables, and meats.

Preparation Time: 5 minutes   **Cook Time:** 1 hour   **Makes:** 2 cups

Ingredients:

- 32 ounces full-fat plain yogurt
- 1 cup water
- ½ teaspoon sea salt

Method:

1. Place the yogurt in a non-stick pot over medium heat. Fill the yogurt container with water, adding it to the pot. Stir and bring to a gentle boil.
2. Reduce the heat to medium and simmer for 1 hour, stirring occasionally to prevent yogurt from sticking to the pot. Shortly before the kashke is done, it will form a cottage cheese texture. It is important to lightly move it around the bottom of the pot every minute or so to prevent from overcooking or sticking to the bottom of the pot. The liquid will almost completely evaporate, and the yogurt will turn a light tan color. Remove from heat to cool for 10 minutes.
3. Pour the yogurt into a nut bag and squeeze out as much liquid as possible.
4. Process the yogurt in a blender with 1 cup filtered water and ½ teaspoon salt until it resembles a sour cream consistency. The texture will be slightly grainy. Transfer to a container and refrigerate for up to 3 days.

Wisdom from Sohiela's Kitchen:

To preserve for up to 3 months, fill ice cubes trays with the kashke and freeze. Pour the frozen kashk into a freezer bag and use as needed.

You can use kashke to thicken soups and stews, enhance roasted vegetables, or drizzled over meats and roasts for a gentle hint of sourness.

Recommended for:

Kashke Bademjan (page 171).

Za'atar

by Laurie Kerkinni - USA

Za'atar is an aromatic herb blend that combines a variety of healthy herbs and spices to create an exotic mix of flavors with countless uses. Za'atar is an Arabic word for "thyme" and is widely used in Mediterranean and Middle Eastern cooking. Although you can find Za'atar in many grocery stores, it is difficult to find the fresh, dramatic flavor that burst from a freshly made batch of Laurie's savory spice blend.

Preparation Time: 20 minutes

Makes: approximately 7 cups

Ingredients:

- 4 cups organic dried thyme
- ½ cup olive oil
- ½ cup black sesame seeds
- 2 cups organic sesame seeds
- 3 tablespoons black cumin seeds (black caraway or nigella sativa)
- 2 tablespoons organic quinoa
- 2 tablespoons sumac
- 1 ½ tablespoons chia seeds
- 1 tablespoon hemp seeds
- 1 tablespoon Himalayan salt or Celtic salt

Method:

1. Place the thyme and olive oil in a bowl. Using your hands, massage the oil into the thyme until it becomes slightly wet and darker in color. Add a little more olive oil if needed, being careful that the mixture does not get too wet.
2. Add in the remaining ingredients and continue to massage until the herbs are well blended. Transfer the za'atar to a large jar, cover, and store in a cool dry place for up to 6 months.

Recommended for:

Za'atar has many delicious uses including as a dip with oil for bread, sprinkled it over salads, massage it into meats and fish, tossed with roasted vegetables, sprinkled over popcorn, or in a grilled cheese sandwich.

Rice Spice

by Shaya Chatraei - Iran

Rice Spice is a mix of five aromatic spices to add a warm, fragrant flavor used in a variety of Persian dishes including Kuku Sabzi.

Preparation Time: 10 minutes

Makes: 5 teaspoons

Ingredients:

- 6 tablespoons dried rose pedals, powdered
- 4 tablespoons cinnamon
- 2 tablespoons cumin
- 1 teaspoon cardamom
- 1 teaspoon nutmeg

Method:

1. Place the rose petal powder, cinnamon, cumin, cardamom, and nutmeg in a mason jar with a lid and shake to combine the spices. Store in your pantry for up to 1 year.

Recommended for:

Kuku Sabzi (page 143)

Mix with rice or grains or sprinkle over baked desserts to add a warm fragrant flavor.

Cajun Spice

by Lisa Soldo-Johnson - USA

Cajun spice is a versatile blend of zesty, spicy, and savory flavors that enhance the essence of heat on vegetables, rice, meats, seafood and more.

Preparation Time: 5 minutes

Makes: approximately ½ cup

Ingredients:

- 2 ½ tablespoons Himalayan salt
- 1 tablespoon cayenne pepper
- 1 tablespoon garlic powder
- 1 tablespoon paprika
- ½ tablespoon dried oregano
- ½ tablespoon thyme
- ½ tablespoon ground black pepper
- ½ tablespoon onion powder

Method:

1. Spoon all of the spices into a jar with a lid and shake until well blended. Store in an airtight container or up to 1 year.

Recommended for:

Cajun Shrimp Pasta with Andouille Sausage (page 131)

Cajun Spice is the perfect addition to your spice pantry. Add to meats, soups, rice dishes, sauces, marinades and so much more.

Bahārāt - Middle Eastern Spice Blend

by Lisa Soldo-Johnson - USA

"Bahārāt" means "spice" in Arabic. You can often find this spice in Middle Eastern grocery stores, but why not make your own? Bahārāt is an aromatic combination of spices that gives a warm, sweet, spicy essence to meats and other dishes. There is a slight variation in this spice depending on the culture and region which makes it. In Turkey, Bahārāt is made with dried mint and other spices, while in North Africa dried rose petals are incorporated into this exotic spice to give it a distinct cultural flavor. The combination of spices I have chosen for my Bahārāt are ingredients you can easily find in your spice pantry.

Preparation Time: 5 minutes

Makes: approximately ½ cup

Ingredients:

- 4 tablespoons paprika
- 4 tablespoons ground black pepper
- 1 tablespoon ground coriander
- 1 tablespoon ground cloves
- 1 tablespoon ground cumin
- 1 tablespoon ground cinnamon
- 1 tablespoon ground ginger
- ½ tablespoon ground allspice

Method:

1. Spoon the spices into a jar with a lid and shake until well blended. Store in an airtight container in a cool dark place.

Recommended for:

Moussaka (page 112)

Enjoy on meats, as a marinade for vegetables or sprinkled a bit over your rice or grain dishes. Also, use Bahārāt to enhance the flavor of your soups and stews with just a small amount of Bahārāt.

Rachel's Everything Sauce

by Rachel Huang - China

I call this sauce, "Rachel's Everything Sauce" because you can use it on almost everything. From rice to noodles, as a dipping sauce for egg rolls and pot stickers, a marinade over fish or chicken, to flavor soups or sauces, or a light and zesty salad dressing. The possibilities are endless. I keep a jar of this sauce in my refrigerator at all times for a quick and easy solution for flavoring any dish.

Preparation Time: 5 minutes

Makes: approximately ½ cup

Ingredients:

- 1 cup water
- 1 cup granulated sugar
- ⅔ cup white vinegar
- ½ cup fish sauce
- 3 small red chili peppers, seeded and minced
- 1 tablespoon fresh garlic, minced

Method:

1. Whisk the water, sugar, vinegar, fish sauce, chili pepper, and garlic in a small bowl. Transfer to an airtight container and refrigerate up to 2 weeks.

Recommended for:

Spicy Chicken Noodle Bowl (page 73).

Pan Fried Garlic Shrimp (page 123).

Sichuan Peppercorn Oil

by Rachel Huang - China

Peppercorn oil adds a fragrant pepper flavor for sautéing, stir-fry, dipping sauces, or anywhere you'd like to add a little zing to your meal. It's a quick and easy oil to make and stores well in your pantry for months. That is of course if it lasts that long!

Preparation Time: 3 minutes

Cook Time: 12 minutes

Makes: approximately ¼ cup

Ingredients:

- ½ - cup light olive oil
- 2 tablespoons Sichuan peppercorns

Recommended for:

Spicy Sichuan Beef (page 117)

Method:

1. Heat a medium saucepan over high heat for 30 seconds.
2. Add the peppercorns and reduce the heat to medium-low. Move peppercorns around the pan for 20 seconds or until they start to smoke and become aromatic. Be careful not to let the peppercorns burn. Transfer the peppercorns to a bowl. Once cooled, lightly crush the peppercorns with the back of a spoon to break the shell.
3. Using the same pan, heat the oil over medium heat 1 to 2 minutes or until it begins to smoke. Carefully pour the oil over the peppercorns and store in your pantry.
4. If you prefer a more subtle flavor, marinate the peppercorns in the oil for 30 minutes, strain the peppercorns from the oil and store the oil in a jar at room temperature for up to 3 months.

Chinese Spicy Chili Sauce

by Rachel Huang - China

Add a kick of spiciness to meats, fish, vegetables, and rice with this flavor-packed Chinese Spicy Chili Sauce.

Preparation Time: 5 minutes

Makes: approximately ½ cup

Ingredients:

- 1 teaspoon Sichuan peppercorn oil (chapter 10)
- ½ teaspoon Sichuan peppercorns
- 1 garlic clove, minced
- 2 tablespoons Spicy Chili Crisp
- 1 ½ tablespoons Premium Soy Sauce, or Tamari
- 1 teaspoon Chinkiang Vinegar, or rice vinegar
- ½ teaspoon granulated sugar
- ¼ cup cilantro, chopped
- 1 tablespoon water
- 1 tablespoon green onions, minced

Method:

1. Whisk the peppercorn oil, peppercorns, garlic, spicy chili crisp, soy sauce, vinegar, sugar, cilantro, water, and onions in a small bowl.
2. Pour the sauce in an airtight container and refrigerate up to 3 days.

Recommended for:

Spicy Sichuan Beef (page 117).

Elderberry Syrup

by Lisa Soldo-Johnson - USA

The great Greek philosopher, Hypocrites, was considered "the father of medicine" because of his incredible insight understanding food and how it plays a significant role in the health or illness of our bodies. He called elderberries "his medicine chest" because of the tremendous healing properties built into each tiny berry. Elderberries are considered an effective natural medicine that aids in boosting the immune system and curing many ailments. I keep a few bottles in my refrigerator at all times. In addition to its medical value, it's easy to make, economical, and delicious.

Preparation Time: 5 minutes

Cook Time: 30 minutes

Makes: 6-7 cups

Ingredients:

- ½ cup dried elderberries
- 6 whole cloves
- 2 cinnamon sticks
- 1 tablespoon freshly grated ginger
- 6 cups water
- 1 cup raw honey

Method:

1. Place the elderberries, cloves, cinnamon sticks, ginger, and water in a medium pan and bring to a boil on high. Reduce the heat to medium-low and simmer for 30 minutes.
2. Place a mesh strainer over a bowl and strain the contents of the pan. Using a spoon, press the berries to strain as much liquid as possible. Discard the berries and cinnamon sticks.
3. Stir in honey until dissolved. Pour the elderberry syrup in a mason jars and refrigerate up to 90 days.

Wisdom from Lisa's Kitchen:

Homemade elderberry syrup makes a wonderful gift for friends and family.

It is recommended to take 1 tablespoon per day for optimal health, take 2 tablespoons per day, 2 to 3 times per day to speed up healing and recovery from colds and flu symptoms.

(Disclaimer: The information, including but not limited to, text and images contained in this recipe are for informational purposes only. It is not intended to be a substitute for professional medical advice, diagnosis or treatment. Always seek the advice of your physician or other qualified healthcare provider with any questions you may have regarding a medical condition or treatment and before undertaking a new health care regimen. Never disregard professional medical advice or delay seeking it because of something you have read in this book.)

Pomegranate Molasses

by Lisa Soldo-Johnson - USA

Pomegranate molasses is a flavorful ingredient used in many Middle Eastern and Mediterranean dishes. The natural sweetener enhances the flavor of dressings, sauces, marinades, beverages, and desserts.

Cook Time: 1 hour

Makes: approximately 1 ½ cups

Ingredients:

- 48 ounces 100% POM pomegranate juice

Method:

1. Bring the pomegranate juice to a boil in a saucepan over medium-high heat. Reduce the heat to low and simmer for approximately 1 hour or until the juice reduces to a syrup. The syrup should coat a spoon when it is done.
2. Remove from the heat and cool before transferring to a glass jar. The syrup will keep in the refrigerator for up to one month.

Recommended for:

Lentil Salad with Pomegranate Dressing (page 49)

Zeytoon Parvardeh - Pomegranate Walnut Dip (page 17)

Drizzle pomegranate molasses over ice cream or desserts, use in smoothies, malts, salad dressings, and more.

Lime Crema

by Lisa Soldo-Johnson - USA

Lime Crema is a light and flavorful topping perfect for fish and chicken tacos, beef, and lamb, rice, soups or chili, chip or vegetable dip. The versatility of Lime Crema is endless.

Preparation Time: 5 minutes

Makes: approximately 1 cup

Ingredients:

- 1 cup plain sour cream
- 1 tablespoon fresh lime juice
- 1 teaspoon lime zest
- ½ teaspoon garlic powder
- ½ teaspoon sea salt

Method:

1. Whisk the sour cream, lime juice, lime zest, garlic powder, and salt in a small bowl.
2. Cover and refrigerate until ready to use.

Recommended for:

Fish Tacos with Pineapple Island Salad (page 127).

Creamy Caesar Dressing

by Laurie Kerkinni - USA

Since learning to make Laurie's homemade Caesar dressing, I will never buy bottled Caesar dressing again. I use this creamy dairy-free dressing to drizzle over a bowl of romaine lettuce or kale salad, as a light dip for veggies and chips, or tossed with my favorite herb roasted potato recipe.

Preparation Time: 15 minutes   **Cook Time:** 1 minute   **Makes:** 6 servings

Ingredients:

- 2 ½ tablespoons lemon juice
- 2 ½ tablespoons lime juice
- 2 cloves garlic, minced
- 1 tablespoon Worcestershire sauce
- 1 tablespoon balsamic vinegar
- 1 teaspoon Dijon mustard
- ¼ teaspoon dry mustard
- ½ teaspoon salt
- ¼ teaspoon pepper
- ⅔ cup olive oil
- 2 eggs, coddled
- 3 anchovy fillets, minced (optional)

Method:

1. Whisk the lemon juice, lime juice, garlic, Worcestershire sauce, balsamic vinegar, Dijon mustard, dry mustard, salt, and pepper in a bowl. Whisk in the olive oil until emulsified.
2. Coddle the eggs by heating 3 cups of water to a boil. Drop in egg (still in shell) and let stand for 1 minute. Remove eggs from the water and let cool. Once cooled, crack open and whisk eggs into dressing.
3. Mash the anchovies and whisk them into the dressing or set aside for garnish.
4. Refrigerate dressing for up to one week.

Recommended for:

Caesar Tossed Herb Roasted Potatoes (page 145), Kale Caesar Salad (page 52).

Caesar salad, vegetable and chip dip, chicken and shrimp marinade, and more.

Yogurt Cucumber Sauce

by Ameneh Gounilli - Iran

Yogurt cucumber sauce, in my opinion, is the perfect complement to any meal. Serve it with chicken, beef, pork, lamb, fish, rice, tacos, falafel, burgers, baked potatoes, and so much more.

Preparation Time: 10 minutes   **Makes:** approximately 1-½ cups

Ingredients:

- ½ English cucumber, peeled, halved lengthwise, seeded and finely diced.
- 1 cup plain Greek yogurt
- 2 tablespoons fresh lemon juice
- 1 tablespoon chopped fresh dill
- ¼ teaspoon salt
- ¼ teaspoon pepper

Method:

1. Mix the cucumber, yogurt, lemon juice, dill, salt, and pepper in a small bowl, cover and refrigerate until ready to serve.

Recommended for:

Koobideh (page 89)

Kebab in Puff Pastry (page 92)

Moroccan Lamb Chops (page 119)

Israeli Lamb and Beef Kabobs (page 97)

Real Deal Cocktail Sauce

by Laurie Kerkinni - USA

Real Deal Cocktail Sauce creates a fresh flavor explosion when paired with shrimp, crab claw meat, or your favorite seafood. You can easily adjust the ingredients to dial the heat up or down. One taste of this sauce and you may never buy a bottled cocktail sauce again.

Preparation Time: 5 minutes   **Cook Time:** 30 minutes   **Makes:** approximately 1 cup

Ingredients:

- 1 cup organic ketchup
- 1 ½ teaspoon horseradish powder or ½ teaspoon wasabi powder
- 1 tablespoon sweet red chili sauce
- 2 tablespoons lemon juice
- ½ teaspoon Worcestershire sauce

Method:

1. Whisk the ketchup, horseradish powder, chili sauce, lemon juice, and Worcestershire sauce. Cover and refrigerate until ready to use.

No Fail Gravy

by Lorraine Soldo - USA

My mom was the queen of homemade gravy. She made hers exclusively from freshly cooked chicken, beef, or turkey broth using both the bones and the meat to achieve an intense flavor. She would often tell me, "The best gravy comes from a stock with a lot of animal fat." Her method of dissolving the cornstarch in cold water or milk before whisking into the simmering broth creates a thick, creamy, lump-free texture. Add a little salt and pepper for the perfect flavored no-fail gravy every time.

Preparation Time: 2 minutes

Cook Time: 5-7 minutes

Makes: approximately 1 ½ cup

Ingredients:

- 1 cup freshly cooked broth
- 2 tablespoons cornstarch
- ½ cup cold water
- Salt and pepper

Wisdom from Lorraine's Kitchen:

For a darker broth, use water and for a lighter broth use milk.

Method:

1. Strain the fresh stock through a mesh strainer to remove any particles left over from the cooking process. Transfer the stock to a pan and bring a simmer over medium heat.
2. Add the cornstarch and water or milk to a mason jar with a lid and shake until the cornstarch is dissolved.
3. Slowly whisk the liquid into the broth until it thickens. Use more or less cornstarch water to adjust the thickness to your liking.
4. Add salt and pepper a pinch at a time until the gravy is the flavor you prefer.

Recommended for:

Open-Face Roast Beef Sandwich (page 101).

Red Pepper Paste

by Suheyla Kerkinni - Assyria

Red Pepper Paste is a highly concentrated puree used in a variety of dishes including soups, stews, dips, spreads, dressings and more.

Preparation Time: 5 minutes

Cook Time: 30 minutes

Makes: approximately 1 cup

Ingredients:

- 3 large red bell peppers, cored and chopped
- 1 large Haperino or chili pepper, cored and chopped
- 1 tablespoon olive oil
- 1 teaspoon granulated sugar
- 1 teaspoon sea salt

Method:

1. Add the red peppers, Haperino peppers, oil, sugar, and salt in a food processor and blend on high until pureed.
2. Pour the puree into a non-stick pan and simmer on medium-low heat (stirring often) for 20 to 30 minutes or until the liquid has cooked off and paste has formed.
3. Transfer the paste to an airtight container and store in the refrigerator for up to one week.

Recommended for:

Tlavhe Red Lentil Soup (page 59).   Flavor stews, soups, stir-fry, and pastas.

CHAPTER 9

Desserts and Baking

Bulgur & Semolina Cinnamon and Sugar Donut Holes / 192

Decadent Mandarin Orange Cake / 193

Dashisto - Assyrian Rice Pudding / 195

Cheese Borek with Cinnamon and Sugar / 196

Cranberry Bread Pudding Cake / 197

Lemon Zucchini Bread with Sweet Turmeric Glaze / 199

Raspberry and Pear Stuffed Fillo / 201

Caramelized Pears with Crusted Goat Cheese / 202

1942 Sweet Molasses Cake / 203

Almond Cornbread with Orange Caramel Sauce / 205

Tres Leches Cake with Chantilly Cream / 206

Creamy Rhubarb Bread Pudding Bars / 208

Yufka Turkish Flatbread / 209

Kuchen de Nuez - Chilean Walnut Pie / 211

Sopapillas - Mexican Donut / 212

Old-Fashioned Banana Bread / 213

Cheese Burekas - Cheese Filled Pastry / 215

Bulgur & Semolina Cinnamon and Sugar Donut Holes

by Lisa Soldo-Johnson - USA

Bulgur and semolina cinnamon and sugar donut holes are guilt-free dessert/snack. It is made with bulgur and semolina infused with sugar and cinnamon. This healthy treat gives you the same great taste of bakery-style donut holes but with a dense texture that is both filling and satisfying.

Bake Time: 20-25 minutes

Preparation Time: 30 minutes

Makes: 6 servings

Ingredients:

- 1 cup fine or ground bulgur
- 1 cup semolina
- ½ cup granulated sugar, plus 1 teaspoon
- ½ cup cinnamon, plus 1 teaspoon

Method:

1. Soak the bulgur and semolina in a bowl of cold water just above the grains for 15 minutes. Pour the mixture in to a mesh strainer, press out any extra water and return to the bowl.
2. Stir in 1 teaspoon sugar and 1 teaspoon cinnamon to create a soft, grainy dough. Using your hands, knead the mixture into a soft, pliable dough. Refrigerate for 30 minutes.
3. Preheat the oven to 350°F
4. Roll the dough into 1-inch donut holes. Lay the donut holes on a lined baking sheet and bake for 20 to 25 minutes, turning once.
5. Set the donut holes on a cooling rack for 30 minutes.
6. Add remaining ½ cup of sugar and ½ cup cinnamon to a zip lock bag and place 2 to 3 donut holes at a time in the bag and gently shake to coat the holes. Lay on parchment paper to set. Store the donut holes in a container with a lid and refrigerate up to one week.

Wisdom from Lisa's Kitchen:

You may want to refresh the sugar and cinnamon coating just before serving.

Decadent Mandarin Orange Cake

by Laurie Kerkinni - USA

There is dessert, and then there is a decadent dessert that keeps you dreaming about it long after the plate is empty. Laurie's decadent mandarin orange cake is a dessert I love to make when I want to impress my guests. The recipe is so simple and delicious, making it the perfect go-to dessert for any occasion.

Bake Time: 40 minutes **Preparation Time:** 30 minutes **Makes:** 12 serving

Ingredients:

Cake:

- 2 eggs
- 2 teaspoons vanilla extract
- 2 cups all-purpose flour
- 2 cups granulated sugar
- 2 teaspoons baking soda
- ½ teaspoon salt
- 2 cans (11-ounce) mandarin oranges, drained
- 3 tablespoons finely chopped walnuts

Topping:

- 1 ½ cups light brown sugar
- 6 tablespoons heavy cream
- 4 tablespoons butter
- ½ cup walnuts, finely chopped

Whipped Topping:

- 1-pint heavy whipping cream
- 3 tablespoons granulated sugar
- 1 teaspoon vanilla extract

Method:

1. Preheat the oven to 350°F.
2. Beat the eggs and vanilla in a medium mixing bowl.
3. Add the flour, sugar, soda, and salt and continue to mix. (The batter will be dry)
4. With the mixer running, add the mandarin oranges (reserving a few for garnish) until batter is moist, then gently mix in the nuts.
5. Grease an 11x7 baking pan. Pour in the batter and bake 40 minutes or until inserted toothpick comes out dry. Poke holes all over the top of the cake using the end of a wood spoon. Set aside to cool while you make the topping.
6. Melt the butter in a small pan over medium-high heat. Stir in the brown sugar, cream, and walnuts. Bring to a boil for 3 minutes. Pour the sauce over the cake spreading it evenly over the top.
7. Beat the whipping cream, sugar, and vanilla in a cold bowl until stiff peaks form. Cover and refrigerate until just before the cake is served.
8. Plate cake pieces and top with whipping cream and reserved mandarin oranges.

Dashisto - Assyrian Rice Pudding

by Suheyla Kerkinni - Assyria

Rice pudding is a sweet dish often served as a dessert and found in nearly every area of the world. Over time, rice pudding recipes have evolved with each culture and the available ingredients in those regions. Dashisto is a classic Assyrian rice pudding that is simple to make, uses only a few ingredients, and can be enjoyed warm or cold for a light dessert or mid-day snack.

Preparation Time: 50 minutes

Makes: 3-4 serving

Ingredients:

- 3 cups whole milk
- ⅓ cup short grain or Arborio rice
- ¼ cup granulated sugar
- Cinnamon
- Pistachios

Method:

1. Bring the milk to a gentle boil in a saucepan over medium-high heat, stirring to prevent the milk from scorching on the bottom of the pan.
2. Stir in the rice, reduce the heat to low, keeping it at a gentle simmer, and cook for 40 to 60 minutes, stirring occasionally. Mixture will thicken to the consistency of yogurt.
3. Remove pan from the heat, stir in the sugar and let rest for 10 minutes.
4. Pour the pudding into 4 individual serving bowls and refrigerate 2 to 3 hours before serving. Garnish with ground cinnamon and pistachios.

Wisdom from Suheyla's Kitchen:

I grew up in a small town called Midyat, where vanilla wasn't readily available. My family's dashisto recipe did not include vanilla but feel free to add it for extra depth of flavor.

Cheese Borek with Cinnamon and Sugar

by Lisa Soldo-Johnson USA

It is a tradition for many cultures for friends and family to visit unexpectedly. Simple dishes like cheese borek, often found in the freezers of these homes, provides something delicious to enjoy when the guests arrive. I love the artful simplicity of cheese borek. Since this dish is often served for breakfast or enjoyed between meals, I took the traditional approach to this cheese-filled phyllo in a slightly different direction with the addition of sugar and cinnamon layered over the cheese for a combination of sweet and salty. Borek is a welcome addition to any meal or served with a hot cup of tea for those unexpected guests.

Preparation Time: 10 minutes   **Bake Time:** 40-45 minutes   **Makes:** 12 servings

Ingredients:

- 1 pack #4 fillo pastry sheets (use only half)
- ⅔ cup melted butter
- 2 cups finely shredded mozzarella
- ⅔ cup feta cheese, crumbled
- ⅔ cup ricotta cheese
- 2 tablespoons plain yogurt
- 1 medium egg
- ¼ cup granulated sugar
- Cinnamon
- 2 tablespoons sesame seeds

Method:

1. Preheat the oven to 350°F.
2. Mix the mozzarella, feta, ricotta, yogurt, and egg together in a medium bowl.
3. To size the fillo sheets to fit a 9x13 baking pan, gently unroll the sheets, lay the pan on top of fillo, cut and discard the dough from around the bottom of the pan. Cover the sheets with the plastic it is wrapped in and then place a damp towel over the dough to prevent it from drying out as you assemble the borek.
4. Brush the bottom of the baking pan with butter. Begin layering the dough by lightly brushing butter on top of each sheet after you lay it into the pan. Continue to layer until half the sheets are used.
5. Spread the cheese mixture evenly across the dough, being careful not to tear the sheets as you spread. Sprinkle the sugar and cinnamon over the cheese.
6. Continue the layering process on top of the cheese with the remaining fillo dough. Brush the top layer with butter, top with sesame seeds, cut the borek into 12 equal pieces and bake 40 to 45 minutes or until lightly golden brown.

Wisdom from Lisa's Kitchen:

Serve cheese borek as part of a Turkish breakfast, a mid-day snack or topped with vanilla ice-cream for a simple dessert.

You can freeze unbaked cheese borek up to 3 months and bake when you are ready to enjoy them.

Cranberry Bread Pudding Cake

by Laurie Kerkinni USA

Cranberry bread pudding cake is an inspiring combination of creamy bread pudding and a lightly sweet cake. Infused with sour cranberries and topped with a warm creamy sauce to create a wonderful balance of sweet and sour with every bite.

Bake Time: 40 minutes   **Preparation Time:** 10 minutes   **Makes:** 9 serving

Ingredients:

Cake:
- 2 ½ teaspoons baking powder
- 2 cups all-purpose flour
- 1 cup granulated sugar
- 1 egg, beaten
- ⅔ cup milk
- 3 tablespoons butter, melted
- 1 cup fresh or frozen cranberries, chopped

Topping:
- 1 cup sugar
- ¾ cup heavy whipping cream
- ½ cup butter, melted

Method:

1. Preheat the oven to 350°F.
2. Mix the baking powder, flour, and sugar in a large bowl.
3. Lightly beat the egg, milk, and butter in a small bowl. Transfer the mixture to the large bowl and mix well.
4. Lightly mix in the cranberries just enough to incorporate them into the batter.
5. Pour the batter into an 8x8 baking pan and bake 40 minutes or until a toothpick inserted in the middle comes out clean.
6. While the cake is baking, melt the butter in a small saucepan over medium heat. Whisk in the sugar and whipping cream until it becomes a creamy sauce.

Plate individual pieces of cake and generously spoon sauce over the cake to serve.

Lemon Zucchini Bread with Sweet Turmeric Glaze

by Lisa Soldo - USA

Lemon Zucchini Bread with sweet turmeric glaze is my version of my grandmother's classic zucchini bread recipe. Baked with most of the same delicious ingredients, I gave it a delightful lemon flavor that takes her bread to the next level — topped with a sweet turmeric glaze for a touch of international flavor.

Preparation Time: 15 minutes   **Bake Time:** 50 minutes   **Makes:** 2 loaves

Ingredients:

- 3 eggs
- 2 cups granulated sugar
- 1 cup coconut oil, melted
- 1 teaspoon vanilla extract
- 1 teaspoon lemon extract
- 2 cups grated zucchini
- 3 cups all-purpose flour
- 1 teaspoon baking soda
- ½ teaspoon salt
- ¼ teaspoon baking powder
- 1 tablespoon poppy seeds

Glaze:

- ½ cup milk (substitute almond or coconut milk for dairy-free)
- 4 tablespoons salted butter, melted
- 1 teaspoon vanilla extract
- Zest from 1 lemon
- 4 tablespoons lemon juice
- ¼ teaspoon turmeric powder
- 2 cups powdered sugar

Method:

1. Preheat the oven to 350°F.
2. Beat the eggs and sugar in a large mixing bowl until creamed.
3. Mix in the oil, vanilla extract, lemon extract, and zucchini until blended.
4. Mix in the flour, baking soda, baking powder, and salt until it becomes a creamy batter, blending in the poppy seeds at the end.
5. Pour the batter into 2 well-greased bread pans. Bake for 50 minutes or until a toothpick inserted in the middle comes out clean. Remove the bread from the oven and cool on a wire rack completely before glazing.

Glaze:

1. While the bread is baking, prepare the glaze by blending the milk, melted butter, vanilla, milk, lemon zest and juice, turmeric powder, and powdered sugar in a blender until smooth. The glaze should be runny enough to drizzle over the bread. Adjust the liquid if needed.
2. Using a spoon, drizzle the glaze back and forth over the bread.

Wisdom from Lisa's Kitchen:

Zucchini comes in a range of sizes from small to large. I prefer to use a medium size, no longer than 12-inch for this recipe since they tend to have more liquid, helping to make the bread moist.

Raspberry and Pear Stuffed Fillo

by Suheyla Kerkinni - Assyria

Making a pastry that looks like it came from a French bakery is so gratifying. There are three layers to this dreamy fruit-stuffed fillo including raspberries, pear, and a flakey, buttery crust. It looks like a complicated dessert to make, but it is surprisingly simple — a dessert as beautiful as it is delicious.

Bake Time: 30 minutes   **Preparation Time:** 25 minutes   **Makes:** 6 serving

Ingredients:

- 9 half sheets of #4 fillo pastry sheets
- 1 stick butter, melted
- 2 cup fresh raspberries
- 4 tablespoons granulated sugar
- 1-2 pears, cut into ¼-inch slices
- ¼ cup powdered sugar

Method:

1. Preheat the oven to 350°F.
2. Place the raspberries in a small bowl and using a fork, lightly crush the raspberries enough to break them apart. Sprinkle the sugar over the raspberries and gently mix.
3. Cut the pears into ¼ inch slices and set aside.
4. Cut fillo dough in half. Using a pastry brush, lightly butter both sides of a fillo sheet and lightly crunch it into a 2 ½ to 3 inch round. Lay it on a baking sheet lined with parchment paper. Spoon 1 tablespoon of raspberries to cover the base of the dough.
5. Crunch a second buttered fillo sheet and add to the top of the raspberry filling. Add 3 sliced pears and top with a third crunched buttered pastry sheet. Once all of the pastries are assembled, bake for 30 minutes or just until the fillo is lightly golden.
6. Just before serving, sprinkle the tops with powdered sugar.

Wisdom from Suheyla's Kitchen:

You can make this dessert using your favorite fruit in place of raspberries and pears.

Caramelized Pears with Crusted Goat Cheese

by Lisa Soldo – Johnson, USA

Caramelized pears served alongside warm crusted goat cheese are a delicious treat. The satisfying flavors of sweet and salty are such a pleasing combination, especially after a delicious meal.

Preparation Time: 20 minutes
Passive Time: 20 minutes
Cook Time: 12-15 minutes
Makes: 6 serving

Ingredients:

- ⅓ cup all-purpose flour
- 1 large egg, whisked
- ⅔ cup Panko bread crumbs, fine
- 1 teaspoon salt
- 1 (11-ounce) log soft goat cheese, room temperature
- 2 cups avocado oil or grapeseed oil
- 4 tablespoons butter
- ½ cup light brown sugar
- ¼ teaspoon cinnamon
- 2 medium ripe pears, cored and sliced ½-inch

Method:

1. Using three separate bowls: add the flour to one bowl, the eggs to the second bowl, and the combined breadcrumbs and salt to the third bowl.
2. Using 1 tablespoon at a time, roll the goat cheese into 24 balls and freeze for 20 minutes.
3. Working in batches, roll the goat cheese balls in flour, dip in egg, and roll in the bread crumbs, making sure they are completely coated.
4. Heat the oil to 350° in a deep skillet over medium-high heat. Working in batches, gently lay the goat cheese balls into the oil and fry 1 to 2 minutes, turning to brown lightly on all sides. Remove the goat cheese from the oil and drain on a paper towel.
5. Melt the butter in a non-stick pan over medium heat. Stir the sugar and cinnamon into the butter until it dissolves and begins to bubble.
6. Lay the sliced pears in the pan, spooning the glaze over the top and simmer until the pears are lightly caramelized and soft.
7. Divide the pears neatly onto six plates, then add four goat cheese balls and serve immediately.

Wisdom from Lisa's Kitchen:

If your breadcrumbs are coarse, crush them into a finer texture by pulsing in a food processor or high-speed blender.

The goat cheese should be served warm, so they are soft when cutting into them. If needed, heat them in the microwave for just a few seconds before serving.

Serve with vanilla ice cream and freshly brewed coffee or tea.

1942 Sweet Molasses Cake

by Lorraine Soldo - USA

One of the many things I find endearing about my late grandmother, Bertha, is that she wrote the date on each of her handwritten recipes. Thankfully, my mother passed her recipes down so I could learn to make them. Bertha baked everything from scratch, including her sweet molasses cake, which she dated 1942. This is a simple, comforting cake made the old-fashioned way with heart-warming ingredients like cinnamon, nutmeg, cloves, and molasses; you could always smell the fresh scent of grandma's molasses cake baking in the oven just in case someone came to visit. Top it with a scoop of vanilla bean ice cream and enjoy!

Preparation Time: 20 minutes **Bake Time:** 35-40 minutes **Makes:** 12 serving

Ingredients:

- 1 cup whole milk, or half and half
- 2 teaspoons apple cider vinegar
- 1 teaspoon baking soda
- 2 eggs
- ½ cup vegetable shortening
- 1 cup granulated sugar
- 1 cup light brown sugar
- ½ cup molasses
- 2 cups all-purpose flour
- 1 teaspoon baking powder
- 1 teaspoon cinnamon
- ½ teaspoon nutmeg
- ½ teaspoon ground cloves
- 1 cup chopped walnuts
- 1 cup raisins

Method:

1. Preheat the oven to 350°F.
2. Lightly grease a 9x13-inch cake pan.
3. You will need 4 mixing bowls. Whisk the milk, apple cider vinegar, and baking soda in a small bowl and set aside.
4. In a separate bowl, whisk the eggs until slightly foamy.
5. In a third bowl, blend the dry ingredients including flour, baking powder, cinnamon, nutmeg, and cloves.
6. Using a standing mixer or hand mixer, beat the shortening, granulated sugar, brown sugar and molasses in a large bowl until creamy, scraping down the sides of the bowl with a rubber spatula as needed. Add in the eggs and continue to beat until combined. Beat in the milk mixture. Slowly incorporate the dry ingredients into the batter until completely blended. The batter will look slightly grainy.
7. Using the rubber spatula, stir in the walnuts and raisins, mixing lightly until just combined.
8. Pour the batter into the cake pan and bake 35 to 40 minutes or until a toothpick inserted into the center comes out clean. Serve warm with ice cream or whipped cream.

Wisdom from Lorraine's Kitchen:

When it comes to baking, always use the freshest ingredients for the best results.

Almond Cornbread with Orange Caramel Sauce

by Michael Hernandez - Mexico

Most of us love to dig into a buttery piece of homemade cornbread fresh from the oven. It's almost as if a splash of warm comfort is baked into every bite. Michael's Almond cornbread with orange caramel sauce takes that nostalgic experience to an entirely new level of delight. Made with a few simple ingredients and topped with a gorgeous golden orange caramel sauce, this is an impressive side dish or light dessert.

Bake Time: 24-29 minutes   **Preparation Time:** 25 minutes   **Makes:** 12 serving

Ingredients:

Cake:

- 3 cups sifted all-purpose flour
- 1 ¼ cup cornmeal
- 1 teaspoon salt
- ½ cup butter, softened
- 1 cup granulated sugar
- 3 eggs
- 1 ½ cups milk
- ¼ cup toasted or slivered almond slices

Sauce:

- 1 stick butter, softened
- 1 cup brown sugar
- ¼ cup light corn syrup
- ¼ cup orange juice
- Zest of 1 orange
- 1 teaspoon salt
- 1 cup sliced toasted almonds or slivered almonds, divided

Method:

Cake:

1. Preheat the oven to 350°F.
2. Stir the flour, cornmeal, and salt together in a medium bowl.
3. In a separate bowl, mix the butter and sugar until creamy.
4. Using a third bowl, beat the eggs and milk together until combined.
5. Using a standing or hand mixer and a clean bowl, begin to combine the separate ingredient mixes by alternating ⅓ butter and sugar mixture, then ⅓ milk and egg mixture, before adding in ⅓ of the dry mixture. Repeat until all ingredients are combined into a creamy batter.
6. Pour the batter into a greased 9x13 baking pan and bake 24 to 29 minutes or until an inserted toothpick comes out clean.
7. Cut the cornbread into 12 pieces before adding the sauce.

Sauce:

1. While the cornbread is baking, prepare the sauce by melting the butter in a medium saucepan over medium heat.
2. Stir in the brown sugar, corn syrup, orange juice, orange zest, salt, and almonds until combined, stirring and cooking on low 5 minutes until sauce thickens into a light caramel sauce.
3. Spread the sauce over the cornbread and serve warm or cold.

Wisdom from Michael's Kitchen:

Oven temperatures and baking time may vary. Be careful not to overbake the cornbread or it will become dry.

Tres Leches Cake with Chantilly Cream

by Michael Hernandez - Mexico

The first time I tasted Michael's Tres Leches cake with Chantilly cream, I thought I had gone to dessert heaven! This soft buttery cake glides between your lips with a lightly sweet flavor infused into a creamy, moist cake that melts in your mouth with every bite.

Preparation Time: 45 minutes
Passive Time: 2 hours
Bake Time: 25-30 minutes
Makes: 12 servings

Ingredients:

Cake:
- 1 ½ cups cake flour
- 1 ½ teaspoons of baking powder
- ¼ teaspoon of salt
- 5 eggs, separated
- 1 cup of granulated sugar, divided
- ¾ cup of milk
- 2 teaspoons vanilla extract

Sauce:
- 10 ounces evaporated milk
- 10 ounces sweetened condensed milk
- ⅓ cup heavy whipping cream
- 1 teaspoon vanilla extract

Chantilly Cream:
- 2 cups of heavy whipping cream
- ⅔ cup powdered sugar
- 1 teaspoon vanilla extract
- Fresh fruit for topping cake

Method:

Cake:
1. Preheat the oven to 350°F.
2. Mix 1 ½ cup flour, baking powder, and salt, in a small bowl.
3. Separate the yolks from the whites in two separate bowls.
4. Add ¾ cup sugar to the egg yolks and whisk 2 minutes or until mixture becomes creamy and pale yellow.
5. Add ¼ cup sugar to the egg whites and beat 8 to 15 minutes (depending on hand or standing mixer) until it creates a thick meringue-like consistency with soft peaks. It is important to beat the egg whites until they get to this consistency.
6. Fold the light-yellow egg yolk mixture into the flour and with a rubber spatula until it is combined. Fold in the milk, and 2 teaspoons vanilla until the batter is creamy and smooth with no lumps.
7. Taking your time, gently fold in (do not stir) the egg whites using a rubber spatula, a few spoons at a time until all of the whites are incorporated. The batter should be light and airy with no lumps.
8. Butter the bottom of a 9 x 13 glass baking dish and pour the batter into the pan. Gently tap the bottom of the cake pan to bring any air bubbles to the top of the cake. Smooth out any bubbles and bake 25 minutes or until an inserted toothpick comes out clean. Let the cake cool for 30 to 60 minutes.
9. While cake is cooling, whisk sweetened condensed milk, evaporated milk, whipping cream, and vanilla in a small bowl until combined. Cover and refrigerate
10. Using the end of a wood spoon, poke holes into the cake ¾ inches apart.
11. Ladle the milk syrup over the top of the cake beginning around edges of the cake and working your way towards the center until all of the liquid is used. Cover and refrigerate 3 to 4 hours until the cake has completely cooled.

12. When you are ready to frost the cake, mix the 2 cups heavy whipping cream, ⅔ cup powdered sugar, and 1 teaspoon vanilla until the whipping cream forms peaks.
13. Frost the cake with the Chantilly cream and garnish with fresh fruit. Keep refrigerated until you are ready to serve.

Creamy Rhubarb Bread Pudding Bars

by Lisa Soldo-Johnson - USA

Rhubarb is one of my favorite dessert fruits. I love the captivating flavors of sweet and sour in these Creamy Rhubarb Bread Pudding Bars. The combination of flavors mixed into the soft, creamy bars are pure bliss with every bite! An excellent make-ahead dessert that keeps well for up to 5 days in the refrigerator or 3 months in the freezer.

Bake Time: 1 hour   **Preparation Time:** 20 minutes   **Makes:** 12 serving

Ingredients:

- 4 cups chopped rhubarb
- 2 cups granulated sugar, divided
- 6 tablespoons butter, softened
- 1 cup half and half
- 2 cups all-purpose flour
- 2 teaspoons baking powder
- 2 ½ teaspoon salt, divided
- 1 tablespoon cornstarch
- 1 cup boiling water
- Powdered sugar

Method:

1. Preheat the oven to 350°F.
2. Place the rhubarb in an 11x7 baking dish.
3. You will need 3 mixing bowls. Using a hand or stand mixer, blend 1 ½ cups sugar and butter in a medium bowl until creamy. Add in the half and half, beating until creamy.
4. In a second bowl, combine the flour, baking powder, and 2 teaspoons salt. Add the flour mix into the batter. It will reach a thick frosting consistency. Top the rhubarb with the batter, gently spreading out evenly until the rhubarb is completely coated.
5. Using a third bowl, combine the remaining ½ cup sugar, cornstarch, and remaining ¼ teaspoon salt. Spoon mixture over the top of the batter and gently pour 1 cup boiling water over the sugar coating. Bake approximately 1 hour. Remove from the oven, allowing the bars set for 20 minutes. Cut into 12 equal bars and sprinkle with powdered sugar right before serving.

 Wisdom from Lisa's Kitchen:

Use frozen rhubarb when fresh rhubarb is out of season.

You can double the rhubarb quantity if you like a lot of fruit in your dessert.

Serve the bars cool or warm with vanilla ice cream or fresh whipped cream.

Yufka Turkish Flatbread

By Lisa Soldo-Johnson - USA

Yufka Turkish Flatbread is a traditional bread enjoyed with Turkish breakfast. Although the basic recipe is a delicious addition to any meal, I love experimenting with a fresh batch of Yufka by adding a combination of fresh herbs and spices into the dough before rolling it out. For a sweeter treat, I top the classic flatbread with butter, cinnamon, and sugar right after I have cooked it for a fresh take on a classic recipe.

Prep Time: 35 minutes   **Cooking Time:** 12 minutes   **Serves:** 6

Ingredients:

- 2 cups all-purpose flour
- 1 teaspoon sea salt
- 2 tablespoons olive oil, plus extra for brushing
- 1 ⅔ cup warm water

Method

1. Place the flour and salt in a food processor and start the machine. Pour in the olive oil and water, processing on high until the flour turns into a ball.
2. Remove the dough and knead it by hand a few times on a floured surface. Place the dough in a bowl, cover with plastic wrap and refrigerate for 30 minutes.
3. Cut the dough in 6 equal portions, lightly flour a work surface and roll into 6 inch rounds ⅛ inch thick.
4. Preheat a 9 ½ inch skillet on medium-high and lightly brush with oil. Gently lay the Yufka in the pan and cook for approximately 1 minute or until the bread forms dark spots. Flip over and repeat on the other side. Transfer Yufka to a paper towel and cover it with a towel to keep warm. Wipe the pan clean and continue this process until all of the Yufka is cooked.

Wisdom from Lisa's Kitchen:

Roll out Yufka no thicker than ⅛ inch or it will burn before it is cooked through.

Be sure to brush the pan lightly with the oil. Too much oil will prevent the Yufka from cooking into a light bread texture.

Kuchen de Nuez - Chilean Walnut Pie

by Ignacia Paredes - Chile

One year our family hosted Ignacia, a beautiful exchange student from Chile. I learned so many wonderful things about her culture, including how to make a traditional Chilean dessert called Kuchen de Nuez. This decadent treat is a dense walnut pie made with a thick buttery crust and a creamy walnut filling that is simply divine.

Bake Time: 15 minutes   **Preparation Time:** 20 minutes   **Makes:** 12 serving

Ingredients:

- 2 cups all-purpose flour
- 1 cup butter, softened, (2 tablespoons reserved for filling)
- ½ cup granulated sugar
- 1 can sweetened condensed milk
- 200 grams walnuts, finely chopped

Method:

1. Preheat the oven to 350°F.
2. Combine the flour, sugar, and ⅞ cup butter in a medium bowl. Using your hands, begin to knead the ingredients until a dough is formed. Transfer the dough to a lightly floured work surface, kneading the dough until it becomes smooth and pliable. Using a floured rolling pin, roll the dough out to ⅛ inch thick. Press the dough evenly into the bottom and up the sides of a 9 inch pie pan and trim extra dough hanging over sides. Bake 15 minutes or until lightly golden brown.
3. Melt remaining 2 tablespoons butter in a skillet over medium heat. Stir in the sweetened condensed milk to combine. Add the walnuts, continuing to stir until a thick paste forms.
4. Pour the filling into the crust and using a spoon, press and spread the filling evenly over the crust. Cover and refrigerate 30 minutes before serving.

Wisdom from Ignacia's Kitchen:

Kuchen de Nuez is very sweet. I recommend cutting the slices thin when serving.

Keep the dessert refrigerated and bring it to room temperature 10 minutes before serving to prevent the filling from becoming soft and runny.

Sopapillas - Mexican Donut

by Michael Hernandez - Mexico

Sugar coated Sopapillas (so-pa-pias), also known as the Mexican Donut, is a popular Hispanic dessert served in South America and New Mexico. Easily made using a few simple ingredients, these puffed fried pastries are the quintessential mid-day or after dinner treat.

Preparation Time: 15 minutes
Passive Time: 30 minutes
Cook Time: 2 minutes
Makes: 12 servings

Ingredients:

- 2 cups all-purpose flour
- 1 ½ teaspoons baking powder
- 1 teaspoon salt
- 2 teaspoons vegetable oil
- ¾ cup warm water
- Vegetable oil for frying
- ½ cup granulated sugar
- 1 tablespoons cinnamon
- ⅛ teaspoon ground anise
- ⅛ teaspoon nutmeg

Did You Know?

Sopapillas were most likely created in New Mexico, about 200 years ago and can be stuffed with cheese, meats, beans, or your favorite filling.

Method:

1. Combine the flour, baking powder, salt, and vegetable oil in a medium bowl.
2. Add the warm water and mix until it forms a sticky dough. Knead the dough on a floured work surface until it forms a smooth ball of dough. Set the dough in a lightly greased bowl and let it rest for 15 minutes.
3. Heat 2 inches of oil to 400°F in a medium pot over medium-high heat. Cut the dough in half and cover one piece with plastic wrap to keep it from drying out as you roll out the other piece. Lightly flour your workspace and roll out the dough to ⅛ inch thick. Cut the dough into 3 to 4 inch squares or triangles. Do not overwork the dough or the sopapillas will become tough.
4. Working in batches, fry the dough until they are evenly golden. Most of the sopapillas will puff up as they cook, some will not.
5. Using a slotted spoon, remove the sopapillas from the oil and drain on a paper towel.
6. While the pastries are still hot, mix the granulated sugar, cinnamon, anise, and nutmeg in a medium bowl and toss the warm sopapillas in the mixture to coat. Repeat with the other half of dough. Serve warm or cooled with chocolate sauce or enjoy them as they are.

Wisdom from Michael's Kitchen:

Keep Sopapillas warm in a 200° F. oven for up to 1 hour or refrigerate and reheat at 350° F. for 10 to 15 minutes before serving.

Discard the scraps of dough or fry them as they are. Re-rolling the dough prevents the sopapillas from frying correctly in the oil.

Sopapillas are best when eaten immediately after they are made.

Old-Fashioned Banana Bread

by Laurie Kerkinni - USA

Banana bread always reminds me of my mom. She would spend an entire Saturday making fresh baked banana bread to store in the freezer so we could enjoy it for months to come. Laurie's banana bread is a welcome reminder of what fresh, moist, flavorful, old-fashioned banana bread should taste like. If you prefer gluten-free bread, you will be delighted with the results using the gluten-free flour recommended in this recipe.

Preparation Time: 15 minutes   **Bake Time:** 30-35 minutes   **Makes:** 2 loaves

Ingredients:

- 2 cups all-purpose flour, or King Arthur gluten-free flour
- 2 teaspoon baking soda, divided
- 1 teaspoon salt
- ½ teaspoon cinnamon
- 2 eggs
- 1 teaspoon organic vanilla extract or organic vanilla powder
- ½ cup olive oil or sunflower oil
- 1 cup organic Florida Crystals (a raw organic cane sugar)
- 4 tablespoons half and half, or milk alternative
- 1 tablespoon apple cider vinegar
- 4 ripe bananas
- ⅓ finely cup chopped walnuts (optional but recommended)

Method:

1. Preheat the oven to 350°F.
2. You will need 5 mixing bowls. Mix the flour, salt, 1 teaspoon baking soda, and cinnamon in a medium bowl and set aside.
3. In a small bowl, beat the eggs and vanilla and set aside.
4. Using a separate large bowl, cream the oil and sugar.
5. In a fourth bowl, beat the half and half, apple cider vinegar, and remaining 1 teaspoon baking soda and set aside.
6. In the fifth bowl, mash the bananas and set aside.
7. With the mixer running, begin incorporating each bowl of ingredients into the creamed sugar starting with the egg mixture. Add in the milk mixture. Mix in the dry ingredients. Add in the mashed bananas and continue to beat until everything is well blended. Stir in the walnuts until just combined.
8. Pour batter into two greased 8.5 x 4.5 bread pan and bake 30 to 35 minutes or until an inserted toothpick comes out clean.
9. Place bread on a cooling rack for 30 minutes, wrap the bread in tin foil and freeze immediately.

Wisdom from Laurie's Kitchen:

Freezing banana bread immediately after it is baked and cooled gives the bread a richer flavor when it is thawed.

King Arthur gluten-free flour, which has no xanthan gum, makes a delightfully moist banana bread. Baking time may increase when using gluten-free flour.

Cheese Burekas - Cheese Filled Pastry

by Vivi Mizrahi - Israel

Burekas is a traditional Israeli pastry stuffed with a variety of ingredients including meat, vegetables, and cheese. I fell in love with Vivi's Cheese Burekas after trying them for the very first time at her house. These stuffed hand pies are the perfect marriage between a light and airy puff pastry and warm buttery cheeses. A match made in heaven.

Bake Time: 15 minutes   **Preparation Time:** 20 minutes   **Makes:** 8 serving

Ingredients:

- 2 sheets puff pastry dough, unthawed
- 1 cup sour cream
- 2 eggs, separated
- 2 cups mozzarella cheese, finely shredded
- 1 cup feta cheese, crumbled
- ½ teaspoon salt
- ½ teaspoon pepper
- 1 teaspoon canola oil
- Butter for greasing baking sheets
- Sesame seeds

Method:

1. Preheat the oven to 350°F.
2. Thaw puff pastry 1 hour before using. Open the dough out flat. Using a pizza wheel or sharp knife, cut the dough into thirds lengthwise and thirds widthwise to make 9 squares.
3. Combine the sour cream, 1 egg, mozzarella, feta, salt, pepper, and oil in a medium bowl.
4. Spoon 1 tablespoon filling in the middle of each square. Fold the pastry over to form a triangle, pressing the edges to seal. Fold the side edges over ½ inch to secure, turn pastry over and lay on a baking sheet lined with butter-greased parchment paper.
5. Separate the remaining egg from its yolk, whisking the whites. Brush the top of the burekas with the yolk and sprinkle with sesame seeds.
6. Bake until golden, about 20 minutes. Cool 5 minutes before serving.

Wisdom from Vivi's Kitchen:

To defrost the puff pastry quickly: Remove from the box, microwave on defrost for 30 seconds, open the ends of wrapper and microwave for an additional 30 seconds.

CHAPTER 10

Beverages

Turkish Coffee / 219

Creamy Chocolate Oat Milk / 220

Carbonated Grape or Pomegranate Molasses / 220

Sweet Canela Tea - Mexican Cinnamon Tea / 221

Coconut Water Strawberry Lemonade / 223

Doogh - Persian Yogurt Drink / 225

Coconut Sugar Lemon Drop Martini / 227

Jamaican Piña Colada / 228

Meyers Lemon Coconut Margarita / 228

Old-Fashioned Hot Buttered Rum / 229

Turkish Coffee

by Laurie Kerkinni - USA

Turkish coffee has been a preferred beverage enjoyed by many cultures around the world since its introduction into Turkey around the 1540s. This strong velvety coffee is traditionally prepared using a "cezve" (pronounced "jezz-va"), which is an excellent conductor of heat and creates the most authentic Turkish coffee taste. Laurie incorporates cardamom and cacao nibs in her coffee grounds, creating sumptuous notes of exotic flavors in every sip of this beverage. One cup is never quite enough!

Cooking Time: 3-5 minutes

Makes: 4 serving

Ingredients:

Coffee grounds:

- ¾ cup coffee beans *(see notes below)*
- 1 teaspoon cacao nibs
- 4 cardamom pods

Other:

- 4 teaspoons sugar, 1 per cup

Method:

1. To make the Turkish coffee grounds, add the recommended coffee bean, cacao nibs, and cardamom pods to a grinder or high-powered blender and grind to a very fine powder. It is important that the grounds are very fine. Store the coffee in an airtight container and freeze for a longer shelf life.
2. Fill the cezve, or a small pot with 1 cup water, bringing it to a gentle simmer on medium heat until you see small bubbles forming at the bottom of the pot and just before the water begins to boil.
3. Stir in 4 teaspoons of sugar until it is completely dissolved.
4. Add 4 heaping teaspoons of Turkish coffee and stir until the coffee raises up to the top of the pot, then stop stirring. Allow the coffee to raise up 3 times (you will see it create a cream on the top as it boils up. Remove the cezve from the heat as the coffee reaches the top, so it doesn't boil over. Continue with this method until it rises 3 times.
5. Fill 4 small Turkish coffee cups with coffee and enjoy black or add a few drops of half and half, heavy whipping cream, whipped cream, or eggnog when in season.

Wisdom from Laurie's Kitchen:

I recommend using African Arabica coffee beans like Ethiopian Harar, either light, medium, or dark roast. I prefer to use Florida Crystals cane sugar in my Turkish coffee.

Serving size will vary depending on the size of cezva and cups you use.

Once you prepare Turkish coffee a few times, you will master the measurements that you prefer best.

Creamy Chocolate Oat Milk

by Lisa Soldo-Johnson – USA

Creamy chocolate oat milk is the perfect dairy-free beverage to have on hand in the refrigerator. This easy to make drink is both economical and healthy. Using only a few simple ingredients and 30 seconds in the blender, add it to smoothies and shakes, freeze it in popsicle molds, or simply enjoy a chilled glass of this goodness any time of the day.

Preparation Time: 5 minutes

Makes: 2 servings

Ingredients:

- 3 cups water
- 1 cup oats
- 2 tablespoons cacao powder
- 2-3 tablespoons agave nectar
- 1 teaspoon vanilla extract
- 2 pinches sea salt

Method:

1. Add ingredients to a blender and process on high for 30 seconds.
2. Strain milk through a nut milk bag.
3. Transfer milk to a container and chill.

Carbonated Grape or Pomegranate Molasses

by Suheyla Kerkinni - Assyria

Carbonated Grape or Pomegranate molasses is a favorite beverage enjoyed by many Mediterranean and Middle Eastern cultures. Grape molasses is made by simmering down extracted grape juice until it thickens into a syrup. Fruit molasses can also be purchased in stores and online. Mix it with plain or carbonated water and pour it over ice for a lightly sweet, effervescent drink that is refreshing and thirst-quenching.

Preparation Time: 5 minutes

Makes: 1 serving

Ingredients:

- ¾ cup club soda or plain water
- ¼ cup grape, or pomegranate molasses (page 186)
- ice

Method:

1. Pour the water and grape molasses in a glass and stir until the molasses has dissolved. Add the ice and serve.

Wisdom from Suheyla's Kitchen:

If you like your drink sweeter, add more molasses. You can also use plain water for a simple flavored beverage without the fizz.

You can purchase grape or pomegranate molasses in Middle Eastern grocery stores or online.

Sweet Canela Tea - Mexican Cinnamon Tea

by Michael Hernandez - Mexico

Sweet canela tea is a traditional Spanish beverage enjoyed both hot and cold by generations of Michael's family. Mexican cinnamon sticks, also known as Ceylon cinnamon, come from Sri Lanka. However, Mexico is the largest importer of this sweet flowery cinnamon which is used as an aromatic spice in many of their recipes. Canela tea is a comforting blend of fragrant cinnamon, sweet honey, and a splash of lemon. My favorite way to enjoy this refreshing beverage is chilled over ice.

Preparation Time: 5 minutes
Cook Time: 10 minutes
Passive Time: 30 minutes
Makes: 8 cups

Ingredients:

- 8 cups water, divided
- 4 cinnamon sticks
- ½ cup lemon juice
- 6 teaspoons honey

Method:

1. Boil 6 cups of water and cinnamon sticks in a medium pot over high heat for 5 minutes. Remove the pot from the heat and add in 2 cups of cold water. Cover and steep the cinnamon for 30 minutes.
2. Remove and discard the cinnamon sticks and reheat the tea to a simmer.
3. Stir in lemon juice and honey adjusting to your preferred taste. Serve hot or cold.

Did You Know?

Cinnamon comes from the bark of the cinnamon tree, which can grow up to 60 feet tall.

Coconut Water Strawberry Lemonade

by Lisa Soldo-Johnson - USA

Coconut Water Strawberry Lemonade is a healthy hydrating beverage blended with natural fruit. A refreshing take on lemonade that is easy to make and a perfect pick me up. Make it with strawberries, pineapple, tart cherries, mango, raspberries, or any of your favorite fruits. Pour it over a glass of ice and enjoy.

Preparation Time: 5 minutes

Makes: 2 serving

Ingredients:

- 4 cups chilled coconut water
- 1 cup frozen strawberries
- ½ cup lemon juice
- 1 teaspoon coconut sugar

Method:

1. Add the coconut water, strawberries, lemon juice, and coconut sugar to a blender and process on high for 30 seconds.
2. Pour over ice in your favorite glass and enjoy!

Wisdom from Lisa's Kitchen:

Pour the mix into popsicle molds and freeze for a deliciously healthy frozen treat ready to eat in 4 hours.

Did You Know?

The average strawberry contains approximately 200 seeds on the surface.

Doogh - Persian Yogurt Drink

by Mitra Murphy - Iran

Doogh has been a favorite beverage enjoyed with Persian food dating back as early as the mid-1800s. This refreshing drink was named Doogh after the Persian word Dooshidan, meaning "milking." The versatility of this pungent beverage allows you to adjust the ingredients to suit your taste. Add a little more salt, use fresh or dried mint, choose milk or yogurt, mix it with plain or carbonated water. The best way to enjoy doogh is to have fun and make it your own.

Preparation Time: 5 minutes

Makes: 2 servings

Ingredients:

- 1 cup whole milk yogurt
- 1 teaspoon finely chopped fresh mint or ½ teaspoon dried mint
- ½ teaspoon salt
- ¼ teaspoon black pepper
- 1 ½ cup chilled club soda, or chilled plain water for no fizz
- Mint leaves for garnish

Method:

1. Whisk the yogurt, mint, salt, and pepper in a container with a pouring spout.
2. Pour in club soda or water, stirring until the yogurt is dissolved.
3. Adjust the flavor with salt and pepper if desired.
4. Pour into individual glasses over ice and garnish with mint sprigs.

Did You Know?

Many Persians prefer Doogh over soda pop because of the health properties found in the fermented yogurt.

Doogh is affectionately known as "The Persian Coca-Cola."

Coconut Sugar Lemon Drop Martini

by Ameneh Gounilli - Iran

The fanciest lemon drop martini has nothing on this drink! Coconut Sugar Lemon Drop Martini takes on a unique twist by adding freshly squeezed lemon juice and a coconut sugar rim to create the perfect balance between sweet and sour with every sip. I will warn you though; one glass is often never enough. Once your glass is half empty, don't be surprised if you find yourself planning seconds.

Preparation Time: 5 minutes

Makes: 2 servings

Ingredients:

- 2 shots vodka
- 2 shots Limoncello liquor
- ¼ cup fresh squeezed lemon juice
- Ice
- 1 teaspoon coconut sugar

Method:

1. Fill a martini shaker with the ice.
2. Add the vodka, Limoncello, lemon juice, reserving 1 teaspoon for rimming the glass.
3. Cover and shake for 10 seconds.
4. Using 2 small plates, pour the reserved lemon juice on one and the coconut sugar on the other. Rim the edges of the martini glasses first with the lemon juice, then with the sugar.
5. Pour the martini mixture into each glass and serve immediately.

Wisdom from Ameneh's Kitchen:

Drop fresh or frozen fruit into the bottom of the glass once the martini is poured. I suggest pomegranate seeds, frozen grapes or frozen raspberries.

Did You Know?

Lemons are technically berries classified as hesperidium, which is a berry with a tough, leathery rind.

Jamaican Piña Colada

by Lisa Soldo-Johnson - USA

During my travels to Jamaica, I fell in love with their creamy Piña Coladas. Nutmeg, cinnamon, and evaporated milk aren't your typical piña colada ingredients - but combined with fresh pineapple juice, coconut rum, and my personal favorite, peach schnapps - the results are a lightly creamy, perfectly sweet, authentic Jamaican Piña Colada. As they say in Jamaican Patois, "Enjoy di jink!" meaning "Enjoy the drink!"

Preparation Time: 5 minutes

Makes: 1 serving

Ingredients:

- ⅓ cup pure pineapple juice
- ¼ cup evaporated milk
- 1 tablespoon granulated sugar
- 1-ounce coconut rum
- 1-ounce peach schnapps
- 1 dash cinnamon
- 1 dash nutmeg
- 1 cup ice

Method:

1. Add the pineapple juice, evaporated milk, sugar, coconut rum, peach schnapps, cinnamon, nutmeg, and ice in a blender and process on high for 30 seconds.
2. Pour into your favorite glass, garnish with fruit and pineapple leaves. Enjoy!

Wisdom from Lisa's Kitchen:

The evaporated milk will separate once the drink sits for a while. If it does separate, simply stir or re-blend to make it smooth and creamy again. Make right before you plan to serve.

Did You Know?

Piña colada translates to "strained pineapple."

Meyers Lemon Coconut Margarita

by Soheila Mirsharif - Iran

I'm a big fan of a refreshing margarita any time of the year. Meyers Lemon Coconut Margarita is a unique twist on the usual summer favorite many have come to know and love. It's a little bit sour, a little bit tropical, and a little bit spicy all rolled into one. Cheers!

Preparation Time: 5 minutes

Makes: 1 serving

Ingredients:

- 1 ⅓ cup chilled coconut water
- 1 Meyers lemon, juiced
- 2 shots Tequila
- 1 pinch sea salt
- 1 pinch cayenne pepper
- 3 ice cubes

Method:

1. Add the coconut water, tequila, Meyers lemon juice, sea salt, cayenne pepper, and ice.
2. Shake for 15 seconds and pour into an 8 ounce glass.

Did You Know?

Margarita means "daisies" in Spanish.

Old-Fashioned Hot Buttered Rum

by Lorraine Soldo - USA

There is nothing more charming than a family tradition passed down through generations. In my family, that tradition is old fashioned hot buttered rum at Christmas time. One sip of this sweet, creamy brew and guests are asking for the recipe before their cup is empty. Made with vanilla ice cream, butter, brown sugar, powdered sugar, melted in hot water and passionately kissed with a shot of brandy and rum. This holiday drink will warm you down to your toes. Of course, I haven't forgotten the kids. In our family, the twenty and under crowd sip on an alcohol-free "hot buttered" drink right along with the adults. Cheers!

Preparation Time: 20 minutes **Cook Time:** 5 minutes **Makes:** 16-24 servings

Ingredients:

- 1-quart vanilla ice cream, softened
- 1-pound butter, softened
- 1-pound light brown sugar
- 1-pound powdered sugar
- 1 shot brandy
- 1 shot white rum
- nutmeg

Method:

1. Leave the ice cream and butter at room temperature for about an hour to soften.
2. Using a standing mixer or hand mixer, cream the butter and brown sugar together until creamy.
3. Slowly add in the powdered sugar and mix well.
4. Scoop the softened ice cream into the batter in chunks as the mixer is running. Mix until the ice cream is blended smooth.
5. Transfer the mix to a freezer safe container and freeze until ready to serve.

Assembly:

1. Boil enough hot water for the number of cups you are preparing.
2. Fill each cup with a large heaping tablespoon of batter.
3. Pour ½ to 1 shot each of white rum and brandy over the batter and muddle the liquor until the ice cream has dissolved.
4. Fill the cup with boiling water and stir to blend. Sprinkle nutmeg on the top and serve.

Did You Know?

January 17 is National Hot Buttered Rum day in the United States.

Wisdom from Lorraine's Kitchen:

If you like to go lighter on the alcohol, add one half shot each of brandy and rum.

You may want to microwave the filled cups for 20 seconds if the drinks cool down from the ice cream. It is best to enjoy this drink hot.

It Begins
AT THE TABLE

CHAPTER 11

Stories and Pantries

United States of America

The Great Melting Pot of Flavors

"Everyone has a story to tell that can make a difference in someone's life, yet few people tell it. Don't waste your life experience in silence. Share your wisdom with the world."

- Unknown

Butterflies are one of the world's most beautiful and fascinating creatures. These delicate flying insects are created with distinctive behavioral patterns. Some butterflies lay eggs on only one or a few plants; others lay their eggs on many. The United States of America is the "great melting pot," where nearly every region of the world has left an indelible mark on the fabric of the nation — creating a beauty of diversity that sets this land apart from any other place on earth.

In the United States, we are living in a global culture. If you look around, you will notice people from every nation, tribe, and tongue who can fill our lives with their profound life stories. In the pages of every culture's story are recipes and life experiences waiting eagerly for a passing of the baton. They are a treasure trove of knowledge — a gift to the world. There is an entire world of neighbors, friends, and strangers ready to share their stories with you.

American cuisine is a melting pot of ideas — a place where recipes from around the world, the old and the new, come together to celebrate the past and the present. It is this profound connection we share that makes America beautiful.

An American Toast: *"May we look forward with happiness and backward without regret."*

Meet Laurie

Multicultural Pantry

- [ ] Allspice
- [ ] Avocado oil
- [ ] Baking powder
- [ ] Baking soda
- [ ] Baharat
- [ ] Black pepper
- [ ] Brown sugar
- [ ] Bulgur
- [ ] Cardamom
- [ ] Cayenne pepper
- [ ] Cinnamon
- [ ] Cloves
- [ ] Chicken bouillon paste
- [ ] Chicken broth
- [ ] Chickpeas
- [ ] Coriander
- [ ] Couscous
- [ ] Cumin
- [ ] Curry
- [ ] Garlic
- [ ] Ginger, dried
- [ ] Grape seed oil
- [ ] Italian breadcrumbs
- [ ] Long grain rice
- [ ] Olive oil
- [ ] Onions
- [ ] Paprika
- [ ] Pomegranate molasses
- [ ] Puff pastry
- [ ] Red wine vinegar
- [ ] Sesame seed
- [ ] Sugar
- [ ] Sumac
- [ ] Tahini
- [ ] Tamari
- [ ] Turmeric
- [ ] Tomato sauce
- [ ] Salt
- [ ] Sour cream
- [ ] Yogurt
- [ ] Za'atar

Assyria

An Ancient Affair with Love

"Spread love everywhere you go. Let no one ever come to you without leaving happier."

- Mother Teresa

In many cultures, a butterfly is a symbol of endurance, hope, life, and love. Each of the 17,000 different species has distinct features that set them apart from the others. Thousands of tiny scales overlapping in rows cover their tiny wings. Arranged in colorful designs unique to each species, these details help to give the butterfly its beauty.

Much like the diversity of the butterfly, there are over 7,102 known languages spoken around the world, each with its own distinct style and purpose. Aramaic is the native language of the Assyrian culture. It's an ancient language with approximately 3,100 years of written history and the language Jesus spoke during his public ministry. One of the oldest civilizations in the world, Assyria's stories and traditions remain an essential part of who they are.

Suheyla was born to an Assyrian family in Midyat, a small town in Turkey established by the Assyrians as far back as 3000 BC. It is located in the Mardin Province of Southeast Turkey. In Aramaic, Midyat is known as the Tur Abdin region, meaning "The Mountain of Slaves." The land has deep roots in the Christian faith and a rich history of food, family, and tradition. The Assyrians were one of the first people in the region to convert to Christianity, tracing their people's original conversions back to Christ. Over the eons, a long list of various leaders and nations ruled Midyat. In 1979, the political and religious winds shifted once again, changing the land of Midyat forever.

Suheyla speaks with a soft buttery accent. She has a sincere voice that draws you in as though you could hear to her talk for hours. She exudes a feeling of wisdom, making the listener know that there is something to learn within her words. Her stories of childhood and everyday life in her small village of Midyat draw you in as if you had walked those dirt roads alongside her.

Suheyla describes her childhood in vivid terms: "As a child, life in Midyat was uncomplicated. We shared a courtyard with my grandparents who lived next door. Summer days meant soccer in the courtyard, spending time with friends, and helping my mother around the house. Our home was filled with savory smells of traditional cooking and memorable aromas of fresh herbs and spices that permeated the rooms of our modest home. It was like a messenger carrying good news through the air; especially during the holidays where my mother made many of our traditional recipes found in this book. Traditional food is like language. It doesn't vary much from street to street. The change happens from region to region. A fusion of cultures and regions inspired many recipes we enjoy today and are now part of our own story. Assyrian food is simple and honest."

I admire Suheyla's unwavering commitment to her heritage. With each generation, she continues to pass along her time-honored family recipes, the age-old Aramaic language and cultural traditions that keep the history of the Assyrian culture alive.

There is a beautiful irony in the meaning of Suheyla's homeland. As she and her family migrated from Midyat to the United States in 1979, her journey brought her from the "Mountain of Slaves" to the "Land of the Free."

Assyrian Pantry

- [ ] Allspice
- [ ] Bay leaves
- [ ] Bulgar
- [ ] Cayenne pepper
- [ ] Cinnamon
- [ ] Crushed
- [ ] Cumin
- [ ] Dried marjoram
- [ ] Dried mint
- [ ] Dried oregano

- [ ] Dried thyme
- [ ] Sesame seeds
- [ ] Fresh Herbs
- [ ] Grape leaves - jarred
- [ ] Grape molasses
- [ ] Italian seasoning
- [ ] Long grain rice
- [ ] Olive oil
- [ ] Orzo
- [ ] Black pepper

- [ ] Pomegranate molasses
- [ ] Red and brown lentils
- [ ] Salt
- [ ] Sesame seeds
- [ ] Sumac
- [ ] Tomato paste
- [ ] Turmeric
- [ ] Vegetable oil
- [ ] White wine

Meet Suheyla

Iran

A Celebration of Food and Life

"Open the door of your heart. Love is waiting on the other side."
- Lisa Soldo-Johnson

Like people, God created butterflies with a stunning mix of colors, shades, sizes, and features. Each person set on this earth has a particular purpose and calling, unlike anyone who has ever come before them. Similarly, each butterfly species has unique color patterns and markings that set them apart from the others. Like the butterfly, it is the diversity of people that make us unique.

Iran is a land of beautiful people, exotic foods, and a genuine spirit of hospitality. Food is an integral part of this ancient culture, including traditional recipes passed down over hundreds of generations. While Persian cuisine is one of the most exquisite styles of food in the Middle East, it is the people of Iran who bring flavor, beauty, and excitement to the table. Their spirit of celebration has helped to define the modern taste of Persian cuisine from centuries past.

Sohiela, Ameneh, Mitra and Shaya, each born in Tehran, Iran are four inspiring friends who have become like sisters to me. Their friendship has given me an intimate glimpse into the charm of the Persian culture. I marvel at people who passionately celebrate life with a deep love for family and friends. They embrace life as an opportunity to celebrate special moments filled with music and dancing, while surrounded by cuisine as exotic to the eyes as it is to the palate. By experiencing the resiliency and joy of this steadfast community, I am inspired to look deeper into my soul and see Iran and the Persian culture through the eyes of love.

Many of my Persian friends are first-generation immigrants from Iran and have encountered immense changes as they settled into their new homeland here in America. They experienced a noticeable difference in language, climate, political and religious ideologies, and often significant variations in food. Some of these changes include the unavailability of fresh herbs, spices and ingredients easily found in street markets in Iran and throughout the Middle East. This limitation sometimes results in a slight departure from traditional recipes, leaving the interpretation and result up to the cook and the quality of the ingredients they use.

The same is true with recipes passed down from generation to generation. Soheila, for example, prepares her food by limiting the spices she uses to keep the food as close to its natural flavor as possible. While Ameneh prefers the sour taste of lemon to enhance many of her dishes, both Mitra and Shaya have their take on traditional Persian cooking. Influenced by their upbringing and how they learned to prepare food is evocative of their mother's kitchen in Iran.

Food nostalgia refers to the memories we make from food. Like a great story that draws you in, each of these friends infuses a taste of their Persian heritage in every dish they make. Like most cuisines, traditional recipes change. Some of the Persian recipes in this book are reminiscent of their classic version. Others have experienced a metamorphosis. Persian cuisine, inspired by the love and passion of its people, is one of the greatest gifts given to the American dinner table.

A Persian Toast: *A traditional toast in Farsi is "Be salamati" meaning "Cheers!"*

Wisdom from a Persian Kitchen:
"Moderation is the key to life. If you have just enough food, just enough work, and just enough love – your life will be good."

- Jamila Motmadie

Meet Ameneh

Meet Sohiela

Meet Mitra

Stories and Pantries | 241

Meet Shaya

Nowruz, Traditional Celebration of the Persian New Year

Nowruz has been celebrated as far back as 555 BC. Nowruz translates to "New Day" and marks the beginning of spring. This secular holiday is observed in many countries, including Iran, Afghanistan, Azerbaijan, India, and is celebrated by about 190 million people across the world. Nowruz usually falls on March 21st, and the celebrations begin at the exact moment of the spring equinox when the sun passes above the equator, or when night and day are the same length. Nowruz marks the first day of the Persian calendar.

One of the most significant traditions that Persians follow during this special season is setting up a Nowruz table called Haft-seen. This symbolic table includes seven objects that begin with the letter "S" because seven is considered a lucky number in Iran. Although other countries may celebrate this tradition differently, in Iran a typical Nowruz table might include these items:

- Sabzeh: A dish of wheat or lentils to represent rebirth.
- Samanu: An Iranian sweet paste made from germinated wheat representing the renewal of nature.
- Seeb: Apples which represent health and beauty
- Senjeb: The fruit of the lotus tree representing love.
- Seer: Fresh garlic bulbs to represent medicine or good health.
- Somaq: A Persian spice representing sunrise and light overcoming darkness
- Serkeh: Vinegar representing age and patience

Preparing for Nowruz begins long before the holiday arrives and includes many meaningful traditions, including:

- The spring cleaning of a home called "Khoneh Takooni" in Farsi, which translates to "shaking of the house;"
- Shopping for new clothes to celebrate Nowruz to look one's best for the new year; and
- Painting eggs that represent fertility.

The Persian Festival of Fire, Chaharshanbe Suri, is celebrated on the eve of the last Wednesday before Nowruz. The celebration begins in the evening when people make bonfires and jump over them, representing purification and letting go of sickness for good health. Finally, on March 21st or March 22nd, depending on where in the world Nowruz is being celebrated, the family comes together to celebrate life, blessings, and the Persian New Year.

Happy Nowruz: *Nowruz Mubarak*

Persian Pantry

- [ ] All-purpose flour
- [ ] Avocado oil
- [ ] Baking powder
- [ ] Baking soda
- [ ] Barberries, dried
- [ ] Basmati rice
- [ ] Black olives, pitted
- [ ] Black pepper
- [ ] Brown lentils
- [ ] Cayenne pepper
- [ ] Celery seed
- [ ] Chicken broth
- [ ] Chickpeas
- [ ] Coriander, ground
- [ ] Coriander seeds
- [ ] Cumin
- [ ] Curry
- [ ] Dried crushed lemon
- [ ] Dried mint
- [ ] Garlic
- [ ] Golpar
- [ ] Grape seed oil
- [ ] Green Olives, pitted
- [ ] Himalayan sea salt
- [ ] Kidney beans
- [ ] Lemon pepper
- [ ] Olive Oil
- [ ] Panko bread crumbs
- [ ] Paprika
- [ ] Pomegranate molasses
- [ ] Salt
- [ ] Sumac
- [ ] Tomato Paste
- [ ] Turmeric
- [ ] Vegetable oil
- [ ] Walnuts

Israel

Abundant Aromas from the Mediterranean

"We delight in the butterfly's beauty, but rarely admit the changes it has gone through to achieve that beauty."

- Maya Angelo

Throughout history, the land of Israel has gone from barrenness to abundance in the culture, food, and land itself. Israel's diverse population is interspersed with various customs and cultures, contributing to a cuisine that is as bountiful as Israel itself.

Israel rests on the Mediterranean Sea and shares land borders with seven countries including Egypt, Saudi Arabia, the Syrian Arab Republic, Yemen, Jordan, Palestine, and Lebanon. This tiny country is only 270 miles long and 85 miles wide at the longest and widest points. Built on the slopes of Mount Carmel is a port city called Haifa, on Israel's Mediterranean Coastline, which is the third largest city in Israel. Vivi was born in Haifa twenty years after Israel gained its sovereignty from Turkey and became an independent state in 1948.

As providence would have it, I met Vivi almost two decades after she moved to the United States with her husband, Eli. I knew instantly we would be friends. Her bubbly personality mixed with outspoken humor and a kind spirit was a charming introduction into the heart of the Israeli culture. Her nostalgic memories as a child in Israel may explain why Vivi extends her hand of hospitality and love to those around her.

Vivi shares her experiences: "Growing up in Israel, my family lived in a high-rise, and on Fridays, everyone would cook. Climbing the stairs of my building, you could smell the aromas permeating the air from each apartment as families prepared their meals before sunset on Friday, which is when Shabbat begins. Shabbat is a day of rest and celebration that begins on Friday at sunset and ends on the following evening after nightfall. Shabbat in Hebrew means sabbath or a day of rest — an ancient tradition honored throughout Israel and in many Jewish communities all over the world." Shabbat commemorates the day that God rested from creating the world. The Torah teaches in Exodus 34:21, "Six days you shall labor, but on the seventh day you shall rest." While some Jews follow this command strictly, others observe this holy day by relaxing and enjoying time with family.

Traditionally, a Shabbat dinner involves family and friends gathering around a table with multiple courses including fish, soup, meat or poultry, sides, a traditional bread called challah, and a dessert. Israeli food is a potpourri of many cultures influenced by the abundant aromas and flavor found in fresh herbs, fruits, and vegetables, whole grains, chicken, lamb, and beef, nuts, bread, and oils. You will see some traditional Israeli dishes Vivi taught me to make in this book. Spending time in the kitchen with Vivi and learning the techniques and flavors of authentic Israeli cuisine is worth every adventurous minute behind the stove.

Inspired by Vivi's journey from Israel to the United States, the love and admiration she expressed for her new homeland is a humble reminder of the blessings we have. She will tell you, "I am proud of this country just as I am of Israel. America is the most amazing country on earth. If you work hard, you can succeed — and I am honored to be a part it."

An Israeli Toast: "*L'chaim*," meaning "for life," is a traditional toast in Hebrew. It is a 2000-year-old wish to those you are toasting for an abundant and healthy life.

Israeli Pantry

- [ ] Allspice
- [ ] Avocado oil
- [ ] Baking powder
- [ ] Baking soda
- [ ] Baharat
- [ ] Black pepper
- [ ] Brown sugar
- [ ] Bulgur
- [ ] Cardamom
- [ ] Cayenne pepper
- [ ] Cinnamon
- [ ] Cloves
- [ ] Chicken bouillon paste
- [ ] Chicken broth
- [ ] Chickpeas
- [ ] Coriander
- [ ] Couscous
- [ ] Cumin
- [ ] Curry
- [ ] Garlic
- [ ] Ginger, dried
- [ ] Grape seed oil
- [ ] Italian bread crumbs
- [ ] Long grain rrice
- [ ] Olive oil
- [ ] Onions
- [ ] Paprika
- [ ] Pomegranate molasses
- [ ] Puff pastry
- [ ] Red wine vinegar
- [ ] Sesame seed
- [ ] Sugar
- [ ] Sumac
- [ ] Tahini
- [ ] Tamari
- [ ] Turmeric
- [ ] Tomato sauce
- [ ] Salt
- [ ] Sour cream
- [ ] Yogurt
- [ ] Za'atar

Meet Vivi

Uncomplicated Meals

"A thing isn't beautiful because it lasts — it's beautiful because it doesn't."
- Unknown

Butterflies are an important symbol in Chinese culture, representing young love and long life. Although a butterfly's life, from beginning to the end, lasts only weeks, this gentle creature reminds us that life is an ever-evolving chain of events that take us from one experience to another.

Over the centuries, Chinese cuisine has experienced a metamorphosis as its population has increased. As meat became scarce, meals became uncomplicated and often comprised mainly noodles and rice. Despite the limited ingredients, Chinese food is famous for its carousel of vibrant flavors from salty to spicy, sour to sweet, and bitter.

Rachel was born near the Sichuan province in the southwest of China over four decades ago. This first-generation immigrant experienced transformation when she settled in the United States in her early twenties. After starting a successful business and learning the English language, this gentle soul became an inspiring example of the American dream.

My friendship with Rachel has allowed me an intimate look at the Chinese culture and cuisine she calls her own. Learning her way around the kitchen was a skill Rachel discovered only after starting her family in America. Since then, Rachel has taught me the art of Chinese cooking as she explained her personal approach to food.

Rachel explains, "I learned to cook by experimenting with the flavors and ingredients I like best with the goal of replicating Chinese food I grew up enjoying. As is the tradition in my culture, we waste nothing, especially rice, out of respect for those who worked hard to harvest it. I want food to be quick, simple, healthy, and uncomplicated. Spices, sauces, and flavors should enhance a dish rather than overpower it. For me, this is how delicious food should to taste."

Chinese New Year, one of the most celebrated holidays in China, is when families often come together and share their best cooking. The ancient annual celebration began with the Shang Dynasty around 1766 BC to bring good luck for the coming year. The 16-day Chinese festival is filled with tradition where red is a lucky color, eating a fish with the head and tail included means a full year ahead, and it is customary to consume foods the culture considers lucky. Traditionally, the list of seven lucky foods includes fish, dumplings, spring rolls, sweet rice, citrus fruit, rice cakes, and noodles. However, in southern China, where Rachel was born, rice is considered bad luck to eat on the day of New Year; instead, they eat noodles along with many traditional dishes.

It was Rachel's kind and peaceful spirit that drew me to her as a friend, and it is her simple, uncomplicated approach to food that has influenced my everyday cooking style. There is something liberating about cooking a fresh, healthy meal in only minutes that inspires many a cook who has labored over a meal for hours. I am one. Maybe you are too.

A Chinese Toast: "*Gānbēi*" meaning "cheers" it's the traditional toast in Chinese.

A custom deeply rooted in the Chinese culture implies the more you drink, the more respect you show to the other person who is toasting or being toasted.

Meet Rachel

Chinese Pantry

- ☐ Black pepper
- ☐ Chicken broth
- ☐ Chinking Vinegar or rice vinegar
- ☐ Corn starch
- ☐ Fish sauce
- ☐ Garlic
- ☐ Granulated sugar
- ☐ Jasmine rice
- ☐ Olive Oil
- ☐ Oyster sauce
- ☐ Premium soy sauce
- ☐ Preserved black beans with ginger
- ☐ Red pepper flakes
- ☐ Safflower oil
- ☐ Salt
- ☐ Sichuan peppercorn
- ☐ Sichuan peppercorn oil
- ☐ Spicy Chili Crisp
- ☐ Stevia
- ☐ Thai Chili pepper
- ☐ Turmeric

Russia

Big Flavor Using Simple Ingredients

"All that I am or hope to be, I owe it to my mother."
- Abraham Lincoln

These words of wisdom stand even today with the power and influence a mother has on her child. This quote resonates with me; when I meet the mothers of my friends, I fall in love with them on the spot. It is like meeting that friend 20 years later and giving me a glimpse of what she might be like when she is a grandmother. Meeting Maya, Natasha's mother, I felt as if I had found a genuine connection to a sweet soul. Her infectious smile and quiet inner confidence match her daughter's personality perfectly.

Many years ago, Natasha and her family moved from Kiev, the capital city of Ukraine, to the United States. Fortunately for me, both Maya and Natasha still honor the heritage of Russian cooking and they graciously invited me into their kitchen for a lesson on authentic Russian food. Since many ingredients used in Russian cuisine are common to everyday cooking, I wondered what makes their food and its flavor unique from other cultures.

They say Russian cuisine is the world's most delicious comfort food, inspired by the enduring strength and creativity of its people. Influenced by limited ingredients and a cold climate, Russians have mastered the art of creating big flavors with simple ingredients. But what's the real secret to success in Russian cooking? Maya would tell you, "We try to cook from our heart."

I have found by immersing yourself in the lives and kitchens of other cultures, there is a window of knowledge that opens your heart and reminds you of the goodness of humanity.

There is an old Russian proverb that goes: "Берись дружно, не будет грузно," meaning "many hands make light work" or "take hold of it together, it won't feel heavy."

A Russian Toast: "*Za Lyubov*" meaning, "to love"

Meet Natasha

Meet Maya

Russian Pantry

- [ ] All-purpose flour
- [ ] Avocado oil
- [ ] Bay leaves
- [ ] Marinara sauce
- [ ] Mayonnaise
- [ ] Olive oil
- [ ] Onions
- [ ] Peas and carrots, canned
- [ ] Pepper
- [ ] Pickles, dill
- [ ] Rice
- [ ] Salt
- [ ] Sugar
- [ ] Tomato paste
- [ ] Yukon gold potatoes

Mexico

Vibrant Food in a Vibrant Culture

"If you judge people, you have no time to love them."
-Mother Teresa

Millions of monarch butterflies migrate to Mexico for the winter every year. These gentle creatures use a circadian clock in their brain to determine when to migrate. The miraculous flight from one continent to another while using their antennas and the sun for navigation is a humble reminder that even God's frailest creations are capable of amazing things. What if we loved with our heart rather than judge with our mind?

Vibrant food and vibrant culture are at the heart of Mexican life. Influenced by the indigenous Indians and Spanish settlers, authentic Mexican cuisine combines the fresh, colorful, often spicy ingredients to create flavorful foods that are both beautiful and healthy. While food establishes the building blocks of this festive culture, unity is at the foundation of the Mexican family. Creating delicious food while celebrating life with the family is an inspiring tradition.

Michael's family moved from Mexico City to the United States over eight decades ago, bringing with them age-old traditions of food, language, and unity. With nine siblings and a tenaciously loving mother who poured her heart and soul into feeding and raising her family influenced Michael's upbringing significantly. From the age of three, Michael stood by his mother's side learning the art of Mexican cooking, which became the birthplace of his passion for the culinary arts.

Julia Childs and Graham Kerr became Michael's teachers as he consumed their television shows religiously; he learned to master the art of the knife skills by age ten and how to make the perfect roux shortly after. By the time this budding chef turned fourteen, he had found himself in the kitchens of the historical Forum Cafe in Minneapolis, learning to make advanced recipes from top chefs as he worked his way up behind the scenes. If you ask Michael what he attributes his success in the kitchen, with a glisten in his eye and tenderness in his voice, he would enthusiastically declare, "It was Fermina."

Traditional family recipes are a valuable inheritance often passed down through the generations. Michael's mother, Fermina gave her children something far more significant than her genius in the kitchen. She instilled in the hearts of her children strong values, the importance of education, strong faith, and the love of family.

Michael explains his background. "I come from a multi-cultural family, and my mom taught me to be accepting of others, to see the best in people, and to extend a hand of charity whenever needed. One thing you could count on seeing at my mother's table was a stranger in need. Even with the little we had, she often opened her home and her dinner table to anyone who needed a meal. Through her selfless love, she taught us what matters most in life."

There is something powerful about food. It connects us to the past. To those we love and to strangers. What began as one man's passion as a little boy at his mother's side has evolved into something far more significant. For Michael, food honors and preserves the memory of Fermina. A bridge to connect mother and son. If even for only a moment — in the kitchen.

A Mexican Toast:

A Toast in Mexico: "*Salute di,*" meaning "love, happiness, and lots of money if you can get it."

Mexican Pantry

- [ ] All-purpose flour
- [ ] Almonds
- [ ] Anise seed, ground
- [ ] Baking powder
- [ ] Baking soda
- [ ] Basil, dried
- [ ] Black pepper
- [ ] Butter
- [ ] Bread crumbs
- [ ] Brown sugar
- [ ] Cake flour
- [ ] Celery seed, ground
- [ ] Champagne vinegar
- [ ] Chicken broth
- [ ] Chili peppers
- [ ] Chili powder
- [ ] Cornmeal
- [ ] Cornstarch
- [ ] Corn syrup
- [ ] Crushed red pepper
- [ ] Cumin
- [ ] Evaporated milk
- [ ] Garlic
- [ ] Honey
- [ ] Light olive oil
- [ ] Mexican cinnamon sticks
- [ ] Mustard powder
- [ ] Nutmeg
- [ ] Onions
- [ ] Oregano, dried
- [ ] Red wine
- [ ] Rice
- [ ] Sage, ground
- [ ] Salt
- [ ] Sugar
- [ ] Sweetened condensed milk
- [ ] Thyme
- [ ] Tomato paste
- [ ] Tomato puree
- [ ] Tomato sauce
- [ ] Tortillas, flour or corn
- [ ] Vanilla extract
- [ ] Vegetable oil
- [ ] Vegetable shortening

Meet Michael

CHAPTER 12

Menus and Countdown for Cultural Gatherings

Gathering for a meal with family and friends is an inspiring way to try new foods, explore other cultures, and look beyond our differences to celebrate what makes us the same. An ethnic dinner gathering presents an opportunity to celebrate the world. Whether you are a talented chef or just learning your way around the kitchen, hosting a cultural dining experience doesn't have to be difficult or intimidating. Introduce your guests to an evening of international foods and delightful flavors with complete menu suggestions and simple strategies to create a memorable experience.

In the following chapter, you'll find refreshment and libation options and appetizer, meal, and dessert suggestions built into a preparation schedule to ensure all the food is ready on time. The recommended "Countdown Schedule" will help ensure a successful gathering. I have suggested recipes that require less time to prepare than others. Of course, you can create your own menu by selecting your favorite combination of recipes in this book. Just keep in mind the preparation and cooking time needed for each recipe, so your food will be ready when your guests arrive. What a beautiful way to bring friends and family together at the table.

Assyrian Gathering

Ancient Assyria is one of the oldest civilizations in the world; the stories and traditions of its people remain an essential part of their identity. Assyrian's affectionate approach to food, family, friendship and love are always on display in their generous spirits. They give the same level of enthusiasm to food, pouring their hearts and souls into creating every dish. From stuffed grape leaves to meat-filled pastries, lamb roasts to fruit layered desserts, every recipe is made with love.

The Menu:

Appetizer:
Aprah du zayto *or* Schloof *or* Hummus

The Platter:
Olives, hummus, pita bread, feta cheese, tomatoes, cucumbers, basil sprigs, fresh figs, dried dates

Soup / Salad:
Tlavhe Red Lentil soup *or* Pomegranate Lentil Salad

Main Course:
Spicy Marinated Chicken Thighs *or* Kebab in Puff Pastry

Sides:
Balogh *or* Orzo with Red pepper, Mushroom, and Spinach

Beverage:
Carbonated Grape Molasses *or* Turkish coffee

Dessert:
Dashisto *or* Raspberry and Pear Stuffed Fillo

Countdown Schedule

3 Weeks
Send out the invitations.

2 Days
Shop for ingredients.

Choose music.

1 Day
Prepare the Aprah du Zayto *or* Schloof and refrigerate. (1 ½ hours)

Make the Hummus, transfer to a serving bowl or plate, cover and refrigerate. (25 minutes)

Make the Dashisto or Raspberry and Pear Stuffed Fillo and refrigerate. (1 hour)

Clean the house and set the table.

6 Hours
Marinate the Spicy Chicken Thighs *or* Kebab in Puff Pastry and refrigerate. (30 minutes to 1 hour)

Make Pomegranate Lentil Salad, transfer to serving bowl, cover and refrigerate. (1 hour)

Make Spinach and Mushroom Orzo, transfer to serving bowl, cover and refrigerate. (1 hour)

2 Hours
Make the Tlavhe Red Lentil Soup. (1 hour, 10 minutes)

Make the Balogh. (1 hour)

Get dressed and take a few moments to relax!

1 hour

Remove Aprah du Zayto *or* Schloof from the refrigerator to bring to room temperature.

Remove the Raspberry and Pear Stuffed Fillo from the refrigerator, sprinkle with powdered sugar and bring to room temperature.

30 Minutes

Fill pitcher with ice and beverages.

Plate Aprah du Zayto, Hummus, bread, or other appetizers.

Final clean up

5 Minutes

Bake the Chicken Thighs. (30 minutes) *or* Kebab in Puff Pastry. (1 hour)

Reheat the soup on low. (20 minutes)

Light the candles.

Start the music.

When guests arrive:

Make the Carbonated Grape Molasses.

Make the Turkish coffee at the end of dinner.

Once your guests are settled in with a drink and appetizers, proceed to plate the main meal on decorative serving platters just before the meal is served.

Dessert Prep

Top the Dashisto with Pistachios and Cinnamon and serve with a spoon.

Prepare Turkish coffee.

What to serve it with:

Serve the Schloof *or* hummus with fresh pita bread.

Serve the Tlavhe as a starter before the meal.

Serve the entrée with Basmati Rice *or* Couscous.

Serve the dessert with tea, coffee, *or* Turkish coffee.

Iranian Gathering

The Persian culture is known for its celebration of food and life, inspired by the love and passion of its people. Food is an integral part of Iran's ancient culture and traditional recipes were passed down for hundreds of generations. In medieval times, Persian warriors used their swords to roast meat over an open fire - the original kabobs! Today we use grills to make the same kabobs known as Koobideh. While Persian cuisine is one of the most exquisite styles of food in the Middle East, it is the people of Iran who bring flavor and excitement to the table. Their spirit of celebration has helped to define the modern taste of Persian cuisine from centuries past.

The Menu:

Appetizer:

Borani-e esfanaj *or* Persian guacamole

Fresh Herb Platter - Sabzi Khordan:

Basil, cilantro, tarragon, spearmint, flat leaf parsley, chives, scallions, walnuts, radishes, flat bread.

Salad:

Pomegranate Seasonal Salad *or* Salad Shirazi

Main Course:

Koofteh *or* Joojeh kabob

Sides:

Basmati Rice with Potato Tahdig *or* Salad Olivier

Mast o Khiar Yogurt Sauce

Beverage:

Doogh yogurt drink *or* Coconut Sugar Lemon Drop Martinis.

Black tea *or* coffee

Dessert:

Fresh fruit platter *or* Baklava

Countdown Schedule

3 Weeks

Send out the invitations.

2 Days

Shop for the ingredients.

Choose music.

1 Day

Assemble the Koofteh Meatballs *or* Joojeh Kabob, cover and refrigerate. (45 minutes)

Clean the house and set the table.

6 Hours

Soak the basmati rice in salt water.

Assemble appetizer platter and refrigerate. (15 minutes)

3 Hours

Make the Salad Olivieh and refrigerate. (1 hour, 20 minutes)

Assemble the fruit platter. (25 minutes)

2 Hours

Make the Borani-e Esfanaj *or* Persian Guacamole and refrigerate. (30 minutes)

Cut the potatoes for the Basmati Rice. (5 minutes)

Prepare Mast o Khiar and refrigerate. (15 minutes)

Get dressed and take a few moments to relax!

1 Hour

Start the Basmati rice with Potato Tahdig. (60 minutes)

Assemble the salad and refrigerate (*do not add the dressing until you serve it*). (15 minutes)

Cook the Koofteh Meatballs. (40 minutes) *or* Joojeh Kabob. (20 minutes)

Pre-squeeze lemon juice for margaritas and refrigerate.

30 Minutes

Fill pitcher with ice and beverages.

Plate appetizers and set in their place.

Final clean up.

5 Minutes

Light the candles.

Start the music.

When guests arrive:

Make the doogh yogurt drink *or* Coconut Sugar Lemon drop Martinis.

Once your guests are settled in with a drink and appetizers, proceed to dress the salad, plate the rice, Koofteh *or* Joojeh Kabob on decorative serving platters just before dinner is served.

Dessert Prep

Set the fruit tray *or* Baklava in the middle of the table with dessert plates and forks.

Prepare the tea or coffee.

What to serve it with:

Serve the Borani-e Esfanaj *or* Persian guacamole with pita bread.

Serve the meal with Torshi Liteh and Mast o Khiar.

Serve the dessert with black tea *or* coffee.

Israeli Gathering

Throughout history, the land of Israel has gone from barrenness to abundance in both culture and food. Israel's diverse population is infused with different foods and customs, contributing to a cuisine that is as bountiful as Israel itself. This menu includes a flourishing collection of flavors and foods from this ancient Mediterranean culture.

The Menu

Appetizer:
The Perfect Hummus *or* Cheese Burekas

Soup / Salad:
Sweet Mediterranean Herb Salad *or* Tabouli

Main Course:
King Solomon's Sweet Orange Salmon *or* Chicken Shoshi

Sides:
Lamb rice

Couscous with Mushrooms and Spinach

Beverage:
Carbonated Pomegranate Molasses *or* Meyers Lemon Coconut Margarita

Dessert:
Bulgur and Semolina Cinnamon and Sugar Donut Holes *or* Caramelized Pears with Crusted Goat Cheese

Countdown Schedule

3 Weeks
Send out the invitations.

2 Days
Shop for ingredients.

Choose music.

1 Day
Make the Hummus and refrigerate. (15 minutes)

Make the Bulgur and Semolina Cinnamon and Sugar Donut Holes. (1 hour)

Clean the house and set the table.

6 Hours
Make the Tabouli, cover, and refrigerate. (1 hour, 15 minutes)

Marinate the King Solomon's Sweet Orange Salmon. (10 minutes)

3 Hours
Assemble the Sweet Mediterranean Salad and refrigerate (*Do not add dressing*). (15 minutes)

2 Hours
Assemble the Cheese Burekas and refrigerate (*Do not bake*). (20 minutes)

Make the Chicken Shoshi. (1 hour, 25 minutes)

Make the Lamb Rice. (1 hour, 20 minutes)

Get dressed and take a few moments to relax!

1 Hour
Remove the Hummus from the refrigerator, drizzle with olive oil and paprika and bring to room temperature.

Make the Couscous with Mushrooms and Spinach. (35 minutes)

30 Minutes

Fill the pitcher with ice and beverages.

Bake the Cheese Burekas. (20 minutes)

Final clean up.

5 Minutes

Light the candles.

Play music.

When guests arrive:

Dress the salad just before serving.

Reheat the main course and side dishes if needed.

Make the Carbonated Pomegranate Molasses *or* Meyers Lemon Coconut Margarita.

Once your guests are settled in with a drinks and appetizers, proceed to dress the salad, plate the main course and sides on decorative serving platters just before dinner is served.

Dessert Prep

Freshen up the Donut Holes with cinnamon and sugar just before serving.

Make the Caramelized Pears with Crusted Goat Cheese just before serving.

Prepare the coffee *or* tea.

What to serve it with:

Serve the hummus with pita bread, chips, *or* vegetables.

Serve the main course with rice *or* couscous.

Serve the dessert with coffee *or* tea.

Asian Gathering

Many consider Chinese food to be a favorite choice of cuisines enjoyed around the world. Simple, healthy ingredients combined with aromatic flavors bring excitement to every meal. This menu includes inspiring recipes for quick and easy Asian meals flavored with authentic Chinese inspiration.

The Menu

Appetizer:
Spicy Sichuan Beef *or* Shrimp and Egg Pot Stickers

Soup / Salad:
Asian Coleslaw *or* Ten-Minute Egg Drop Soup

Main Course:
Ginger Chili Pork Ribs *or* Pan Fried Garlic Shrimp

Sides:
Chinese Smashed Cucumber *or* Japanese Soba Noodles with Ginger Peanut Sauce

Beverage:
Sweet Canela Tea *or* Coconut Sugar Lemon Drop Martini

Dessert:
Decadent Mandarin Orange Cake *or* Dashisto rice pudding

Countdown Schedule

3 Weeks
Send out invitations.

2 Days
Shop for the ingredients.

Choose music.

1 Day
Bake the Mandarin Orange Cake but do not add the topping. (1 hour, 10 minutes)

Clean the house and set the table.

6 Hours
Cook the Spicy Sichuan Beef and refrigerate until ready to serve. (1 hour, 40 minutes)

3 Hours
Prepare the Asian Coleslaw (*without the dressing*) and refrigerate. (20 minutes)

Make the Sweet Canela Tea and refrigerate. (40 minutes)

2 Hours
Prepare the Pot Stickers (*uncooked*) and sauce and refrigerate. (1 hour)

Make the sauce for the cake, reheat, and top the cake just before serving. (10 minutes)

Get dressed and take a few moments to relax!

1 Hour
Cook the Pot Stickers. (30 minutes)

Cook the Pork Ribs with Ginger. (35 minutes)

Make the Rice. (45 minutes)

Prepare the Chinese Smashed Cucumbers and refrigerate. (15 minutes) *or* Japanese Soba Noodles with Ginger Peanut Sauce. (20 minutes)

30 Minutes

Fill the pitcher with ice and beverages.

Make the Pan-Fried Garlic Shrimp. (10 minutes)

Make the whipped cream and refrigerate. (10 minutes)

5 Minutes

Light the candles.

Play music.

When guests arrive:

Serve the Sweet Canela Tea *or* Coconut Sugar Lemon Drop Martini.

Add the dressing on the salad just before serving.

Make the Egg Drop Soup just before serving

Once your guests are settled in with a drinks and appetizers, proceed to dress the salad, plate the main course and sides on decorative serving platters just before dinner is served.

Dessert Prep:

Top the Mandarin Orange Cake with heated sauce and fresh whipped cream.

Serve the Dashisto with a spoon.

Prepare the tea.

What to serve it with:

Serve the main course with white rice.

Serve the dessert with tea.

Russian Gathering

Russian cuisine is the perfect marriage between big flavor and simple ingredients. It is known as a culture that celebrates family and life around hearty dishes like Russian stuffed peppers and baked cod in red sauce. Your guests will not leave your table hungry. This chapter gives you an inspiring selection of recipes that will set the stage for an authentic Russian dining experience.

The Menu:

Appetizer:
Russian Baked Cod *or* Bacon Wrapped Medjool Dates

Soup / Salad:
Spicy Fish and Seafood Soup *or* Arugula with Garlic, Ginger, Tamari Mushrooms

Main Course:
Russian Stuffed Peppers *or* Stuffed Bok Choy

Sides:
Salad Olivier *or* Garlic Green Beans with Shallots and Barberries

Beverage:
Carbonated Grape Molasses *or* Vodka over ice

Dessert:
Cranberry Bread Pudding Cake *or* Kuchen de Nuez

Countdown Schedule

3 Weeks
Send out the invitations.

2 Days
Shop for the ingredients.

Choose music.

1 Day
Make the Russian Baked Cod in Tomato Sauce and refrigerate. (45 minutes)

Make the Cranberry Bread Pudding cake. (50 minutes) *or* the Kuchen de Nuez. (35 minutes)

Clean the house and set the table.

6 Hours
Make the Salad Olivier and refrigerate. (1 hour)

3 Hours
Make the Bacon-Wrapped Medjool Dates and refrigerate. (45 minutes)

2 Hours
Make the Spicy Fish and Seafood Soup. (1 hour, 10 minutes)

Prepare the ingredients for the Russian Stuffed Peppers. (30 minutes) *or* Prepare the ingredients for the Stuffed Bok Choy Leaves. (25 minutes)

Get dressed and take a few moments to relax!

1 Hour
Assemble the Arugula Salad with Garlic, Ginger, and Tamari Mushrooms (*without the dressing*) and refrigerate. (15 minutes)

Cook the Russian Stuffed Peppers. (45 minutes) *or* Cook the Bok Choy Leaves. (55 minutes)

30 Minutes

Fill pitcher with ice and beverages.

Cook the Garlic Green Beans with Shallots and Barberries. (15 minutes)

5 Minutes

Light the candles.

Play music.

When guests arrive:

Heat the Spicy Fish and Seafood Soup on low.

Make the Carbonated Grape Molasses *or* serve vodka over ice.

Once your guests are settled in with a drink and appetizers, proceed to dress the salad, plate the main course on decorative serving platters just before dinner is served.

Dessert Prep

Keep the Kuchen de Nuez refrigerate until 30 minutes before serving so the filling doesn't get too soft.

What to serve it with:

Serve the Baked Cod with plates and forks.

Serve the dessert with coffee *or* tea.

Mexican Gathering

Many people across the globe love Mexican food. With classic dishes like roasted pork enchiladas and handmade tortilla tacos, the flavors of this colorful and unique culture are as welcoming as the people itself. This chapter gives you a glimpse into time-honored traditions and easy-to-make recipes that celebrate Mexico's hospitality.

The Menu

Appetizer:
Chimichurri Shrimp *or* Wine and herb Marinated Carrots

Soup / Salad:
Albondigas Soup *or* Salad Shirazi

Main Course:
Fish Tacos with Pineapple Island Salad *or* Mama Hernandez Tacos

Sides:
Fiesta Salad *or* Sesame Garlic Veggie Trio

Beverage:
Sweet Canela Tea *or* Meyers Lemon Coconut Margarita

Dessert:
Sopapillas Mexican Donuts *or* Almond Cornbread with Orange Caramel Sauce

Countdown Schedule

3 Weeks
Send out the invitations.

2 Days
Shop for the ingredients.

Choose music.

Make Wine and Herb marinated Carrots. (40 minutes)

1 Day
Bake the Almond Cornbread (*without the Orange Caramel Sauce*). (45 minutes) *or* Make the Sopapillas Mexican Donuts and store in an airtight container. (25 minutes)

Clean the house and set the table.

6 Hours
Make the Chimichurri Sauce. (15 minutes)

Make the Lime Crema and refrigerate. (15 minutes)

Make the Sweet Canela Tea and refrigerate. (40 minutes)

3 Hours
Make the Orange Caramel Sauce and top the cornbread just before serving. (20 minutes)

Make the Albondigas Soup. (40 minutes)

Cook the filling for Mama Hernandez Tacos and refrigerate. (25 minutes)

Make the tortillas and set aside on the countertop under a dish towel. (25 minutes)

Make the Fiesta Salad (*without the dressing*) and refrigerate. (20 minutes)

2 Hours

Make the fish for the Tacos (*but do to assemble tacos*) and refrigerate. (20 minutes)

Prepare the ingredients for the Pineapple Island Salad (*but do not combine*) and refrigerate. (20 minutes)

Finish preparing and assemble Mama Hernandez Tacos. (25 minutes)

Get dressed and take a few moments to relax!

1 Hour

Grill the Chimichurri Shrimp. (6 minutes)

Make the Salad Shirazi (*without the dressing*). (25 minutes)

Strain excess liquid from pineapple, assemble the Pineapple Island Salad, and the Fish Tacos. Arrange them on a serving platter and refrigerate.

30 Minutes

Fill pitcher with ice and beverages.

Heat the soup on low.

Make the sesame garlic veggie trio.

5 Minutes

Light candles.

Play music.

Plate the Grilled Shrimp, drizzle the Chimichurri Sauce over the shrimp to serve.

When guests arrive

Serve the Sweet Canela Tea *or* Meyers Lemon Coconut Margarita.

Once your guests are settled in with a drink and appetizers, proceed to dress the salad, plate the main course on decorative serving platters just before dinner is served.

Dessert Prep

Serve the Cornbread *or* Sopapillas with coffee *or* tea.

What to serve it with:

Serve the Mama Hernandez tacos with lettuce, tomatoes, and pickles.

American Gathering

The United States of America is known as the "great melting pot," where nearly every region of the world contributes distinctive flavors to its cuisine. The essence of American food is being redefined to include a potpourri of flavors and ingredients with an international twist. This menu offers you a selection of recipes and flavors inspired by around the world.

The Menu

Appetizer:
Warm Bacon Eggplant Dip *or* Crowd Pleaser Crab Dip

Soup / Salad:
Cruciferous Salad with Creamy Poppyseed Dressing *or* 1938 Tender Leaf Lettuce with Warm Bacon Vinaigrette

Main Course:
Melt in Your Mouth Lemon Butter Chicken *or* German Sauerkraut and Spareribs

Sides:
Sweet and Spicy Cauliflower *or* Caesar Tossed Herb Roasted Potatoes

Beverage:
Coconut Water Strawberry Lemonade *or* Jamaican Pina Colada

Dessert:
Decadent Mandarin Orange Cake *or* Rhubarb Bread Pudding Bars

Countdown Schedule

3 Weeks
Send out the invitations.

2 Days
Shop for the ingredients.

Choose music.

1 Day
Bake the Decadent Mandarin Orange Cake (*do not make the sauce*). (1 hour)

Bake the Creamy Rhubarb Bread Pudding Bars and refrigerate. (1 hour, 20 minute)

Clean the house and set the table.

8 Hours
Bake the Melt in Your Mouth Lemon Butter Chicken. (8 to 10 hours)

6 Hours
Make the Warm Bacon Eggplant Dip and refrigerate. (45 minutes)

Prepare the ingredients for the Cruciferous Salad (*do not add dressing*) and refrigerate. (20 minutes)

3 Hours
Make the Crowd Pleaser Crab Dip and refrigerate. (20 minutes)

2 Hours
Cook the Bacon and make the dressing for the Tender Leaf Lettuce. (20 minutes)

Assemble the Tender Leaf Salad (*without the dressing*) and refrigerate. (10 minutes)

Make the German Sauerkraut and Spareribs. (1 hour, 30 minutes)

Get dressed and take a few moments to relax!

1 Hour

Make the Caesar Tossed Herb Roasted Potatoes. (1 hour, 10 minutes) *or* Make the Sweet and Spicy Steamed Cauliflower. (25 minutes)

Make the sauce for the Decadent Mandarin Orange Cake and top the cake. (10 minutes)

Make the Coconut Water Strawberry Lemonade and refrigerate. (5 minutes)

Make the whipped cream and refrigerate. (10 minutes)

30 Minutes

Fill the pitcher with ice and beverages.

Toss the Cruciferous Salad with dressing and refrigerate.

5 Minutes

Light the candles.

Play music.

Reheat the Warm Bacon Eggplant Dip.

When guests arrive:

Make the Coconut Water Strawberry Lemonade and serve over ice.

Make the Jamaican Pina Colada and serve immediately.

Warm the dressing and toss the Tender Leaf Salad with dressing just before serving.

Once your guests are settled in with a drink and appetizers, proceed to plate the main course on decorative serving platters just before dinner is served.

Dessert Prep

Plate the Decadent Mandarin Orange Cake and top with whipped cream.

What to serve it with:

Serve the Crab Dip with crackers *or* veggies.

Serve the Warm Bacon Eggplant Dip with bread.

Serve the dessert with coffee *or* tea.

Multicultural Gathering

A multicultural dinner gathering presents an opportunity to celebrate the world in an exciting new way. Introduce your guests to an evening of international foods and delightful flavors with a combination of recipes from the seven countries and cultures presented in this book. An appetizer from Assyria, a salad from Iran, a vegetable dish from Israel, a soup from Mexico, a side dish from China, a dessert from America, and a beverage from Mexico. Prepare one dish from each culture or invite your guests to choose and make their favorite for a culinary journey around the globe as you gather together at the table.

The Menu

Appetizer:
Persian Guacamole *or* Cheese Burekas *or* Fresh Figs with Maple Bacon Glaze

Soup / Salad:
Chicken Noodle Soup *or* Pomegranate Seasonal Salad *or* Asian Coleslaw

Main Course:
Joojeh Kabobs *or* Lamb and Beef Kabobs *or* Open-face Roast Beef Sandwich

Sides:
Mast va Laboo *or* Lamb Rice *or* Garlic Green beans with Shallots and Barberries

Beverage:
Carbonated Grape Molasses *or* Coconut Sugar Lemon Drop Martini *or* Turkish coffee

Dessert:
Kuchen de Nuez *or* Decadent Orange Mandarin Cake *or* Raspberry and Pear Stuffed fillo

Countdown Schedule

3 Weeks
Send out the invitations.

2 Days
Shop for the ingredients.

Choose music.

1 Day
Assemble the Joojeh Kabob *or* Lamb and Beef Kabobs and refrigerate. (30 minutes)

Make the Kuchen de Nuez and refrigerate. (35 minutes) *or* Make the Decadent Mandarin Orange Cake (*do not add the sauce yet*). Cover and leave at room temperature. (1 hour) *or* Make the Raspberry and Pear Stuffed Fillo - unbaked (*do not add powdered sugar*) and refrigerate. (25 minutes)

Clean the house and set the table.

7 Hours
Make the roast beef for the sandwiches. (7 hours)

3 Hours
Make the Asian Coleslaw (*do not add dressing*) and refrigerate. (20 minutes)

Make the Mast va Laboo (*do not add the yogurt*) and refrigerate. (1 hour)

2 Hours
Make the Persian Guacamole and refrigerate. (10 minutes)

Assemble the Cheese Burekas (*but do not bake*) and refrigerate. (20 minutes)

Make the Chicken Noodle Soup. (1 hour, 30 minutes)

Make the Lamb Rice. (1 hour, 20 minutes)

Get dressed and take a few moments to relax!

1 Hour

Make the Maple Bacon Glaze. (20 minutes)

Make the glaze for the Decadent Orange Cake and set aside.

Assemble the Pomegranate Seasonal Salad (*without the dressing*) and refrigerate. (10 minutes)

Grill the Kabobs. (20 minutes)

Make the whipped cream for the Mandarin Orange Cake. (10 minutes)

30 Minutes

Fill pitcher with ice and beverages

Bake the Cheese Burekas. (20 minutes)

Make the gravy for the sandwiches. (15 minutes)

Fold in the yogurt and spices in to the beets in the Mast va Laboo and refrigerate. (5 minutes)

Make the Garlic Green Beans with Shallots and Barberries. (15-20 minutes)

5 Minutes

Light candles.

Play music.

Top the fresh figs with the Maple Bacon Glaze.

When guests arrive:

Assemble the Beef Sandwiches just before serving.

Once your guests are settled in with a drinks and appetizers, proceed to dress the salad, plate the main course on decorative serving platters just before dinner is served.

Dessert Prep

Remove the Kuchen du Nuez from the refrigerator 30 minutes before cutting to soften. *or* Heat the sauce and top the Mandarin Orange Cake with sauce and plate each piece before topping with whipped cream. *or* Sprinkle powdered sugar on top of Raspberry and Pear Stuffed Fillo before serving.

What to serve it with:

Serve the Persian Guacamole with chips *or* pita bread.

Serve coffee, tea *or* the Turkish coffee with dessert.

Dedication

"Perhaps the butterfly is proof you can go through a great deal of darkness and yet become something beautiful."

- Unknown

I dedicate this book to my mother, Lorraine Soldo. She was beyond amazing. Most daughters who love their moms will proudly declare the same, but mine really was. As the matriarch of the family, her generous heart, deep love for the family, and ability to bring friends and strangers together over a good meal have inspired my passion to embrace these qualities whole-heartedly. She loved to laugh at her own jokes, even the bad ones, and was resolute with what she believed was right. It was her love in the kitchen that has given birth to my conviction that food, family, friendship, and love connects us as human beings - and given a chance, can mend the world in unexpected ways.

Just a few days before my mother passed away, as she lay in bed with an unwavering strength fading from her fragile body, my brother, who shared her gift of humor, light-heartedly asked, "So mom, what did you do today?" In a faint and delicate voice, she firmly declared, "I lived."

That very moment and those very words stole my breath away and forever changed my life. The act of living took on an entirely new meaning for me. An unrealized truth had permeated my soul and shook me to the core, reshaping my perspective on the value of our days. A two-word sentence that humbled my heart and drove a profound revelation into my spirit that every day we get to live, every single breath God has given is a gift.

I now understand each day I awake to a new sunrise — is the most important day of my life. To comprehend the gift of breath and the life-altering difference we can make within those breaths - that's where true wisdom lives. Seeing life through the eyes of someone whose breath on this earth was limited to a few is to understand what's most important. It's not counting our differences but embracing them.

Someone once asked me why I wrote this book. My answer was simple. There is an important story to tell. A redemptive tale of seeing life through the eyes of love. A verb that can create providential change in the world, in the lives of the 7.7 billion people who live on planet earth. The butterfly effect. I have resolved to tell this story while I still have breath in my lungs. So, when the moment arrives, and someone asks me, "What did you do today?" I can firmly declare three of the most important words I will ever say, "Today, I lived."

This book is in loving memory of my beautiful Mother - Lorraine.

"What the caterpillar calls the end of the world, the master calls a butterfly."

- Richard Bach

Acknowledgments

To Duane, Jean-Marc, and Isabella,

Thank you for your support and encouragement. Your willingness to taste-test the recipes, including my successes and failures, is an essential part of helping to make this book a reality. Thank you for giving me grace during the busy seasons of cooking and writing with a messy house, cold dinners from mini photos shoots, and those nights when I couldn't make one more meal. Most of all, thank you for being my biggest fans.

To Lexi and BJ,

Thank you for cheerleading me through this process and believing in my vision for this book. Your support and love are an integral part of what makes the journey of discovery in the kitchen all worthwhile. You are such a gift!

To my friends and recipe contributors,

Suheyla Kerkinni, Ameneh Gounilli, Sohiela Mirsharif, Mitra Murphy, Shaya Chatraei, Laurie Kerkinni, Vivi Mizrahi, Rachel Huang, Natasha Baig, Maya Pugachevsky, and Michael Hernandez for your patience and time teaching me the art of cooking in a style that represents your family's heritage and your beautiful culture. You have given me a place in your kitchen and a seat at your table to discover the undeniable connection we each share through food, family, friendship, and love. It has been a privilege and pleasure to spend this time with you. I am a better person for it.

To my creative team,

Taylor Smith (food stylist) for your artistic food styling eye and meticulous attention to detail in bringing the essence of each dish to life. Thank you for being willing to take on an important piece of this project. Your generosity in going the extra mile to help this book come to life is a testament to the goodness within you.

Christine Armbruster (food photography) for your peaceful spirit and incredible patience while capturing each dish you photographed with artistic perfection and editing genius. I am blessed to have worked with you.

Rick Fisher (RJF photography) for capturing the essence and beauty of my friends and many of the stunning food and lifestyle photos. You are a creative genius.

My daughter, Isabella, (book trailer) for your beautiful editing and video creation. You helped to bring my vision to life on screen for the world to see. You have a bright future ahead of you, and I am excited to see what the Lord has in store for your life.

Loralee Erickson (contributing editor) for generously giving up valuable time to help me articulate the heart of this book on paper. Thank you for humoring me as I walked through the book writing process for the first time, gently steering my thoughts and words in the right direction.

Melinda Ruben (editor) for your meticulous attention to detail. Your insightful perspective has helped shape my work, give deeper meaning to my thoughts, and made me a better writer. You are a gift to anyone with a story tell.

To my family,

Desiree, Michelle, Buddy and Toni, Terry and Debbie, Pauline, Venessa and Spencer, Cassie, Hannah, Megan, Jason and Barb, Josh and Shannon, Malia, Hailey and Denver, all of my nieces, nephews, cousins and extended family who are part of a beautiful family heritage that has taught us to love deeply, give generously, be kind, and show hospitality to anyone who sits at our dinner table.

A special thank you to my mom - Lorraine,

Thank you for raising me to see the importance of a generous spirit and the blessing of hospitality. It was your passion for food, family, and love that has etched a deeper story of love for others in my heart.

Finally, to my Creator,

You have blessed me with the desire to see with my heart rather than my eyes. A passion for looking beyond our differences and celebrating what makes us the same. To love your creation just as you made them. There are times I may fall short in seeing the world as you do, yet you continually extend forgiveness and grace. For that, I am eternally grateful.

Universal Conversion Chart

Oven Temperature Equivalents

250°F = 120°C

275°F = 135°C

300°F = 150°C

325°F = 160°C

350°F = 180°C

375°F = 190°C

400°F = 200°F

425°F = 220°C

450°F = 230°C

475°F = 240°C

500°F = 260°C

Measurement Equivalents

Measurements should always be level.

⅛ teaspoon = 0.5 mL

¼ teaspoon = 1 mL

½ teaspoon = 2 mL

1 teaspoon = 5 mL

1 tablespoon = 3 teaspoons = ½ fluid ounce = 15 mL

2 tablespoons = ⅛ cup = 1 fluid ounce = 30 mL

4 tablespoons = ¼ cup = 2 fluid ounces = 60 mL

5 ⅓ tablespoons = ⅓ cup = 3 fluid ounces = 80 mL

8 tablespoons = ½ cup = 4 fluid ounces = 120 mL

10 ⅔ tablespoons = ⅔ cup = 5 fluid ounces = 160 mL

12 tablespoons = ¾ cup = 6 fluid ounces = 180 mL

16 tablespoons = 1 cup = 8 fluid ounces = 240 mL

Index

A
Aprah Du Zayto, 15
Asian Coleslaw, 43
Arugula with Garlic, Ginger, Tamari Mushrooms, 39
Albondigas Mexican Meatball Soup, 61
Ashe Berenj, 63

B
Bacon Wrapped Medjool Dates, 21
Banana Bread (old fashioned), 213
Binge Worthy Nut Brittle, 31
Borani-e Esfanaj, 25
Beef Khoresht Bademjan, 118
Borek, 105
Basmati Rice with Potato Tahdig, 159
Balogh, 161

C
Cheese Burekas, 215
Creamy Cashew Cheese, 29
Creamy Chocolate Oat Milk, 220
Creamy Chocolate Oat Milk and Turmeric Smoothie, 11
Crowd Pleaser Crab Dip, 125
Chimichurri Shrimp, 133
Cajun Shrimp with Andouille Sausage, 131
Chicken and Vegetable Pot Pie, 70
Chicken Shoshi, 69
Chicken Khoresht Bademjan, 83
Cruciferous Salad with Creamy Poppyseed Dressing, 45
Clo Hay Red Lentil Soup, 57
Couscous with Mushroom and Spinach, 151
Chinese Smashed Cucumbers, 155
Caesar Tossed Herb Roasted Potatoes, 145
Coconut Sugar Lemon Drop Martini, 227
Coconut Water Strawberry Lemonade, 223
Carbonated Grape Molasses, 220

D
Dolmas, 32
Dobo, 99
Doogh, 225

F
Fresh Figs with Maple Bacon Glaze, 20
Fish Tacos with Pineapple Island Salad, 127

G
Garlic Cinnamon Tilapia, 134
Ginger Chicken with Spicy Steamed Cabbage, 72
German Sauerkraut and Spareribs, 103
Ghormeh Sabzi, 91

H
Healthy Turkey Chow Mein, 81

I
Israeli Lamb and Beef Kabobs, 97
Israeli Tabouli, 41

J
Joojeh Kabob, 75
Jamaican Pina Colada, 228
Japanese Soba Noodles with Ginger Peanut Sauce, 146

K
Kale Caesar Salad with Pomegranate, 52
King Solomon's Sweet Orange Salmon, 135
Korean Style Baked Chicken, 80
Koofteh, 95
Kebab in Puff Pastry, 92
Khoresht Karafs, 106
Kuku Sabzi, 143
Kashk-o bademjan, 171

L
Lentil Salad with Pomegranate Dressing, 49
Lamb Rice, 153
Lufka Turkish Flatbread, 209

M

Melt in Your Mouth Lemon Butter Chicken, 77

Maldoum, 98

Moroccan Lamb Chops, 119

Moussaka, 112

Mama Hernandez Tacos, 114

Mast va laboo, 164

Mexican Fiesta Salad, 163

Mast o khiar, 169

Meyers Lemon Coconut Margarita, 228

N

Now, *This* is Chicken Noodle Soup!, 56

O

Open-Face Hot Beef Sandwich, 101

Orzo with Red Pepper, Mushroom, and Spinach, 142

Old Fashioned Hot Buttered Rum, 229

P

Pasta Genovese, 113

Persian Guacamole, 24

Pan Fried Garlic Shrimp, 123

Pork Ribs with Ginger and Chili, 96

Pomegranate Seasonal Salad, 47

Persian Salad Olivieh, 141

R

Russian Baked Cod, 129

Russian Stuffed Peppers, 111

Roasted Pork and Green Chili Enchiladas, 108

Russian Salad Olivier, 168

S

Shrimp and Egg Pot stickers, 19

Salmon Asparagus Pinwheel with Goat Cheese, 137

Spicy Marinated Chicken Thighs, 76

Spicy Chicken Noodle Bowl, 73

Saffron Chicken, 79

Shaami Kabab, 90

Spicy Sichuan Beef, 117

Stuffed Bok Choy Leaves, 107

Sweet Mediterranean Herb Salad, 40

Salad Shirazi, 51

Spicy Fish and Seafood Soup, 55

Shirin Polo, 149

Schloof, 147

1890 Slow Baked Pinto Beans, 154

Sesame Garlic Veggie Trio, 167

Sweet Canela Tea, 221

T

The Perfect Hummus, 23

Turmeric Salmon with Capers and Dill, 124

Tass Kebob, 102

1938 Tender Leaf Lettuce with Warm Bacon Vinaigrette, 46

Ten-Minute Egg Drop Soup, 65

Tlavhe Red Lentil Soup, 59

Torshi Liteh, 165

Turkish Coffee, 219

W

Wine and Herb Marinated Carrots, 35

Warm Bacon Eggplant Dip, 27

Y

Yufka Turkish flatbread, 209

Z

Zeytoon Parvardeh, 17

*"This story is about truth, beauty, freedom;
but above all things, this story is about love."*
— Moulin Rouge